HOTTER THAN A PEPPER SPROUT

HOTTER THAN A PEPPER SPROUT

A HILLBILLY POET'S JOURNEY FROM APPALACHIA TO YALE TO WRITING HITS FOR ELVIS, JOHNNY CASH & MORE

BILLY EDD WHEELER

FOREWORD BY
JANIS IAN

INTRODUCTION BY
DOUG ORR

BMG

HOTTER THAN A PEPPER SPROUT:
A HILLBILLY POET'S JOURNEY FROM APPALACHIA TO YALE TO WRITING
HITS FOR ELVIS, JOHNNY CASH & MORE

Cover design by Christopher Miles.

Book production by Adept Content Solutions.

Song lyrics reprinted courtesy of the following publishers. Words and music by Billy Edd Wheeler, except where noted.

"Gunnertown" (words and music by Dr. Henry W. Jensen) © 1958; "Rock Boll Weevil" © 1959; "I Ain't Goin' Home Soon," "Love to My Love," "Sassafras," "Farewell Brother" © 1961; "A Wedding Song for Mary and Billy Edd Wheeler" (words and music by Dr. Henry W. Jensen) © 1963; "Mississippi Magic" (words and music by Will D. Campbell) © 1969; "Buckskin Buddies" © 1978; "In Your Spanish Eyes" (words and music by Billy Edd Wheeler and Chet Atkins) © 1978; "The Ballad of Edsel Martin" © 1980; "Asheville" © 1981.

Above titles published by Sleepy Hollow Music. Used by permission. All rights reserved.

"Desert Pete" © 1962; "Blue Roses," "Coal Tattoo," "High Flyin' Bird, "Winter Sky" © 1963; "Red Winged Blackbird," "The Coming of the Roads," "Ode to the Little Brown Shack Out Back" © 1964; "They Can't Put It Back" © 1966.

Above titles published by Quartet Music, All Rights Administered by BMG Rights Management (US), LLC. / Words West LLC, d/b/a Butterfield Music. Used by permission. All rights reserved.

"The Reverend Mr. Black" (words and music by Billy Edd Wheeler, Jerry Leiber and Mike Stoller) © 1962; "Jackson" (words and music by Billy Edd Wheeler and Jerry Leiber) © 1963.

Above titles published by Sony/ATV Music Publishing LLC / Words West LLC, d/b/a Butterfield Music. Used by permission. All rights reserved.

"A Baby Again" © 1968; "Having a Baby," "Little Lucy" © 1969; "Love" © 1970.

Above titles published by EMI U Catalog Inc. Used by permission. All rights reserved.

"Gimme Back My Blues" © 1977 Universal Music Corp. Used by permission. All rights reserved.

"Chain Gang of Love" (words and music by Billy Edd Wheeler and Roger Bowling) © 1979 Universal Music – MGB Songs / Sleepy Hollow Music Corp. / Universal Music – Careers. Used by permission. All rights reserved.

"Step Lightly on the Earth" © 1993 Chinkypen Music. Used by permission. All rights reserved.

"Swannanoa" (words and music by Janis Ian) © 2016 Rude Girl Publishing, Inc. Used by permission. All rights reserved.

ISBN: 9781947026025

Published by BMG
www.bmg.com

CONTENTS

FOREWORD

by Janis Ian

"A Hill-Billie is a free and untrammeled white citizen of Tennessee, who lives in the hills, has no means to speak of, dresses as he can, talks as he pleases, drinks whiskey when he gets it, and fires off his revolver as the fancy takes him."
—New York Journal, April 23, 1900

To call Billy Edd Wheeler a "hillbilly" is to say that a man is only as good as his beginnings. Yes, he was raised in a coal mining town, and his speech still carries the lilt of Boone County, West Virginia. And, yes, he still "dresses as he can," though I have yet to see him fire off a revolver. This early description is heavy on negative stereotypes but also captures a glimpse of the celebrated American values of self-sufficiency and independence. That romanticized duality is the only aspect of this "definition" where I catch a glimpse of Billy Edd. Hillbillies are not always what you might expect.

What do you do with a child like this, who spends his time dreaming of words and sounds no one else can see or hear? His yearning to "get out," to become something more than his surroundings, is the same longing John Travolta felt in *Saturday Night Fever*, restless to become something bigger than the life laid out for him would allow. It's the same hunger I felt as a young

girl in New Jersey, staring at the Manhattan skyline and vowing
I'd live there one day, with "people like me."

Here is a man who can call the birds with a whistle. He writes
legendary songs with the ease that you or I would write down
someone's telephone number. His garden is filled with sculptures
carved from trees and rocks painted with faces you wish you
knew. The walls of his home are hung with art I long to slip
under my coat and steal like a thief in the night. The only thing
holding me back is the certainty that he will visit my own home
at some point and recognize the stolen works. He'd probably let
me keep them, but one never knows....

My favorite work at the Wheeler home is an intricate
sculpture of metal on prominent display in an airy room
as comfortable as Billy Edd himself. It makes me think of
swallows in flight. It makes me feel like I'm dancing. Every
time I look at it, I see something new. When I asked Billy
Edd about it, he said, "Well, when I first went up to New
York, there was nothing in my little apartment except some
wire hangers. I was so bored and so discouraged, I took those
hangers and made that."

Hangers. Who makes a work of art from hangers? For that
matter, who writes a hit song about an outhouse? I'll tell you
who. A "hillbilly" who takes himself off to college at the age of
sixteen, graduates, joins the navy, and ends up at Yale University
a few years later studying to become a playwright. An artist who
pens classic songs like "Jackson," writes operas commissioned by
the National Geographic Society, and creates books and plays too
numerous to go into here.

Among writers, it's common to say someone "owns" a
particular subject matter. If one of us says, "I think I'll write a
book about the summer when I was twelve," another writer
might say, "Yeah, but Ray Bradbury 'owns' twelve-year-old
summers." You might say, "I think I'll write about a great

white whale and the man who hunts it down," but someone
will tell you to go read *Moby Dick*, because Melville "owns"
the great white whale. Frank Capra and Jimmy Stewart
"own" the holiday-themed "what-if-I'd-never-lived?" story.
Charles Dickens "owns" greedy rich men at Christmas, their
punishment, atonement, and redemption. And Billy Edd
Wheeler "owns" coal, and coal country, and yes, God help me,
little brown outhouses.

When I look at Billy Edd I see two people. The scared
little boy who walked a mile through an unlit train tunnel at
the age of eleven, with only a sapling he rubbed along the rail
to guide him in the dark. He'll say he was running from his
abusive stepfather, but he was really running from the life laid
out for him, the assumption that it was the only life he could
ever live.

Then I look again, and I see that incredibly brave little boy
from coal country, who left it for the bigger world beyond but
kept the best of it alive in his heart. He kept it alive so he could
write it and sing it and paint it—and teach people like me about
it. As a twelve-year-old songwriter, just starting out, I listened to
"Coal Tattoo" and heard:

Blood veins blue as the coal...

I began to understand that you could use beautiful words to
write about something ugly, sneaking in under the radar before
the listener even knew what had happened.

Or take my personal favorite, "High Flyin' Bird." My grandfather
bought me a little transistor radio, and I'd listen to music way after
bedtime, with the covers over my head and the speaker pressed
against my ear. I heard Judy Henske sing that song, and the day her
album came out I was at the record store, clutching my hard-earned
babysitting money and flying home to study the lyrics:

Now I had a man, and he lived down in the mine
He never saw the sun, Lord, but he never stopped tryin'
Then one day my man up and died
I said my man up and died—oh, yeah, my man up and died
Oh, he wanted to fly
And the only way to fly was to die

Just think about it. My grandfather had joined the union and gotten his head busted open for it. My parents worked for the civil rights movement and were under surveillance by the FBI throughout my childhood because of it. I'd visited migrant families with my other grandmother to hand out extra food and pamphlets urging them to band together for the common good. It was all very noble, but all very distant.

But there was nothing distant about "High Flyin' Bird." It was all too easy to hear those lyrics and see a person like my own father or brother. It was terrifying to think of them spending all their daylight hours in darkness. It was awful to imagine that the only release from darkness was death. It wasn't distant at all. It was uncomfortably close, and it's part of what made me the songwriter I became.

Billy Edd Wheeler is a creative spirit, the sort of which this world has rarely seen. He lives it and breathes it. Surrounds himself with it. Whether sitting in a dark, depressing room fiddling away the time making sculptures from wire coat hangers or accepting the very first Doctor of Humane Letters from Warren Wilson College, he is a true one-of-a-kind.

Before introducing us for the first time, Chet Atkins said to me, "Now, Janis, don't use too many big words. Keep it simple. He's just a hillbilly from the mountains, y' know."

Two meals and several hours later, after listening to Billy Edd quote the Greek playwrights and discuss the history of art during the Renaissance, I confronted my friend: "Chet Atkins! You knew

I'd make a fool of myself treating this brilliant man like he was practically illiterate. How could you do that to me?!?!"

Chet, never one to miss a practical joke, just smiled and said "Well, it was pretty good while it lasted, wasn't it? I sure enjoyed watching you try to 'dumb down' for him."

I've never made that mistake again. And neither should you.

INTRODUCTION

by Doug Orr

President Emeritus, Warren Wilson College, and coauthor, with Fiona Ritchie, of *Wayfaring Strangers: The Musical Voyage from Scotland and Ulster to Appalachia*

B illy Edd Wheeler was born a storyteller and now, after an eight-and-a-half-decade life journey, he is sharing his own story. His hardscrabble origins in the West Virginia mining camp of Highcoal, which disappeared from the map long ago, seemed to hone his ear for life's bittersweet moments. Despite the isolation of the remote Appalachian mountain coves, where in the mountain vernacular, "you have to lie down and look up to see out," Billy Edd absorbed it all, from the depths of the miners' existence to the mysteries and inspiration of the ancient, time-worn mountains.

Billy Edd is part of a continuum of troubadours who have given expression to an age-old culture tracing back to the eighteenth-century Ulster Scots who emigrated from a similarly challenging life of carving a living off the land. As those intrepid wayfarers reached their ports of embarkation to cross the unknown darkness of the "Western Ocean"—to a new home advertised as "A Land of Milk and Honey"—they carried most of their worldly possessions in a single trunk. Yet their most prized and lasting possessions resided in their hearts and voices—the songs and stories of home—repeated aboard ship, thereafter at dockside arrival, and along the wagon trails heading west into the southern Appalachians. There they settled amidst the hills and "hollers" and carried on the singing and storytelling as an integral part of their daily lives, gathered on mountain cabin porches and hearthside. Surely Billy Edd's unerring talent for stories and songs originates deep within his ancestral DNA from across the sea. It is no wonder that the music emanating from his pen, and the pens of those who came before and since, are all part of a family tree of song, often described as "the music that America comes home to."

Billy Edd Wheeler's productivity is staggering: song compositions recorded by over 150 artists (selling over 75 million units), twenty-one plays, four outdoor dramas, books of humor, and novels, poetry, paintings, and stories beyond counting. For good measure, there are also the many ASCAP songwriting awards, his induction into the Nashville Songwriters Hall of Fame and the West Virginia and North Carolina Music Halls of Fame, and the honorary doctorates of humane letters awarded by his alma maters, Warren Wilson College and Berea College.

I first met Billy Edd in 1991 after arriving at Warren Wilson College as its newly appointed president. I knew of him by reputation, and since my wife, Darcy, and I were folk singers—indeed having met through the music—I immediately sought out the Appalachian balladeer. I was intent on launching a traditional music summer camp at the college, and he was already hosting a singer-songwriter workshop, "The Great Smokies Song Chase." I wanted to fold it into an extended and more varied summer music program, the Swannanoa Gathering, which we accomplished with Billy Edd's support. We immediately became friends and kindred spirits. As his experiences as a student at Warren Wilson College were transformational, the songs and stories he wrote gave expression to the college's values and distinctive mission in the heart of the Southern Appalachians.

Subsequently we shared music get-togethers at the president's home, on campus, or at his house.

An artist's genius derives from a wellspring of personal qualities and life experiences. Billy Edd's music colleagues attest that his creative life has been characterized by an abiding interest in people and places, humor—including the self-deprecating kind—a generous spirit, honesty, and a good heart. When we celebrated his eightieth birthday some years ago at Warren Wilson College, I was asked to emcee and in doing so solicited testimonials from a number of talented and well-known musicians who have shared the journey with Billy Edd. Fellow artists such as Kathy Mattea, Tom Paxton, George Grove of the Kingston Trio, and Judy Collins spoke of him in the most moving and reverent of ways.

There are many others who could give testimony to Billy Edd's impact. Through a lifetime he has drawn from deep within his musical soul and touched so many lives beyond measure. This memoir is not only the chronicle of a life. It is a winding journey through those years in which a folk music renaissance emerged and was sustained in America. And it is recounted for us through the significant people, places, and events this son of West Virginia's mountains vividly portrays with a tapestry of story and song that will inspire other troubadours for years to come.

HOUSE OF DREAMS

After hors d'oeuvres and lots of food and wine served by white-gloved wait staff, my wife, Mary, and I stood in the reception line to shake hands with President and Mrs. Nixon. We were told not to engage the president in conversation. Just shake hands, smile, and move on. But as I shook Nixon's hand, I said, "Mr. President, I'd like to offer you a personal invitation to attend the premiere of an outdoor drama I wrote for Beckley, West Virginia. It's called *The Hatfields and McCoys*. He smiled and said, "You mean…?" He raised his hands as if aiming a rifle and pulling the trigger. "Yessir," I said. He chuckled and looked to the next person in line as we moved on.

Before the evening's entertainment began, President Nixon sat in the center of the front row to my left, and I was beginning to feel a little sorry for him. He didn't seem to be nearly as popular as the lady sitting between my Mary and me. Ruth Graham was gracious to all who made their way over to her. "How's Billy, Ruth?" asked Senator So-And-So. "You tell the reverend I said 'hello,'" belted Congressman What's-His-Name as he took her hand enthusiastically. They kept coming, right up until showtime, dozens of them. I watched the president. After all, we were in his house; he was host; this was a command performance for him, his wife, Pat, and their friends.

We sat on risers in the East Wing of the White House, waiting for the Man in Black to step on stage and growl in his gravelly voice, "Hello, I'm Johnny Cash," sling his guitar around like a sawed-off shotgun in a loose shoulder holster, his back to the audience, then twist this way and that as he established the rhythm for the band. *Chung, chicka-chung, chicka-chung, chicka-chung.* They say he got hyper before a show, pacing around like a caged tiger, wearing his clothes out from the inside. Well, with the president on my left, Ruth Graham on my right, and Johnny Cash smack dab in front of me, I was a little hyper myself. It was a long way from here back to Boone County, West Virginia, where I was born.

Of course, I was not the president's guest; I was Johnny's, because he had recorded a song of mine. He had told me backstage at Carnegie Hall four years before, "When the show starts dragging or the crowd's getting sleepy, I whistle for June and we do 'Jackson.' That wakes 'em up, brings 'em back. I'm gonna record it one of these days."

"One of these days?" Mary asked me, after she'd shaken hands with Johnny in the dressing room of the legendary concert venue. "Don't artists usually record songs first and then start singing them in concert?" I assured her they did. Mary smiled. "I like his hands. They're strong and rough, like his face. He has kind eyes." Then she scrunched her brows together in a mock frown. "But I wish he'd hurry up. We could use another hit." It had been a while since The Kingston Trio had recorded "The Reverend Mr. Black," my first real moneymaker.

"Jackson" filled the bill nicely when Johnny finally got around to recording it in 1967. It went to number 2 on *Billboard's* country chart, won a Grammy for him and June as Best Duet, and turned out to be one of his greatest hits, selling millions of copies from the single, as well as several different album releases. It became his and June's signature duet.

Johnny mentioned my name when he introduced "Jackson" to the White House crowd, which tickled me to death, and prompted Mrs. Graham to ask me after the show how I came to write it. "*Who's Afraid of Virginia Woolf,*" I said. "The play by Edward Albee." Mrs. Graham was incredulous. "You got 'Jackson' from a theater piece like Woolf?"

"Yes. But my couple's sparring is good-natured."

She smiled and shook her head. "The creative process never ceases to amaze me."

During the show, President Nixon was clapping his hands—which caused other people to clap—and swaying to some of Johnny's songs, like "Hey Porter" and "Cry, Cry, Cry," the two that made Sam Phillips sign him to a contract with Sun Records in 1955. That was the year I graduated from Berea College in Kentucky.

Johnny listened to the radio at night while others slept and carried the songs back to the fields, where he sang them with his brother Jack and his sister Reba. I sang while I worked for the coal company, cutting weeds along a tramway high on the side of a mountain, making up crazy lyrics and harmonizing with the big fans that pumped air into the mineshafts. At eighteen Johnny worked for Fisher Body in Pontiac, Michigan. At eighteen I worked for GMC Truck and Coach in Pontiac, Michigan. Johnny quit and enlisted in the air force. I enlisted in pilot training in the navy as an aviation officer candidate.

I pondered the similarities of Johnny's life and mine as Mary and I sat with Mrs. Graham and enjoyed his concert. Both of us had done hard physical work before finding our music. Maybe that's why I admired the man so much. I had written and rewritten songs in the Brill Building on Broadway in New York, which was referred to by many songwriters and publishers as the House of Dreams. I wondered if that's how Nixon felt about

xx House of Dreams

the beautiful place we were sitting, where he rewrote his career. I wondered if Johnny had a specific place he called his House of Dreams, or if his "house" was as long as the Mississippi and as wide as a cotton field with an unlimited sky above. We had all built our own version of that house, and our lives were changed forever and ever. Amen.

HOTTER THAN A PEPPER SPROUT

Chapter One

COAL TATTOO

Traveling down that coal town road
Listen to my rubber tires whine
It's goodbye to buckeye and white sycamore
I'm leaving you behind
I've been a coal man all my life
Laying down track in the hole
Got a back like an ironwood
Bent by the wind
Blood veins blue as the coal
Blood veins blue as the coal

Jarrolds Valley, West Virginia, 1936. When I was four-and-a-half years old (as far back as I can remember), I was a velveteen puppy being petted by a loving family in a halcyon place called Jarrolds Valley in Boone County, West Virginia. Our house stood by the railroad tracks. My grandfather, Samuel M. "Step" Wheeler, could go to work by taking a few steps beyond the front gate and swinging up onto the moving coal train. This was before the C&O Railroad had the luxury of cabooses. If he came back when it was dark, I could tell it was him by how the lantern swung to his loping gait. When he picked me up to hug me, he smelled like tobacco juice and coal smoke. His railroad smell.

1

He always wore a buttoned-up vest, with a big round watch in its right pocket that he could fish out by hooking his forefinger under the plaited leather chain anchored in a pocket on the other side. It made a great arc over his big belly.

My grandmother, Leda Jane, was the caregiving Mother Goose to a family of four girls and three boys, including Sister, who was my mother, Mary Isabelle Wheeler. But for a long time I thought she was my sister, since that's what everyone called her. A collection of clues gradually informed me that she was, indeed, my mother. For instance, when they all tired of petting me, they deferred to Sister. When I knocked Aunt Shirley Faye down during rough play—she was a year younger than I—it was Sister's job to spank me. But if I skinned a knee or cut my foot, my grandmother doctored me. Just like she saved my life when the hospital in Charleston sent me home to die. I was a blue baby, I was told later, and the doctors had given up on me. Nobody told me what a blue baby was. They just said my grandmother cured me, using old-time remedies and concoctions. But I'm convinced it was the old-fashioned love of Mommy, as I called my grandmother, and her warm, encompassing hugs that did the trick.

She was also handy with a switch when Shirley Faye and I used curse words, showed disrespect to our elders, or got into food fights. The fighting didn't bother her as much as wasting food. She'd say, "We're not poor. We just don't have any money to throw away. And food is money."

Uncle James was handy with a switch, too, the time I stole a dollar from his pocket and ran to a neighbor's house to buy candy. He was there before I left their porch and made me walk in front of him back to our house, flicking the switch at my bare legs.

Vincent was the jokester uncle. When Shirley and I sat on the ground watching him milk our cow, Bessie, he would aim one of the teats at us. Our faces would be bathed in foamy milk, some of which actually got into our mouths. It tasted to me like a meadow full of clover and wild honeysuckle. Sometimes he took Shirley Faye and me for a ride in his coupe, letting us sit in the rumble seat, laughing when it rained and we got soaked.

But the greatest thrill of all was when Vincent let me sit on his lap and take over the steering wheel. It made me feel older than almost five, and I loved him for it, not to mention the hotdogs he bought me. I heard Mommy tell people, "If you buy Vincent hot dogs and gas, he'll drive you anywhere on earth."

Uncle Babe—real name Joseph Garland—worked on cars at the Esso gas station in Whitesville, where I was born in 1932. It was just across the river from Jarrolds Valley. He was kind and generous, as were my aunts Jean, next to youngest, and Louise, the oldest. If I timed it right I could go down the tracks and walk across the river on the swinging bridge, arriving at the gas station soon after the Valley Bell milk truck got there. Vincent would buy me a half-pint of chocolate milk. Nothing in this world ever tasted as good as cold chocolate milk. Well, unless it was Mommy's strawberry shortcake, which was so moist and delicious words cannot describe it.

Once, Granddaddy came home drunk after we'd all gone to bed and saw four rounds of pound cake Mommy had baked and laid out to cool. He ate two of them and boasted the next morning, "Best damn cornbread I've ever eat!" Mommy gave him hell.

In that wonderful place I learned to entertain with simple props, standing in Uncle Vincent's tall boots that reached to my knees, doing a wobbly drunk man's walk, falling at last into the arms of whoever was closest. I was always being hugged.

One day a dark blue Ford drove into Jarrolds Valley and parked by the wire fence near our front gate. A man with slicked-down dark hair, wearing a white shirt buttoned at the top, came calling on Sister. His face was sharp-edged, and his smile was quick and perfunctory—at least when he smiled at me. It was warmer when he smiled at Sister or Mommy. Even in my young innocence I had a funny feeling, as if I smelled trouble coming to paradise.

They told me he was Arthur Stewart, come here from Kentucky. He made a good living working for Anchor Coal Company, up at Highcoal, wherever that was. If things worked out, they said, he would make me a good daddy. He would be the daddy I never had. They seemed happy for Sister. I felt sorry for myself and hoped things wouldn't work out. I didn't want to leave paradise.

But I decided to give happiness a shot. What choice did I have? The Ford did intrigue me. Sometimes, when Arthur was in the house, I would sit behind the wheel pretending to drive and shift gears. It was as clean inside as Arthur's white shirt. On his third or fourth visit, I managed to touch the clutch with my left toes, holding on to the knob of the tall shifter stick for balance, causing it to pop out of gear. The car started rolling slowly, and I couldn't reach the brake pedal well enough to stop it. Fear in the form of goose bumps shot up my arms and the back of my neck. Fortunately, because the ground was almost level, the car came to rest halfway between our fence and the railroad tracks, just ten feet from where it had been parked.

Sister and Arthur were strolling toward me, and when Arthur saw what had happened, he dashed ahead and yanked the door open. "Here, now, what're you doin'?" His voice was low but stern. "You could've wrecked my car."

Sister asked what was wrong as she approached the car, and Arthur's tone turned to sweetness. "Why, nothing. But I may have to give little Billy a ticket for speeding." He laughed and leaned into the car. "Ain't that right, honey?"

"The name's Billy Edward, not honey or little Billy," I said to myself. "But that don't matter anyhow. You're just trying to impress Sister."

The train and car rides are now dim in my memory. But one incident from that summer has stayed with me, frozen solid for all these decades. It had just got dark. I was in bed with Uncle James and couldn't get to sleep because of his snoring. So I got up to discover that Sister was still up, entertaining Arthur in the living room. I went back to bed. But after some time had passed, with Uncle James still snoring, I decided to sneak around the house and take Arthur's Ford for another imaginary drive. He had brought me candy earlier, which I took to mean he was trying to be nice. He wouldn't mind.

But the Ford wasn't there, which was strange. It was usually parked in front of the fence near the gate. Off to the side, though, through the tall corn, I caught a glimpse of something shiny, about twenty yards away. It was the car's windshield, gleaming in the moonlight. I would have my ride after all. I walked through the corn, glad the stalks reached above my head, until I came to the parked car. With my foot in a square of the wire fence, I was ready to swing up and over when I heard muffled noises, like sighing or heavy breathing, and the rustle of clothing.

It made me shiver all over.

I stepped back down, causing the fence to screech a little, and ducked back into the corn as I heard Arthur say, "What was that?" Sister said she didn't hear anything. I stood mummified and saw Arthur straighten up to look out the window toward the house. His hair looked ruffled, like he'd been asleep. He settled back, almost out of sight, and turned toward the passenger side. I saw his arm arc and disappear, heard him mumbling in that tone of sweetness and honey, sounding like he was trying to be persuasive. Sort of begging-like.

I was afraid to bat an eyelash.

Then I heard a crescendo of soft voices and muffled activity in the front seat, heard the car creak on its springs, heard Sister say "huh-uh" or something, and heard Arthur's talking grow more desperate until Sister said, "Huh-uh," more clearly this time. She seemed to be trying to get herself back to a sitting position, reaching back to pull up her clothing, trying to cover herself. Arthur exhaled loudly and sat up, blocking my view, for which I was thankful. But I'm sure I would have continued to look, in spite of feeling some kind of distaste, because what I saw happening was Arthur being intimate with my mother. In bright moonlight, for God's sake. It was a feeling too adult for me to comprehend. It felt extremely dangerous. *I shouldn't be here.* If they started the car and began to drive away, I could run back through the corn. But running now was more risky than staying put. I was trapped, forced to watch and hear. I remember trembling, wanting to move, wanting to cry out, but knowing I had to be brave and control my nerves. I stood as still as the corner post.

"Why'd you push me away?" Arthur's voice was sober, with an edge of meanness.

Sister's response was meek, barely audible. "I don't know."

"I didn't see you push them hotdogs away I bought you for supper."

No reply.

"You should've stopped me sooner if you wasn't going to—"

"I know, I know. I'm sorry."

"I'll not put up with gettin' pushed away, I'm John Brown if I will. I may just stop coming around. Where'll you be then?"

Sister's voice lost some of its meekness. "I said I'm sorry."

"You'll be more than sorry, honey. You don't seem to know which side your bread's buttered on. Huh?"

"I don't want to do nothing yet. You've been good to me, but . . ." She had to pause to clear her throat, rubbing her eyes with the back of her hand. "I don't want to get, you know, in trouble, and have another—uh—"

"Little bastard?"

"Don't you call him that," she snapped, as defiantly as I had ever heard her speak. "You could at least say *accident*, or *a big surprise*, or something."

I didn't fully understand this talk. "Bastard" and "surprise" meant nothing to me, except I'd heard people get mad and say *bastard*. It was a cussword. Yet I had heard my name. The conversation involved me, too.

"You're not gonna be nice to me, huh?" The timbre of
Arthur's voice was changing. Some of the meanness was gone,
but it didn't sound friendly, either. He was laying down rules and
making it plain he ruled the roost. "You think about it, and you'll
see you ain't got many choices."

"I don't care," Sister said, trying to be firm, but still in a voice
so feminine and vulnerable it made my heart ache. "I won't do
that again—I won't go all the way 'til . . . 'til I'm married."

"We'll see about that. You may not *get* married. Who'd have
you, except somebody like me? And I ain't sure I want you. You
understand that?"

"Yes."

"Well, what do you say about it?"

"You've never said you love me."

"I may not, either, the way you . . . " A long silence. "I don't
think you appreciate what I could do for you and—uh, your boy."

Looking back, in an odd way this sounded like a proposal. I
think Arthur was glad Sister had turned him down. And so was
she. After another silence he said, "Well, give me a kiss, then. I'll
let you out at the gate. Straighten up your clothes. And you better
think about what I been tellin' you. Huh?"

She sat still for a brief moment, as if digesting it all, and then
turned her head toward him. "I wouldn't fool around on you."
She sounded sorrowful and meek again. "Like Daddy does on
Mommy. He never gave her a wedding ring. I'd never marry
without a ring. That's all there is to it."

Chapter Two

≡ I AIN'T GOING HOME SOON ≡

It's been a long time since I've been home
And I ain't going soon, no I ain't going home soon

When Sister and Arthur Stewart got married, in 1937, I found myself living with them in Highcoal, West Virginia, in a coal company house without running water or an indoor bathroom. Just an outhouse. Later in life, I would glorify outhouses by writing "Ode to the Little Brown Shack Out Back," my only hit as a recording artist. But then, in Highcoal, I hated them.

> *I was born in a coal camp, stars at my head*
> *And the sun didn't shine all the day*
> *But the banjo in the night and the star's big light*
> *Was a pleasure that I wanted to stay*
> *How could anybody know that the next day or so*
> *We would all be roaming over mountain and plain*
> *Trying to plant our roots again*

Most of Highcoal was divided by a creek, with the road and a row of houses on the left and a row of houses on the right, where we lived. The lower end was populated by blacks. The upper end, where the poolroom and company store were, the houses were

9

nicer, occupied by managers, mine bosses, and foremen. The three nicest houses of all, by far, were enjoyed by the superintendent, Van B. Stith, Doctor Whitaker, and Mr. Clyde Carter. He was second in command, I'd heard, but I never knew what his job was. I guessed it had to do with hiring and firing, and when miners had any trouble getting money with their scrip cards, he would take care of it. The most important thing to me, though, was that his wife Sylvia was my first- and second-grade teacher.

Arthur enrolled me, and on my first day of school, Sister kissed me and handed me a poke (paper sack) with my lunch in it—a sandwich of baloney, fried almost black, with mustard and onion, and an apple. I must have looked scared. She said, "Nobody's going to bite you. Want me to go with you?" I shook my head. "OK. You're a big boy. Go on, now."

As I walked up the hill to the school house, I felt a combination of being scared and excited. Really excited. Mrs. Carter opened the door before I could get my hand on the knob. She was as pretty as Sister, but because she was dressed in clothes that looked really expensive and her hair was so soft-looking and wavy, it made her look prettier. She smiled. "Well, you would be Mister Billy Edward Wheeler." I nodded. "Your mother is married to Arthur Stewart."

"Yes, ma'am. But he's not my daddy."

"I'm aware of that," she said, continuing to smile.

"I was a accident."

Now her smile was accompanied by twinkling eyes, as she managed to suppress a chuckle. "You were *an* accident."

"Huh?"

"Never mind. Come on in."

Some girls giggled as I followed Mrs. Carter, and I could feel their eyes on me.

In the center of the room was a pot-bellied stove, and on the wall a very large blackboard showed examples of cursive writing, and words printed in capitals and lowercase. I remember the first book I learned to read there. It was about a tree, a lumberjack, and an ocean. I think I remember it so clearly because I loved the colorful illustrations.

As winter came on, I was grateful for that big fat stove. I was cold all the time in our house, where the main source of heat was a coal-burning fireplace. Warm only when you stood close to it. I had an unlined mackinaw that was made to last, but not to hold in body heat. I had unlined brogans you would outgrow before you could wear them out. When I went sleigh riding and stayed out too long, my feet felt as if some icy fire deeper than freezing was making them too painful to walk on. I'd have to go to bed to thaw them out and get warm.

Mrs. Carter told a second-year student named Paul Morton to take me with him to the coal house to get a bucket of coal for the pot-bellied stove. "When you leave here to enter third grade at Whitesville Jr. High, maybe Billy Edward can take over your job of feeding the fire." She looked to me for an answer.

"Yes, ma'am. I'd like that," I said, and she nodded.

I followed Paul to a small, six-by-eight-foot shed with an opening on one side the size of a big window, and an open door on the other side that faced the school. As he shoveled coal into the bucket, he said, "I expect you noticed they's one of these in front of ever house in Highcoal. The company dumps a big load next to 'em, and it's somebody's job to shovel it on into the coal house. At my home it's me." He looked at me, as if saying, "You up to it?"

"I ain't never shoveled no coal."

He laughed, showing a good row of front teeth. Mine were uneven, with rust-looking spots in between them. "You'll learn, I reckon. Hard dang work, but it'll put meat on your bones, my daddy says." He squeezed my bicep with a grip that almost hurt. "You could use some."

I knew right off I would like Paul Morton. He took me under his wing and got me into marble games. I lost a lot of marbles for him, but he didn't care. One time, Sister gave me a dime and let me go with him all the way up to the poolroom. It was a great big cinder block building, with about eight cheap-looking car garages off to the side, next to the creek, and two gas pumps in front. People were coming and going, kids older than me, young and old adults, lots of them smoking cigarettes.

"This here's where 'bout ever' thing happens," Paul said. We walked through two open doors. "This is the barbershop. Up them stairs is where the boxers work out, after they get off work." We walked into a large smoky room, with candy cases and a soda fountain on the left, a long bar on the right, and beer signs lit up. Men stood along the bar, nursing beers, almost all of them smoking cigarettes or cigars. I bought Tootsie Rolls, jawbreakers, and a double-scoop cone of ice cream.

At school, I took to the building blocks of reading and writing like our calf at Jarrolds Valley took to sucking its mother's teats. I was hungry for it, spurred on by Mrs. Carter, who had a gentle but firm way of making you want to succeed. If she had a paddle or switch, I don't remember seeing it. But one Friday after lunch, a boy named Benny Murphy started pinching girls, making them cry out or laugh. Or he'd throw spitballs. When Mrs. Carter stared at him, he would point at another boy, causing that boy to shout, "It weren't me, it was him!" Giggles would erupt. When Mrs. Carter asked him to quiet down and be good, he would obey, with a triumphant grin. Ten or fifteen minutes later, he'd start another ruckus.

Mrs. Carter sat in silence, shaking her head. After a while, she closed a book, put papers into a file, and stood. "Class," she said calmly, "this afternoon you're getting out early. You can thank Mr. Murphy." A few girls clapped and there were a few subdued "Yeas," but Mrs. Carter's gaze cut it short. "Have fun this weekend, and I'll see you bright and early Monday morning."

Walking off the hill with Paul Morton, I told him I didn't like the way that Benny guy acted, making it hard to study. Who was he anyhow? "He's the son of the man that looks after the poolroom," Paul said. "The boss. Benny's what you call a clown, or somebody that thinks they're funny—always trying to make people laugh."

"I didn't think he was funny, did you?"

"Naw. I think he's crazy. You know, touched in the head." Benny looked to me like he was big enough to be in the third or fourth grade. "He'll prob'ly settle down when his carryin' on gets old to ever' body," Paul continued. "You ever played baseball, Whiller?" I shook my head. "You ain't never done nothin', have you?"

"Yeah, I've drove a car." He looked at me, shook his head, and laughed. Paul then introduced me to a whole lot of his buddies, all of them older than us. They were waiting for one of the gang to get back from the company store with some black tape. They didn't have a baseball. Paul and I watched as the tape guy took a small rock and wrapped it with paper and rags. Then used almost the whole roll of tape, making it tight and round. They did have one old bat. The ball field was an open space next to about ten car garages, like the ones at the poolroom. I mostly watched from the "outfield" as they took turns hitting. I ran down a few balls and threw them back toward the "infield." They said I had a good arm, and one day would make a good player. But, of course, I didn't have an arm. Still, I had a feeling, as remote and crazy as it seemed, that I would take to baseball like I was taking to book learning.

On Monday morning I expected to find Mrs. Carter in a tougher frame of mind. And I wondered what she'd do if Benny carried on the way he did Friday. But there was not a peep out of him. He kept his head down, eyes glued to his book. And Mrs. Carter gave him no more attention than any other student.

After class, as we walked down the hill, a boy who sat next to him in class asked him, "Why you so quiet, Benny?" No response. He just kept walking. The boy said, "Aw, come on, why you in a hurry? What's wrong, cat got 'cher tongue?" I couldn't keep up,

so I couldn't hear his reply. But Paul told me later the desk mate
told him that Benny's dad had beat the shit out of him. Said he'd
lose his poolroom manager's job if Benny didn't behave. Paul said
he bet Mr. Carter was behind it. But, looking back, I can't believe
that Mrs. Carter would have asked her husband to take care of
her school problems. I'd rather believe that Benny was crazy
enough to brag about getting the class out early, and his dad got
wind of it.

Part of the untold story about Benny came to light when one
of Paul's older buddies invited us to join him and two other guys
to sneak into the top of the poolroom to watch a black-and-white
Frankenstein movie. When people started filling up the big
room below us, mostly noisy kids, we dropped down through an
opening in the attic floor, like Greek soldiers coming down from
the belly of the Trojan horse. All of a sudden a man's booming
voice was calling for silence, as he began a speech, walking through
the puzzled crowd. In a mournful, tortured voice, he said, "I'd walk
through blood up to my knees to know who gave morphine to
my son." Paul whispered, "That's Benny Murphy's dad."

Mr. Murphy finished by begging someone, anyone, to tell him
what he wanted to know. Paul whispered, "I guess Benny ain't
just crazy, he's taking that…whatever it is…that makes him that
way. I feel sorry for 'em both." I told him I did, too.

One of my jobs was to carry water from the pump up at
the end of our row of houses, which is right where we played
baseball. A gallon bucket of water is heavy for skinny arms. I
thought it might put some meat on my bones, as Paul said, so I
told myself it was a good thing.

By the time the fourth of July rolled around, we got some
real baseballs. Anchor Coal Company had a team that played
other coal companies. Miners who had cars drove to the ball field
down on the Big Coal River, about eight miles beyond Sylvester
and Dog Patch. But kids and some parents would ride standing
in the bed of a big truck. That was more fun. Sister and Arthur

didn't think I was old enough to ride that way. But Paul Morton's parents let him do it, and Paul convinced my parents that he'd look after me.

It was all-you-could-eat hotdogs and ice cream, handed out from stands decorated with American flags. The most festive thing I'd ever seen. We'd eat 'til we popped, then sit in the stands and watch some of the game. When a foul ball came back over the stands and landed in the woods not far from the river, we boys would light out. We'd plunge into thickets, scrambling in the dirt for the ball. Sometimes a fistfight broke out between our gang and the black guys, who were fast as lightning. But we got our share of barely used baseballs. I say "we," but I contented myself by being a spotter.

Watching those pitchers throw the ball to the catcher with such lightning speed was a dazzling experience for me. I was a long way from being a baseball player, but I loved hearing the leathery sound of the ball plugging into the catcher's mitt, and the brittle crack of the bat. The sound of umpires yelling, *Yer out!* or *Safe!* almost made me flinch. Yes. I was going to take to baseball.

There was no music in my life, except for the hymns I heard at church on Sundays. But I think I missed it; I just didn't know it yet. Just like I think I missed the father I didn't have, but didn't realize it consciously. I was too busy studying and doing chores, like carrying laundry water from the creek for Sister and tending the fire under the big tubs. She stretched small sheets made from feed sacks over the tubs to strain out dirt and an occasional minnow.

I did miss Mommy, Shirley Faye, and my aunts and uncles. But I got to see them more by the time I finished the second grade at Highcoal and was riding the school bus to Whitesville to start third grade. The Wheelers had moved to Whitesville by then and now lived in a big white house up on the hill across from the Funeral Home.

FRENCH SCENE: A scene in a play in which the beginning and end are marked by a change in the presence of characters onstage.

My life in Highcoal was about to be changed—big time. On February 11, 1939, a new member of our family arrived by the name of Robert Arthur Stewart. My half brother Bobby was born, and the dynamics in the Stewart household changed, forever and ever. I was six years old, and I wasn't sure how I felt about having a younger brother. I had flashes of jealousy. Not because little Bobby had a daddy and I didn't, but because he was now the focus of Sister's attention. Who'd want a daddy anyhow, if he'd be like Arthur Stewart? On the other hand, as I would soon find out, Arthur's attention would also be centered on his son. Maybe he would stop finding fault with me. And, in fact, that is what happened. Right away, I began to see a tender side of Arthur, even though I felt like throwing up, seeing him pick up Bobby, kiss him, and call him honey.

But my life had actually improved dramatically. Whitesville Jr. High was just a quarter of a mile from the center of town. At lunchtime a lot of us would walk to Speedo's Hot Dogs, buy two dogs and a soft drink for fifteen cents, and make it back in time for afternoon classes. And on Fridays, Sister and Arthur let me walk to Mommy and Granddad's new house and spend the weekend with them. When summer came, I stayed with them for weeks at a time.

Summers in Whitesville were different from life in Highcoal, where everything was the color and smell of coal. Coal roads, coal trucks, coal smoke, and the rattle of coal buckets on wheels overhead, full of coal and riding cables from the mountain over to the tipple. Anytime you went to the poolroom or company store during working hours, those flat bins were rolling up there, occasionally sprinkling coal dust and slack onto hats and hair below.

Whitesville was a bustling metropolis compared to Highcoal. It had a movie theater, a Piggly Wiggly grocery store, furniture stores and restaurants, a bank, and Uncle Babe's Esso station. Miners from coal camps like Highcoal, Red Dragon, and Montcoal came there to shop. There was also a swimming hole on Big Coal River that was deep enough for diving from the biggest rock. Uncle Vincent taught me how to swim and hold my breath underwater there. He also taught me where to look for crawdads and how to bass fish with them. Shirley Faye and I would make kites from newspapers, using flour and water for glue. We sat on the floor to watch Mommy make dresses on her Singer sewing machine, listening to the *Amos 'n' Andy* radio show at night. Sometimes, on Saturday night, it was *The Grand Ole Opry* from Nashville.

Mrs. Carter remained an important part of my life. She hired me to clean out her chicken houses, sometimes paying me as much as twenty-five cents an hour. More importantly, she encouraged me to do well in school, telling me I would amount to something someday, and she would be proud of me. Nobody else except Mommy told me things like that. Those two beautiful women were a huge boost to my self-esteem. I had no illusions of grandeur, nor did I have any goals, unlike most of the boys I knew, who wanted to be big league baseball players.

Whitesville Jr. High was an impressive building, and as the years passed, I got chosen to appear in blackface minstrel shows, when male teachers or coaches would blacken their faces and mimic "Negroes," as they were called back then, or "colored people," exaggerating their dialect. An interlocutor, who stood at center stage, would set up jokes that minor characters like me could easily respond to, with "Sho nuff," or "At's rat, Boss." My name was Rastus.

It never occurred to me that these minstrel shows were a cultural thing, and we were making fun of a whole race of people. That sank in several years later when I was on a bus to Florida, to work for Uncle Babe at his service station in Crestview. When the bus stopped in small towns, I noticed there were "white only" and "colored only" signs by water fountains and restrooms. Once, I saw a well-dressed older black lady standing by one of these signs. In some way she reminded me of Mommy and Mrs. Carter, and I imagined this insult being done to them. It made me weep, and I saw that dignified and beautiful face in my dreams for a long time.

It was at Whitesville Jr. High that I began signing my name as Billy Edd. I don't know how it happened, but I got accustomed to telling people, "There's two d's in Edd."

My fifth grade teacher was a good-looking, extremely well-built young woman who sat on the front of her desk, with her legs crossed, to lecture to us. Her dress covered only half her legs, and of course, every boy's eyes were focused on that twelve or thirteen inches of bare female skin.

Unlike Mrs. Carter, the teachers at Whitesville *did* have paddles. When our teacher paddled, she made us bend over a desk, and, with our butts bristling, she swung that wooden paddle as only an athlete can, hitting each of us seven times in a row. She waited a few seconds after each blow, to let the blood return to our burning bottoms. By the time number seven was done, water was popping out of my eyes. And I didn't want to sit down for a long time.

In 1941, the movie *Gone with the Wind* was playing in Whitesville. It had premiered nationally in 1939. I was absolutely blown away by it. The color, the sets, the music, and the acting stretched my mind into realms I could not have imagined. It was magic, a gigantic reminder to me that there was another world out there. It inspired me, but not to the point of thinking, at that time, that someday I might be a small part of it.

Chapter Three

PAPER BOY BLUES

They say, good morning mister paper boy
Man, it ain't no good morning for me
They say good morning mister paper boy
Man, it ain't no good morning for me
Cause I hear that wind a-blowing thru them hickory trees

This was the first song I ever wrote, and it certainly isn't memorable. But it was born out of personal experience. Delivering papers in Highcoal was a hell of a tough job. I had to get up at 5:30 a.m., while it was still dark, and walk down to where the *Charleston Gazette* dropped off its papers under a porch. In freezing rain or snow, I had to fold papers with hands so cold they didn't want to work. Then walk with a very heavy bag all the way down to my black customers, putting papers behind screen doors, and finish at the last row of houses in the upper part of town. All this before eating breakfast in time to get on the bus and ride twenty miles to Sherman High School.

I had a fourteen dollar Sears & Roebuck guitar I got for Christmas. An arch-top Kay. A coal miner named Gene Green showed me those first three chords. G, C, and D. Gene could sing Eddy Arnold's "Cattle Call" exactly like Eddy. I'd never heard anything like it. I was barely able to make the chords it took to play my "Paper Boy Blues" because the strings were so high off the fret board. The tips of my fingers actually bled, and the pain was so intense I gave it up. Several times. But I really wanted to play, so I kept at it until my fingertips got callused.

> *Yes, I'm a gittar playing paper boy*
> *It hurts my fingers when I play*
> *I'm a gittar playing paper boy*
> *Hurts my fingers when I play*
> *But I feel good when I'm playing*
> *So I keep playing every day*

Paul Morton used to take me with him when he wandered around after supper. Until then, I was not allowed to stay out late. When we heard music coming from a porch, we'd sit on the steps and listen. Hearing someone play guitar and sing had a magical effect on me, especially when it was a voice like Gene Green's. I got goose bumps up my back and arms. That's when I had first started lobbying for a guitar. I was saving the money I earned from Mrs. Carter, but it would take a whole lot of chicken shit— she called it poop, or droppings—to pay for a store-bought guitar.

Before I got that guitar, things happened so fast in my life it is hard to write them down in proper sequence. It was as if I just turned around and my aunts had all got married, except Shirley Faye. Louise married a coal miner named Ben Anderson in Red Dragon, and started having the first of five boys. I could walk to their house from Whitesville Jr. High, which I did often, and she would treat me like one of her kids. I bathed in a washtub in the same water as the baby, then the second and third in line. She rinsed our heads with warm water from the stove. I wasn't ashamed to get naked in front of her and her other sons.

Aunt Jean married a scoundrel named Claude Jarrell. They lived at Peach Creek. The last time I stayed with them, I was terrified to wake up hearing them fighting in the kitchen. Dishes were breaking, and

from Jean's screams I realized that Claude had a knife and was chasing
her around the table. I ran from the house down the road in the dark
until I came to a fork, where, just by chance, Claude's mother was
walking. She shined her flashlight on me and asked what in the world
was wrong. I was still crying as I told her what was happening. She
just shook her head and said, "Claude's crazy. Ain't got a god-damned
lick-a sense. Don't worry, honey. He ain't kilt her yet. You can come
up to the house and stay all night with me, if you want to."

Uncle Babe had joined the army. Uncle James had joined the
navy. And Uncle Vincent had married June Cook and was living
with the Cooks in Dorothy.

I could never feel comfortable in the house with Sister and
Arthur. It is hard to express feelings of love in the presence of
someone you dislike, especially the lord and master of the house, so
I could not be affectionate with my mother. I resented Arthur for
denying me that privilege. And I outright hated him for the times
I saw him slapping Sister. The worst was when he stopped the car,
ran around to her door, jerked her from her seat, and dragged her
out in front of the headlights. He was scolding her in a mean tone
of voice as he slapped the left and right sides of her face, open
handed and back handed. She never let out a sound, while I cried
wildly and cursed him, hitting the back of his seat with my fists
until my knuckles felt burned and raw. Even now, as I look back, it
seems bizarre that he would want her in the headlights. Unless it
was to hurt me and teach me some kind of lesson.

After I graduated from ninth grade at Whitesville, I started riding
the bus twenty miles to Sherman High School at Seth. My favorite
class was English, especially when the emphasis was on public
speaking. I did well enough to be invited by a senior girl who was
putting together some kind of big show to which parents were
invited. She gave me the lyrics to "Dark Town Poker Club," a song
by Phil Harris, and played his record over and over so I could learn it.
There was no melody, just rapid-fire speaking. The way he performed
the song would be called rapping today. It was about a guy playing

poker in the black section of town, with a one-eyed dealer who was cheating. So the singer gets fed up after a while, rises, and says, "I'll refrain from mentioning the party's name, but if I catch him cheating just once again, I'll take my fist and close that other eye."

I was so nervous before I walked on stage I had to go to the bathroom twice. My legs felt frozen. But I did make it to center stage, and once I got a little bit into the song and saw how people were smiling I relaxed. It tickled me to death that my performance went over so well. Even Arthur paid me a compliment. He said, "I didn't know you could get up in public and do something like that." I said, "I didn't know it, either." I'm certain that song had a huge influence on my future songwriting, especially songs with spoken verses, like "The Reverend Mister Black."

We dressed up for Sunday school and church. I wore knickers and knee-length socks and tried to sing along with the hymns, like "The Old Rugged Cross," but I couldn't figure out if I was a bass or was supposed to sing the melody higher. But one summer a black preacher, or choir leader, was teaching shape note singing in the evenings. He was short of stature, but he was full of fire about singing. I had never heard anything like it, everybody singing do-re-mi's instead of words. But the preacher was so enthusiastic, jumping up and down and waving his hands, conducting, he made it fun. He was full of compliments and praised us to high heaven when we sang to please him.

I got into a new job when Gerald Stewart, Arthur's first cousin, became manager of the company store. I was a delivery boy. The store was about twenty-five yards above the road, a steep climb for many customers, so many of them just placed orders. We boys had to carry heavy bags or boxes to their houses. When we got an order from the doctor's house, or from other big shots, the anticipation of a big tip was exciting to think about. But it seldom paid off. It was the poor people who tipped the most. Usually a dime.

Once, when I was returning from a delivery, I heard a siren wailing so loud you could hear it all over Highcoal. A sound

every woman dreaded, because it meant a bad accident had
happened, and one of them might have lost a husband, a son, or
some other relative. Usually because of a slate fall in the mine.
As I reached the path, I saw three or four men up ahead, one
kneeling and the others standing in the road next to the steps of
the store. They were looking down at something. Some people up
on the porch were looking down too, but nobody was talking.

I hurried up to see that two more men were kneeling; it was
"Uncle" Gerald (as I called him, since he was my stepfather's cousin)
and a man with a first aid kit, both looking down at the miner lying
on a stretcher. The miner's black face was cracked and broken, in
contrast to the white skin next to his hair line, where his hard hat
had been. As the first aid man poured some sort of liquid into a gap
in the miner's forehead, I almost fainted when I saw it drain out of a
crack in his jaw, mixed with blood. I cringed and turned away. Gerald
got up and led me gently to the steps, where we sat in silence. He
put his arm around me. Soon an ambulance came and took the man
away. Gerald said, "It's an awful thing, seeing something like that. You
just have to put it out of your mind." I nodded, as if agreeing with
him. But I had a feeling I would never forget that man's dying face.

RED WINGED BLACK BIRD

Oh don't you see that pretty little bird
Singing with all his heart and soul
He's got a blood red spot on his wings
All the rest of him's black as coal
Of all the colors I ever did see
Red and black are the two I dread
For when a man spills blood on the coal
They carry him down from the coal mines dead
Fly away you red winged bird
Leave behind the miner's wife
She'll dream about you when you're gone
She'll dream about you all her life

As if to change the subject, so to speak, from what we'd seen, Gerald told me that when I took groceries to the boardinghouse, near the bottom of the road, I could take a shower in the bathhouse there. If there were miners showering, he said they wouldn't pay any attention to me. But I paid attention to them. The first time I did it, I was amazed at the sight of men with black faces and arms, with pure white bodies. They kidded me a lot when I was shy about getting naked in front of them, but I soon got over it. They shared their soap and towels with me.

A few of the miners were boxers for Anchor Coal Company, and one of them, a young man of about twenty, invited me to come and train with him. His name was Willie, but he boxed by the name of Wild Man Morton, famous for howling like a catamount when he was close to beating his opponent. Sometimes I timed him with a stopwatch. But most of the time I threw a basketball-sized padded leather ball at his gut. He called it his medicine ball.

The trainer was a professional named Johnny Protan, the nationally ranked number two boxer in his class in America. After seeing me helping Willie work out for a while, Johnny asked me if I'd like to work out myself. I said sure, flattered as all get-out. So I worked out for a week or so, and he set me up for three rounds against Eddie Joe McConnell. When I won the match, Johnny said, "I think you're a natural. How's about I set up another three rounder?" I was elated. Two weeks later, Johnny introduced me to a slender black kid named Dexter Johnson. He was soft-spoken and well mannered. I looked at him and thought, *This guy's a pushover.* But I was wrong. Dead wrong. Within two minutes, Johnny had to stop the fight. My nose was gushing blood. I said, "Johnny, I don't think boxing's my sport. My nose bleeds too easy."

"Aw, don't worry about it," he said. "You get your nose broke a couple of times, and that gristle in there'll toughen up. I know from experience." I stopped working out, and by the end of the next year, Dexter Johnson won the featherweight Golden Gloves championship of West Virginia.

By the time I turned eleven, brother Bobby was four, and we were good friends. That Christmas, he and I went hunting for a Christmas tree. We climbed up to the railroad and headed down toward Fern Dale, a half mile or so, before I spotted a nice tall tree with a perfect top. But by the time I had climbed to the top with my hatchet, Bobby was getting cold. So I cut the tree top off, as quickly as I could, and watched it fall into the snow below.

When I got to the ground, Bobby's lips had turned blue and he was shivering badly. There was no way I could drag that tree with one hand, and Bobby with the other, so I left the tree. We started home. After a while, Bobby's feet and legs were so cold he couldn't walk. I helped him onto my back. He put his arms around my neck and I held on to his legs. I carried him the last half mile back up the tracks, and then down to the house. Arthur was not pleased that his baby had suffered so, and he let me know it.

The atmosphere was still frigid in the house on Christmas morning. I could not fully express my joy at getting that guitar from Santa Claus, aka Arthur Stewart. Sister didn't let me off the hook. "What do you say to your stepdad?" she said. When I thanked Arthur, he flipped a hand at me and said, "That's all right. Now, you can take that money you got from Mrs. Carter and start you a bank account down in Whitesville. You're not too young to start saving."

In spite of the hardship I endured delivering newspapers, collecting the money from my customers was even harder. I would go to the back porch and knock, and when the lady of the house came out, and I told her I was collecting, a typical reply would be, "Honey, I ain't got no money. You'll have to get it from my husband. He's prob'ly at the poolroom, drinking and gambling."

At the poolroom, Mr. Murphy would let me go in the back and talk to the husband, who would say something like, "That lyin' hussy. She handles all the money. Don't let her tell you no different."

I lost my paper boy job, and was glad of it. It gave me more time to chase girls. The first one I dated was Helen Anderson, but we didn't call it dating. I was "going with" her. Paul Morton was going with Cookie Henderson. It started on the school bus, going to Sherman High and back, twenty miles, one way. A school bus could get rowdy. The girls would let you know they liked you by hitting you over the head with a book or by jabbing you in the ribs with an elbow, screaming like a banshee with laughter. Sometimes a fight would break out, and the driver would kick us off the bus. We'd have to walk or hitchhike home. When it snowed, we'd pair up and sleigh ride down the hill. Helen and I would double up on one sled, taking turns being on the bottom. We had lots of clothes on, but it was still exciting to have such close contact.

When I was twelve-and-a-half years old, a woman came to Highcoal to teach vacation Bible school. She didn't call herself a missionary, but Sister told me she was from the Presbyterian Board of National Missions in New York City. Her name was Shirley Jo Smith, and her brother, Walter, looked to be four or five years older than me. Well dressed and very polite. I guess they spoke with a New York accent—how would I know? But where I said caint, poosh, and boosh, they said can't, push, and bush. In addition to Bible studies, Miss Smith and Walter took us on hikes, and we played softball. Once, Walter invited me to accompany him to their apartment, located on the top floor of the company store, so he could put on his hiking shoes. As we entered, he said, "Please excuse the way this place looks. We're still settling in." Why was he apologizing? It made me think, once again, there was a world out there that I knew nothing about.

Miss Smith reminded me of Mommy and Mrs. Carter. She had kind eyes and a pleasant way of speaking. And listening. It made you feel like you'd known her forever. Time and again she told us about a Presbyterian-related school called Warren Wilson in a beautiful valley in North Carolina. They had a high school and two years of college, all together. And if you couldn't afford the $250 for tuition, you could go a few weeks early and work on the farm or dairy. Then they would knock off a big chunk of it. I told her it sounded like a good deal, but there was no way my stepdad would pay for even half of it.

As she talked, a gleam appeared in Paul Morton's eyes I'd never seen before. He asked, "Do they have a baseball team?" She said they did, and they were working on putting in a swimming pool. He said, "I'd like to go right now. This summer. Could I, if my parents agreed?"

Miss Smith said she thought so, but she'd have to make some calls to be sure. And just like that, I said goodbye to my best friend and mentor as he got on a Greyhound bus in Whitesville. I felt sorry for myself immediately. But before I could sink deeper into depression, I found out that the Wheelers had moved yet again when Granddad came to Highcoal to visit us. He said Shirley Faye needed someone to play with over there in Eskdale, in Kanawha County, where they'd moved. Sister and Arthur said I could go with him to stay with Shirley Faye and the family for a while, so I put some clothes in a shopping bag and followed him up the steep path through the weeds until we reached the railroad.

After walking about thirty yards, we tiptoed across a cattle guard and entered a big tunnel. When we rounded a curve and it got darker, Granddad took the tip off a flare and rubbed the scratchy part of it across the end, causing it to burst into a searing red flame. It lit up the walls of the tunnel like some sort of candle from hell, the smoke from it smelling acrid. It burned my eyes. He said, "This fuzee'll last till we reach yon end, about a mile. We got to walk fast." Water dripped from the ceiling, making the cross ties slippery. When we reached the end, we walked down a rocky path past the Kayford tipple and got a ride to Eskdale from one of Grandad's friends.

Mommy's welcoming hugs filled my heart with joy. And Shirley Faye couldn't wait to tell me about some friends she'd met, one of whom, Jack West, was about my age. He played the guitar. The new Wheeler house was a nondescript, two-story, dark brown building, the first of three in a row. The last one was near the creek, beyond which the mountain went straight up. There was a pump in the yard, with an outhouse standing out at the edge of the large property.

Just like Jarrolds Valley, the house was close to the railroad tracks, and it faced a dirt lane. The first evening, after eating pinto beans and cornbread, Shirley Faye and I lay on top of the bed, on each side of Mommy, while she read to us. She held a thick book I had seen back in Whitesville, but never tried to read, called *For Whom the Bell Tolls*. I liked stories from *Reader's Digest* or *Farmer's Almanac*. In spite of being excited, I dozed off several times.

The next day, Shirley Faye took me to meet Jack West and his older sister, Rose. Jack was shy and wasn't too keen on playing his guitar for me. Jack handed me the guitar and asked me to play something. When I started singing the "Paper Boy Blues," he smiled and his attitude changed. I figured he was thinking, *Well, shit, I'm way better'n he is*. He asked me to play something else, but I told him it was the only song I knew. He took the guitar and began playing, obviously better than me. When I started to leave to return to Mommy's house, Rose gave me a hug and told me to please come back. Much older than her little brother Jack, Rose was a large woman. I'd heard it said, "fleshy." To me, she was chubby, handsomely so, and carried it well.

Within a week, Uncle Vincent came to Eskdale from Highcoal. As soon as he got out of the car, he held up my guitar and said, "I betche you been missing this." He laughed, seeing my smile. "I knowed ye did." Vincent was the most good-natured man I ever met. And generous. He also knew where the hotdogs were. The next afternoon, he took Shirley Faye and me down the lane to pick up my new guitar-playing friend, Jack. Rose not only said it was OK for Jack to go with us, I think she wanted to go, too. Vincent favored chubby women, and I think Rose felt it. There was a shine in her smile when she said, "Now, don't you let these young'uns founder on hotdogs. I'll cook 'em a good supper, and you're invited."

Jack had an older brother, Carl, who could *really* pick a guitar. He played riffs and runs up and down the neck that dazzled me. He was a coal miner, but I learned he had also had a career as a professional softball player. But after a short and successful career, Carl decided he'd rather mine coal and be happy than live in the big city and be homesick. West Virginia called him home, and he answered.

Sometimes a small crowd would gather next to the covered porch when Carl was showing me and Jack how to make chords on the guitar. Two brothers, Tom Black and his brother Ben, would always stay the longest. I found out that they lived in the house where I sometimes heard preaching in the evening after supper, on my way to Jack's house. We became good friends, and thirty years later, after my Kingston Trio hit, "The Reverend Mister Black," Tom called me from Charleston and said he needed a favor. He was running against a rich man for Kanawha County Commissioner and was thirty-five points behind. He said if I'd make him a short tape, saying the song was about his dad, it might be a big help. I told Tom I couldn't outright lie, but I would make the tape. Almost overnight, the polls shifted in Tom's favor.

The next time I went to Jack's house, he and Carl were playing and talking about some songs they'd learned from a group over in another county. Carl said they met often to sit around in a circle, playing old tunes like "Worried Man Blues" and some traditional folk songs. I asked Carl what "traditional" meant. He said, "It's songs handed down from one generation to the next.

'Pretty Polly' and 'Barbry Allen' and such. Lots of 'em go back to the old countries, England, and so on. Ain't much tradition in coal camps, people coming and going, not settin' down roots, 'specially foreign workers, Hungarians, Poles, and such. But here's one old tune that every gittar player in the world learns how to play, whether they can sing or not. It's 'Wildwood Flower,' and it sounds traditional, but it ain't, 'cause somebody wrote it to start with. Way back in the eighteen hundreds, I heard from the group. Because the song is so long, one guy in the group took part of the first verse and combined it with one of the last verses. Goes like this..." He played and sang:

> I'll twine with the mingles of my raven black hair
> The lilies so pale and the roses so fair
> I'll live yet to see him regret the dark hour
> When he won then neglected the frail wildwood flower

"The Carter family had a hit with it, and Maybelle Carter played it the 'Carter scratch' way," playing the melody and the rhythm at the same time. Now, boys, that's some trick, and I ain't learned it yet."

I said, "Uncle Carl, you're the best I ever heard."

"Hear that, Jack?" Carl said. "Billy respects his elders. Listen to him and take lessons. Now, boys, I'll sing you one that is pure-out traditional, 'Froggy Went a-Courting.'"

I'd never heard it, so I listened carefully. I think I fell in love with folk music right then and there. Jack and Carl advanced my musical ability and knowledge by leap years. And, living in Eskdale with a loving family filled me with a contentment I hadn't felt since Jarrolds Valley. I felt blessed, and one of those blessings was a little white dog named Sugar, an Eskimo spitz. We had no dog in Highcoal, so I had never witnessed how much joy a dog could bring to a family. I noticed that when relationships get strained, even between people who love each other, they can always pet the dog and show affection. Dogs are ambassadors of love, and when Sugar got run over by a car and died, I cried and walked the railroad tracks for days.

I thought I understood sadness when Sugar died, but when Mommy died, on December 31, 1946, I found out what *real* crying was about. Shirley Faye and I wept on each other's shoulders. Our fountainhead of joy and happiness was gone. Walking the railroad tracks didn't help this time. Only being in the woods made me feel a little better. For a while. But nothing could go deep enough to offer me real solace.

After the funeral, Granddad sent Shirley Faye to Florida to live with Uncle Babe. I rode back to Highcoal with Bobby and Sister in Arthur's car, and was really surprised to find that Paul Morton was home from Warren Wilson on Christmas break. It raised my spirits immensely to hear him tell how much he liked the school, the showers in the dorm, and the mountains of North Carolina. He said I'd be a plain fool not to find some way to come down and join him.

On the way home from Eskdale, even though I was still in mourning for Mommy, I decided to work harder at getting along with Arthur. And it really worked…for about two weeks. Then one night, after I dried the dishes, Sister said she would finish with the pots and pans for me. Arthur came into the kitchen and told me I wasn't done. When I said I couldn't stand doing the greasy pots and pans, and besides, it was girls' work, Arthur said, "I told you to do it, so do it." When I protested, and said that Sister volunteered to help, he slapped me. He had never hit me before. I was stunned. He went to the sink and grabbed the dish towel.

He threw it at me. I let it drop to the floor. He slapped me again, so hard it caused me to lose my balance and fall down. I got up, crying, and yelled, "You shitass!" I had never cursed at an adult in my life. Arthur threw a punch at me, but I was already reaching down for the dish towel, so it just grazed the side of my head. Arthur turned and went into the living room. Sister came and took the dish towel from me. It was an act of bravery. But I tried to make her give it back, afraid of what Arthur might do. She wouldn't, so I let it go and hoped for the best.

The next morning, I left the house, my school lunch bag in hand, and headed down toward the poolroom, as if to catch the school bus. Across from Mrs. Carter's house, I instead climbed a faint path through the weeds up to the railroad tracks and turned back toward the tunnel. I'd made up my mind I was getting away from Arthur and going back to Granddad's. I broke off a small limb from a poplar sapling and used it to rub along the rails in the dark. Without a light or a flare like Granddad had used, it was slow going, and I fell several times. But I didn't care.

Twenty minutes later, the far end of the tunnel had become the size of a basketball, but suddenly it went dark, and I heard an unmistakable noise. A big cold hand squeezed my heart so hard it made me shiver. A train was coming. Without a light I couldn't run back, and walking fast on the slippery ties, with only a poplar branch for a guide, was impossible. I had to make a decision— stand with my back to the wall of the tunnel, or lie down in the watery ditch. Standing was preferable, I thought, but if it was a C&O coal train, there might be metal rods or something sticking out. My belly could be sliced open. Or I could be hooked and dragged along with the train, or sucked under the steel wheels.

The rails set up a humming vibration that was enough to make the crosstie I was standing on start to shake. I figured I had maybe a minute left, but the debate was over. I lay in the ditch, resting my head on one forearm, with the other across my head, my elbow partly covering my face. This hand held my lunch sack away from the water. The rails were now about a foot above my head, resting on ties laid across a bed of heavy, egg-sized gravel that sloped down to where I lay.

As the train thundered over me, the crossties jolted up and down spastically, knocking chunks of gravel loose that sometimes hit my elbow or my side. I could see sparks shooting from the rails. I smelled coal smoke, thick and acrid all around me, hot in my nostrils. After the train was gone, I rolled up onto the gravel, but stayed down for several minutes, hoping the smoke would clear or rise to the top of the tunnel, allowing me to get up and walk without having to breathe much of it.

When I stood up, the sandwich and apple rolled out of my lunch bag, along with the piece of gravel that had shot into it, causing it to tear. I heard the apple bounce and plunk into water. But the sandwich, wrapped in waxed paper, landed safely on a crosstie. I picked it up and stuffed it into a front pocket, felt around in the water until I found the apple, and put it in my other pocket, the one containing twenty-five cents. I would eat a good lunch later. First, I had a half-mile of smoky tunnel left to negotiate.

I walked and caught rides from Kayford to Eskdale, wondering all the way what Granddad would say. Would he be home? Would he let me batch it with him? He was home but was too tired, he said, to talk about it tonight. He was saved from telling me his decision when Sister and Arthur drove up the next day. Granddad told me it was best for me to go back with them. Reluctantly, I got in the car. Once again, I told myself I had nowhere else to go, and I'd better make up my mind to try harder to live peacefully with Arthur. But all the way home he chided me with comments like, "You know which side your bread's buttered on. Huh? You better think twice about running off. We might not come after you the next time. Huh?"

The next morning, history repeated itself. But this time I had a flashlight. Granddad listened to me tell him how miserable I was, living in Highcoal under Arthur's thumb. He studied my face for a long time, as if he'd never seen me before. Then he gave a nod and went to bed.

I played hooky more than I went to school. The truant officer left notes for Granddad several times. He ignored them. But when the vegetables we planted in Granddad's garden just barely started popping up, he got impatient and bought some green beans from Mexico, or Central America, at the grocery store. He made me watch carefully as he washed the beans, put them in a pan half-filled with water, and added a chunk of fat back. He said, "Now, Billy, I want you to let these beans simmer real slow, and ever' half hour to a hour, add some water. We'll have 'em for supper with some corn bread. My, my, that'll be good eatin'."

It was a weekend, so Tom and Ben, those two Mexican boys, and a couple of their friends came by, and we ended up playing football with an empty Carnation milk can. It was a rough and noisy game, and I forgot all about the green beans. Until I smelled them. My heart sank. I rushed in and pulled the pot of beans from the stove. I was frantic. I added cold water and started lifting out the unburned beans. I scraped the pot and tossed away the burned beans, put the good beans back in with the fat back, put the pot back on the stove, and prayed. When Granddad came in that evening, his nose wrinkled and twitched. He knew the beans were burned, and I knew I was in deep trouble. He sat down and lowered his head, shook it sadly, and told me I had to go home. He said, "I cain't trust you no more. And you need to be with Sister."

The next morning, I hitchhiked to Kayford, walked through the tunnel, and with my tail tucked between my legs walked down the path from the railroad. Every step jarred my innards and burned my heart.

Sister was glad to see me, but she knew I was hurting inside. I think Arthur actually felt sorry for me. He didn't gloat or rub it in. And when I said I wanted to talk to Shirley Jo Smith about going to Warren Wilson next year to continue my high school education, Sister told me Arthur would help, if I went early and worked off half of the tuition. Miss Smith helped me write a letter to Dr. Henry W. Jensen, Dean of Warren Wilson Jr. College.

In mid-June, 1948, I got on a Greyhound bus, leaving the hills of home bound for the mountains surrounding a college town with the funny name of Swannanoa. The president of the college, Dr. Arthur M. Bannerman, said Swannanoa was an Indian name that meant "beautiful valley." Some of the college boys said Swannanoa was an Indian name that meant "last stop for beer this side of Knoxville."

All I know is that as soon as I boarded the Greyhound in Whitesville and sat down, a man reached across the aisle and offered me a drink of whiskey. I said, "No thank you, sir." And I thought, once again, *Yep, it's a big world out there, and I've sure got a lot to learn.*

Chapter Four

ASHEVILLE

If I could write a love song to a city
I'd pretend that Asheville was my girl
Then I could say of all the lovely ladies I have seen
Asheville, you're the most beautiful in the world
—Look homeward angel, hmmm—

I walked through the stone gates of Warren Wilson and headed toward a large red brick building. A man was ambling toward me who obviously was not sent to meet me. But he introduced himself as Bill Diehl, younger brother of the minister, Irving Diehl. He took me into the building and introduced me to an elderly lady who was the dorm manager, Eila Carson. Her room was quite dark, but not too dark for me to miss her winking at me. A nervous tick, I supposed. She took me upstairs to my room and pointed out the bathroom and showers. I was deliriously happy to have my own room. And thrilled to be able to take a shower anytime I wanted to.

My first job was cutting thistles on the hillside pasture, between the dairy and two women's dorms above. I had a feeling this was make work. But the next week I cleaned out stalls in the barn by shoveling manure-soaked straw, and the following week helped put shingles on a section of small barn roof down at the farm. I was earning my tuition, and I loved it.

The dining room was downstairs below the first floor, and the food was just as Paul Morton said: delicious. I was eating combinations of food I'd never had before, salads and vegetables from the college gardens. There was lots of meat, also from the college farm, with green beans, butter beans, and mashed potatoes, and always fresh bread daily (and occasionally pastries) baked by a Danish dietician, Catherine Laursen. We ate family style. If you took the last helping of something, you carried the bowl back to the kitchen counter and someone, usually a student, would refill it.

In addition to Paul Morton, I met some other guys from West Virginia. One night, when a pickup basketball game was going on in Bryson, the gym, near Sunderland Hall. Roland Pettry, from Pettus, West Virginia, headed up one team. Nathan "Sharpie" Sharp, from Ridgeview, headed up the other. As the odd man out, I was appointed referee. The players pretty much refereed themselves, but when the action got hot, I called a hefty guy named Sam Owens for walking. He approached me and said, "I wasn't walking." I told him he took more than two steps, so it looked like walking to me. Without any warning, he punched me hard in my right eye. I was totally shocked. He threw another punch, but I managed to see it coming in time to make it a glancing blow. I started punching him back, using all the boxing advice Johnny Protan had given me, but with only one eye I was not doing well. I was relieved when Paul grabbed Sam from behind, and Sharpie stepped in between us. Sam was trying to get free of Paul's grasp, and Paul barked something in his ear that sounded like, "Back off, you sucker-punchin' bastard."

By morning my eye was black and swollen, and I was in a funk. For some reason it made me feel homesick. Ashamed to go down to breakfast, I had the urge of old to go for a walk in the woods. But I had not yet become acquainted with the woods bordering the campus. So I walked down to the farm, in the dwindling rain, and found a spot with a good view of the mountains. Fluffy patches of white clouds swirled up out of the coves, and I suddenly had the oddest feeling that I had witnessed this scene

before. Maybe in the Scottish Highlands. But I had never heard of
the Scottish Highlands. In a past life? It was a puzzling sensation,
but a welcome one. In those moments, I had forgotten about my
black eye. It was ugly, but I could live with it now.

I did go to the infirmary, and Miss Jones rubbed something on
my eye that smelled funny. She said it was the arnica in the salve,
and it had healing qualities. But only time would make the black
go away. She said, "Have you been to the dentist lately?" I shook
my head. "Have you ever been to a dentist? I said, "No, ma'am."

"Well, those three front teeth need to be looked at. My guess
is they'll need to come out. I told her I was horrified at the idea
of losing three front teeth, not just because it was bound to hurt
something awful, but because I could never smile again. She said, "Of
course you can. Nobody will see you without those teeth. Before
the dentist pulls them, you'll be fitted for three new teeth. As soon as
those rotten ones come out, your brand-new ones will be put in."

"I'll be wearing false teeth? Like old people?"

"It's called a partial. Don't worry, you'll be proud of your new
smile. We'll do it first thing when you get back from the holiday."

"Uh, I don't think I'll be going home for Christmas. It's a
awful long ride on the bus, and you have to change two times,
and wait and wait." She nodded understandingly, but I was sure
she knew the real reason was that I couldn't afford a dentist and
a new set of teeth. She said it could wait until after the summer
break. But not any longer.

> Asheville, land of the sky, fed by rushing mountain streams
> Asheville, you're a southern lady, and you're the girl of my dreams
> We got cloggers here and loggers, bear hunters & football punters
> By the score
> Got tobacco growers and pottery throwers, painters, thinkers
> Writers, weavers, we got nationalities galore
> From the winos and the ladies on Lexington Avenue
> To the Biltmore House and Gardens, there is no place like you
> —Look homeward angel—hmmmm—

The summer melted into August. I started exploring the hills north of Suicide Ridge, just above the baseball field, crossing over into a community with a wonderful view of the mountains to the west. I sat on a big well-worn log for about ten minutes one day when a little girl plopped down on the end of it, jarring me out of my reverie. About seven or eight, and cute as a button, she said, "Are you from the college?" I said yes. "My mom said she bet you was." She pointed up the hill. "I live up there." She sat and looked at the view with me for a few minutes, then said, "That big tall mountain is Mount Pisgah. And that part of it, lower down, Mom says, is the Rat. Mount Pisgah and the Rat." I nodded and sat looking. Then I looked over at her and said, "You know what?" She shook her head. "I think I'd like to paint a picture of Mount Pisgah and the Rat." Her eyes lit up, and she asked if I was a...a whatchamacallit. I said, "Artist?" She said yes, that was it. I said, "No, but I'm thinking I might like to be."

Before school ended the following May, I went to the dean's office and asked Dr. Jensen if I could return early again. He surprised me by saying that if I came even earlier, I could attend tuition free. And with a little twinkle in his nervous eyes, he said, "Perhaps you could use some of the money you'll save to pay for your new front teeth." That flabbergasted me, and I left the office smiling big and saying to myself, "Thank you, Miss Jones."

Uncle Vincent came to give me a ride home, and I just about talked his ear off about all the things I was learning, and even though the work was hard, I was enjoying it. He said, "That's good, but wait till you use a double-handled scythe seven or eight hours a day." My puzzled look made him laugh and say, "Arthur talked to Mister Carter, and he's giving you a job cutting weeds." I asked how much I'd get paid. "Buck an hour. You'll have to get a pair of hard-toed shoes at the company store. Sister said Arthur said they'd give you some scrip to buy 'em with."

We came to the base of a mountain, and he said I had to help him. His carburetor wasn't pumping enough gas going uphill.

He placed a piece of plywood on the rear bumper and had me kneel on it. He took the gas cap off. "I want you to blow into the tank as hard as you can. Don't you dare breathe in with your mouth. Just your nose, and blow hard, like you're blowin' up a big balloon. Can you do it?" I gave a nod, eager to help.

My brother Bob acted like he was really glad to see me. There weren't many boys to play with up where they lived. Bobby and I walked down the railroad tracks to the place where I cut down the Christmas tree, then carried him home on my back when he got so cold he couldn't walk. He couldn't get enough of my stories about Warren Wilson, and in a way, he looked upon me as extra special, like a celebrity or something. Bobby told me he was getting to like basketball at Whitesville Junior High and thought that when he got bigger and started going to Sherman High, he was going to try out for the team. He said his dad didn't like the idea, afraid he might get hurt. But he was going to do it anyway. I said, "Good for you, brother Bob. Stick to your guns."

Sister and Arthur were glad I was back home, too, Sister more than Arthur, of course. I was surprised at how much I enjoyed being back in Highcoal. A young staffer at Warren Wilson had congratulated me on "escaping" from West Virginia. I corrected him, saying I was never depressed living in the mountain state. Except for the trouble I had with Arthur, it was my disposition to be upbeat. Even if we had to sweep our yards instead of mowing them, life seemed normal.

Mowing weeds and high grass was not something to brag about, I soon found out. It was really hard work, especially perched on the side of the hill below the company store, swinging a scythe that got heavier and heavier by the hour. For two weeks then, I got on a low-slung motor with an arm that reached up to the heavy wire that provided the juice to run it. I sat with miners and rode thorough a section of mountain to where they let me off, saying they would pick me up on the way back. As they rode away, the motorman yelled back, "Watch your head, boy! Touch that wire and you'll get a hell of a headache, if it don't kill ye!"

This was lonesome work. But worse, that thick, bare, high-voltage wire was always on my mind. It was head high, and between dodging it and watching for snakes, I was way beyond nervous. A big fan ran constantly nearby, pushing air into the mine shaft. To relieve the boredom, I started humming along with it, then harmonizing with it, and making up nonsensical lines and phrases.

> *Hmmmm, here I am on the side of a hill, hmmmm*
> *Makin' mon-mon-money if I don't get killed, yeahhhh*
> *Great big thunderbolt next to my head, hmmm*
> *Fry my brains and kill me dead-dead-dead ah-ummm*
> *Money gonna buy me a brand-new smile, uh huhhhhh*
> *Mouth fulla blood a-chokin' my lungs with bile hmmm*

I got a break from swinging the scythe and was put to washing houses with Eddie Jo McConnell and Harry White. Some other boys got stuck with working on the honey wagon. Being a honey dipper was the worst stinking job imaginable. I finished the summer unloading bags of cement from box cars. Each bag of cement weighed ninety-two pounds. Seven hours of that and I was done in. But it was worth it. All told, I made almost three hundred dollars.

Chapter Five

WINTER SKY

Out under the winter sky / out under the winter sky
Stars come trembling on my eye / stars to tremble my eye
And I feel like something's gonna die / I feel like something's gonna die
I feel like something's gonna die / Hand me wings for to fly

The dentist on Pack Square said to me, "Son, this is not going to hurt much at all. So just relax and enjoy the view." What I saw out the window was a tall monument of granite, or stone. Probably in honor of a Confederate general, I thought, or a governor named Pack. I found out later that the monument was erected to honor Governor Zebulon Vance and that George Pack donated the land.

The dentist was right; it was not too painful. The partial was inserted right into my bloody gums. The dentist shook my hand, and the nurse held a mirror up to let me check out my new smile. I was amazed. I liked it.

Miss Schafer said she liked it too, but was more interested in what it cost. I told her the dentist's bill was ninety dollars, twenty for each tooth, and thirty for the partial. That left me with about a hundred and ninety bucks. She said, "You should bring it to me tomorrow morning. I'll keep it for you in the safe." The next day I took the money to her, but told her I wanted to keep thirty dollars.

A week later when I went to the dentist for my checkup, which went fine, I hurried to the store on the corner and bought the artist's carry box, or one like it. Two weeks later, after I'd read the pamphlet's instructions for beginners, I hiked over Suicide Ridge and sat once again on the log below the house. I was sketching Mount Pisgah and the Rat when, sure enough, the little girl came down and sat beside me. "Who are you?" I asked. She frowned, looking disappointed, and said, "I'm me. Don't you remember?" I shook my head. "No, the girl I remember was smaller and wasn't as cute as you."

She laughed. "You're silly. I'm still me." I gave her an extra big smile and kept sketching. She said, "You look different." I thought she was awfully observant for such a youngster. After a few minutes, she said, "I can draw better than you." I told her I didn't doubt it and asked if she'd like to draw with me? Her eyes lit up like they did last year. I gave her a pencil and pad. She started drawing on the top sheet and soon wanted to paint. I gave her a small brush and two tubes of paint, blue and yellow. She stuck the brush into the tubes and started smearing it onto the paper. When she put yellow on top of blue, she exclaimed, "Look! It's turning green." I said, "So is your dress. I think you'd better go up to the house and let your mom change you into something else." She nodded and her lips pooched out, admitting she'd screwed up. Within half an hour she returned and handed me a warm sweet roll. I thanked her, ate the delicious roll, and started packing up. It was dark when I got back to the campus.

My second year at Warren Wilson I learned how to use the electric milkers and how to strip by hand the cows whose teats were injured or were suffering from mastitis. Within weeks my forearms were muscle bound, as big as my calves. My grip would have held its own with the best insurance salesmen. A boy from Bogota, Columbia, Sammy Loiza, had taken over my job of

climbing to the top of the silo and shoveling silage down to feed
to the cows, along with doling out commercial feed.

When classes began, I was assigned a roommate named Aziz
Sharooz, from Iran. Aziz was high strung, with intense, moist eyes,
and could get emotional in a heartbeat over almost anything. But
he was kind hearted and neat, a good roommate. Right off, he
scrunched his nose and said, "What is it that I smell?" I explained
that it was the dairy work clothes hanging in my closet, which I
would try to keep closed all the time. He waved it off and said,
"No matter. I get...what you say...okay with it."

We had required chapel every week in the log building that
served as the church, a movie house almost every week, and a
stage for putting on plays. It was the time when announcements
were made, and often Dr. Jensen would sing an original song,
playing his guitar left handed and upside down. On one occasion,
he introduced the song by saying:

> *A country road forks at Gunnertown. But there is no*
> *town. From this lonesome spot came one of my students.*
> *A little house at the back of the cove was humble indeed.*
> *But it was home. It was Gunnertown.*

Then he sang:

> *There are few homes in Gunnertown. Folks just moved away*
> *No one rents in Gunnertown. Couldn't make it pay*
> *Timber's gone, the land's wore out, the hills return to God*
> *And broom sedge and field pine, briars and goldenrod*
> *They are the ones in Gunnertown, as reckon they can stay*

He finished the song, and I was entranced. Here was a man
who wrote songs based on real-life experiences. My first thought
was, "Wow, I wish I could do that." To write a song, play it that
well, standing up in front of a crowd with such confidence and

ease, was an accomplishment I could only dream about. And
dream I would. But to "Doc" Jensen, as he was known, it was
almost like an ongoing hobby. With a doctorate from Harvard,
he served as dean, admissions director, botany professor, and,
of special importance to me, he was also an artist. One of the
announcements made that day at chapel was that he was giving
a lecture on painting, and those interested could come and listen
to him talk as he painted. A couple of weeks later, I attended his
demonstration, sitting on the ground with a group that included
two faculty members, a housewife, a student named Robert, and
the president's wife, Mrs. Bannerman. She sat on a low rock wall
directly above me.

At lunch a few days later, Miss Schafer told me that Mrs.
Bannerman would be glad to have me accompany her on a field
trip. She would pick me up, and if I had questions she would
try to answer them. According to Miss Schafer, Mrs. Bannerman
paid a dollar to join a painting class in Asheville every so often.
Of course, I was thrilled and couldn't wait to brag to Paul and
Sharpie that I was going to start learning how to paint. And my
teacher *and* my chauffeur would be the first lady herself. Being
West Virginia boys, they were quick to tell me that if I started
getting the "big head," they would kick my ass up between my
shoulder blades.

What a teacher and what a lady Mrs. Bannerman was! She
put me at ease at once, speaking in a soft but authoritative voice
as I helped her set up her easel. She had me half close my eyes,
as she did, and sort of squint at the scene she was painting. She
said it helped you see what the main objects were, as you figured
out your composition. As she painted, she asked me about my
upbringing and how I got to Warren Wilson. I wanted to ask her
similar questions but was afraid it would be impolite. As if sensing
this, she told me she was a valley girl and how her family, the
Pattons, were descended from one of the first families to settle
here. Pioneers. Before she married Dr. Bannerman, she taught

school. She was so gracious I was not surprised to hear, in later years, that as first lady she had the reputation for entertaining visitors with "elegant simplicity."

After our outing, she invited me in for supper. Dr. Bannerman was as gracious as she had been, and I was introduced to their oldest daughter, Janet, and her red-headed younger sister, Mary, who was nine years old.

It was 1950, and the big disappointment was not graduating from high school. Dr. Jensen called me to his office and said, "You have enough credits to graduate. But if you plan to go on to college, you need more schooling." It was a blow, but after thinking it over, I knew there was wisdom in his remarks. Besides, my respect for him was endless.

But there were many fun moments, too. I made the baseball team, playing left field, and the basketball team as a substitute. There were not enough players to have what you would call a second team. And I was selected by Miss Shock to play a role in Oscar Wilde's play *The Importance of Being Earnest*. It was the most minor role in the play, and I appeared in act one only. I played Lane, Algernon Moncrief's manservant. I enjoyed having even a bit part, but my accent was more West Virginian than English. The laughs I got did not please Miss Shock. She said, "Laughs are good, but not in the wrong place and for the wrong reason."

1950 was a very busy year for me at Warren Wilson, and I felt I was maturing at a rapid pace. But by spring, I felt that something was missing. In spite of the inspiration I got from Dr. Jensen's music and songwriting, my guitar playing had languished from lack of attention, and I had not tried to write any songs. I think one depended on the other. A song idea would have demanded chords and strumming, and playing more guitar would have suggested ideas. But I hadn't *pulled one song out of that guitar*, as I was to hear real songwriters put it a few years later.

But before my mood changed, at that point in 1950, my boss at the dairy, Howard Wheeler, died. My creative stagnation was interrupted by his death that made such questions seem frivolous. Mr. Wheeler was my work supervisor, yes, but he and his wife Eloise had become my friends. Neva Watson and I, the girl I was dating, had babysat for their kids. I found that you can never be prepared for death. It makes everything come to a halt and makes you think about life and the sudden loss of it. I rode with Mrs. Wheeler to her husband's home place in Pennsylvania, and while she was visiting with them, I walked into their apple orchard, sat, and wrote a poem about the tragedy of a child dying before his parents.

At the end of the school year, I was going to return to Highcoal. And if I thought milking cows and laying stone was hard work, I was about to learn that it was nothing compared to what was coming. Waiting for me back in Boone County was the most dangerous and physically demanding job I could have imagined

When Arthur told me I was going to be working with our next-door neighbor, Mr. Oliver Hudson, who was a prospector, I was excited. Arthur said Mr. Hudson and I would open up a little mine of our own, on a mountain in Dorothy, where Uncle Vincent lived. The vein of coal we would be mining ran all the way back to Highcoal. After supper, he introduced me to Mr. Hudson, then left us alone to get acquainted. Mr. Hudson said, "We'll dig and blast our way in about thirty or forty yards, to see how rich the vein is. Are you 'fraid o' work?" I said, "No sir." "Good. Be hard goin'. It's low coal, 'bout forty-two inches high. Be ready to go at four-thirty. Got some things to pick up to take with us."

I was still excited, and in my dreams was a romantic flavor to the image I saw of myself actually working in a mine, decked out like a real coal miner, with a battery-powered light on the front of my hardhat. The gather we made when I got up, way before daylight, included ten sticks of dynamite. I had loved lighting firecrackers and throwing them when I was younger. This was going to be a blast, literally, when we set off explosions.

When we unloaded Mr. Hudson's truck at Dorothy, it was just getting daylight. Into a wheelbarrow went the pouch of dynamite, a long drill and breast plate, a pick and shovel, and our lunch buckets. Mr. Hudson tied a rope to the front of the wheelbarrow and started towing as I pushed. Soon we were going up the mountain slowly. There was no path, and it was so steep, things kept falling out the wheelbarrow. It was high noon before we arrived at the right spot. We both flopped down on the ground, exhausted. How he knew we were at the right elevation was one of his gifts as a prospector, I supposed.

As we ate and drank from our coal buckets, Mr. Hudson talked about his younger days. He started out working on a section crew for the C&O Railroad. He said he was not popular. His coworkers told him to slow down and take it easy. He was making them look bad. But he said he could not make himself cheat the company just because the boss wasn't looking. He wanted to earn his pay, as meager as it was. I liked him for that. It was the Warren Wilson way. I swung the pick, and he shoveled until he looked up at the sun and then checked his watch. He nodded, pleased that he was close to guessing the correct time of day. We put the dynamite and tools under the overturned wheelbarrow, covered it with dead branches and weeds, and walked, partly slid, and stumbled down the mountain.

After turning in our batteries to Arthur at the lamp house, I rode with Mr. Hudson to his house. He said, "You done good today. In the morning we'll leave at 5:30. Don't have too much to pick up." Bobby was all ears when I told him about lugging all those tools up the side of the mountain. He said, "Wasn't you afraid that that dynamite might go off, bouncin' around like that?" I assured him there was no danger, having asked Mr. Hudson the same question myself.

Hiking up the mountain the next morning was quite a contrast to the first day. But I had to carry a pretty heavy electrical cord, and Mr. Hudson had a canvas bag containing a battery and some other stuff. So it was still tiring. We both had lunch buckets, of course, with half a gallon of water in the lower part. It was six hours of hard work before we hit a solid enough seam to need dynamite.

We were only four feet into the mountain. Mr. Hudson put his chest against the breast plate while I cranked away, turning the drill. It seemed like an hour before he pulled the drill out and pushed the first stick of dynamite into the hole, using the blunt end of the drill. It was a perfect fit. Another stick went in. He opened the waxy end of the third stick and inserted a pencil-sized cap into the dynamite. A thin double-wire was attached to the end of the cap. This wire was strung out to the end of the hole. On top of it two more sticks of dynamite were pushed into the hole. The thin wire was connected to a very long black electrical cord that was stretched out to the mine entrance. Then it was uncoiled for about twenty yards off to the left of the entrance. At the end of the cord were two wires, bare at the end.

The big blast happened when Mr. Hudson touched these wires to a battery. Just for fun, he yelled, "Fire in the hole!" as if there were people around who needed a warning. The boom was loud enough to make you flinch, and the mine entrance belched forth smoke and flying debris, mostly small bits and chunks of coal. Mr. Hudson wiped his face with a big bandana-like cloth and said, "That's enough for today. I don't know about you, Bill, but I'm tired. We'll clean this mess up tomorrow."

That night I slept soundly but dreamed a lot about that explosion. When we climbed the mountain at first light, Mr. Hudson and I took turns carrying a four-foot-long one-man crosscut saw. We shoveled all the loose coal into the wheelbarrow and dumped it over the mountain, off to the left of the mine shaft.

Now, picking at the soft coal seam was easy, but loading
the coal into the wheelbarrow was difficult because of the low
ceiling. We had to wear kneepads to pick-pick-pick and shovel.
Wrestle-push the wheelbarrow out in a constant crouched-over
position. Pick-pick-pick and shovel some more until the coal
seam got so hard the sharp-ended pick could hardly pierce it.
Which meant boring another hole into that hard anthracite
with the breast plate and drill and putting in five more sticks of
dynamite. After the boom, Mr. Hudson said, "Let's not put the
cleanup off until tomorrow. Let's get to it and knock off. I'm
plumb wore out. How 'bout you?" I nodded very slowly, not
wanting to waste energy by nodding my heavy head up and
down too rapidly.

Mr. Hudson looked up at the sun and pulled out his watch.
He looked at it, then slapped it against his palm. He shook his
head as if sadly disappointed. "Durn thing's quit on me. I'm fer
sure and certain it's quitting time. Come on." When we reached
the truck we didn't get in. He saw a man walking toward us. He
waited, and said, "Say, mister, what time is it? Got a timepiece on
ye?" The man, obviously a coal miner, reached a dirty hand into
his shirt pocket and pulled out a round watch that looked like
Mr. Hudson's. He said, "Four fifteen." Mr. Hudson thanked him,
and when the man had walked on, he said, "We come off the hill
fifteen minutes early. I'm gettin' rusty. Or old, maybe. Well, we'll
make it up tomorr'." Sure enough, we worked fifteen minutes of
overtime the next day.

Morning came too early. I had gone to bed sooner than
usual, but didn't feel well rested. I carried the pouch that held
ten more sticks of dynamite, five of which were used by noon.
As we got farther into the mountain, the work got harder. The
shaft was only six feet wide and forty-two inches high. Working
on our knees in close quarters with no fresh air being pumped
in made us sweat like crazy and lose twice as much energy. The
ceiling was pure slate, but not totally smooth, as my back found

out. It got scraped and snagged on shard-like bumps. When my legs cramped, Mr. Hudson added a small packet of salt into every fourth or fifth cup of water I drank. When Sister woke me on Friday, every muscle in my body ached. I wanted to call in sick. But of course I couldn't, and we didn't have a phone anyway. It was a pipe dream, and a case of young masculine pride. I had no choice.

As the weeks wore on and we got deeper into the mountain, we had to use the crosscut saw to down some slender trees and use them as posts in the mine shaft to support the slate ceiling. Week after week my muscles had gradually stopped aching and complaining, and I realized I was in the best shape of my life. Mr. Hudson noticed it and tried to compliment me, but I said, "Mr. Hudson, you've matched me shovel for shovel. Considering your age, you're ten times the man I am." I saw a twinkle and a sliver of a smile, when he said, "You ain't callin' me old, are ye?" I said, "No, sir. I got better sense than that." He snorted and mumbled, "Ha. You'll do." That compliment marked the end of our coal-mining days together. The company was pleased with Mr. Hudson's report, and the job was closed down.

Shelby Gene Stewart, Arthur's nephew, boss of the poolroom and the company store, then gave me the soft job of riding along with him when he delivered groceries down along the Big Coal River. And it was not just groceries. Sometimes we delivered refrigerators and bedroom sets, bags of fertilizer and cement— everything you can imagine. Occasionally, he let Bobby ride along with us. The fun part was standing up in the truck bed, leaning over the cab, and enjoying the breeze on the way back. It wasn't true, I'm sure, but I imagined Shelby Gene had heard of my hard work with Mr. Hudson, and this was his way of rewarding me for the company. I always liked him. Like the store manager, Gerald, he was fun.

What I knew as I began classes again was that there was no job at Warren Wilson anywhere near as hard as working in a coal mine in West Virginia. There was no reason why I should not take advantage of it. I would never be too tired to study, or folk dance, or play baseball. Or date, something I needed to catch up on. I started dating Neva Watson, from Indiana. Walking her to the girls' dorm almost every night after supper provided lots of places for necking. The path led down from behind the log chapel into a swale, and then up to where we crossed the highway. From there it was another twenty-yard climb. Trees on each side of the path were made to lean against, if you could find one unoccupied. The days getting shorter and dark earlier helped too, creating spots of privacy. You could go as far as your date would let you, which was never all the way. At least with Neva and me. It was called dry humping. But now and then a guy would come in with a dark spot on the front of his pants, which didn't mean that he had had sex. A couple of guys who didn't believe in masturbating complained of having the stone aches—whatever that was.

When I graduated from high school in May, my good friend Donald "Zummy" Zumstein had just finished his first year in college. He told me he and his friend, Fred, had rented a duplex in Detroit for the summer. Zummy assured me I could get a good-paying job and said I could stay with them until I found a room of my own. He gave me an address and told me I was a chicken-shit coward if I didn't show up. I decided to do it. It would be an adventure. No more coal mining. I rode the bus home and announced my intentions. Sister was doubtful and begged me not to do it. Brother Bob said the idea scared him to death, but he admired me for doing it. He asked how I would get to Detroit. I said I would hitchhike. Arthur did not take kindly to such a "dumb-fool risk," partly, I think, because I didn't ask him first for permission or advice. He said, "If you think you're old enough to leave home, don't come back." Sister burst into tears when I said, "Don't worry, I won't be back."

Uncle Vincent and Aunt June drove me to Cincinnati where he got us a room for the night in a cheap motel, after a supper of, what else, Cincinnati hot dogs. He declared they were OK but couldn't hold a candle to West Virginia hot dogs. He said he didn't trust his car to last all the way to Detroit and back. So after breakfast at a pancake house, and a bunch of teary hugs, they left me standing with my suitcase on the side of the road. I was scared, but my mind wouldn't let me admit it. What if it rained? What if? What if? When big trucks roared past, I did the same thing I did on that tramway on the side of a mountain in Highcoal, where I harmonized with the sound of the fans, pushing air into the mine shafts, making up crazy lines.

> *Hmmm, where you going there, big ole truck?*
> *Hmmm, come on, come on, buddy, change my luck*
> *Hmmm, yeah-yeah, pick me up and save me a buck*
> *Zoommm, this hitch-hitchhiking really, really sucks*

I could not possibly name every town, big or small, where people stopped to give me a lift. But one thing I do remember: almost every male driver—no women—told me to hang in there when I told them I was working my way through college, after working my way through high school. But often it was women who started the conversation. None of them had heard of Warren Wilson. But that didn't matter. They all wished me luck, some saying they wished they had stayed in school. Many of them went out of their way to let me out at a good spot to keep hitchhiking. Some of them asked if I needed money. When I said, "No thanks, I'm OK," they nodded approvingly, and several times made me take a few bucks. What I learned from this was, when people see you're working hard toward a goal or taking a chance to better yourself, they'll try to help you. That's a truism, I believe, and you can quote me on it.

The last ride before Detroit was with a big trucker who let me out at the city limits. He said, "Go on down this street for 'bout eight miles. That's the center of town. There's a bus strike on. You can't catch a bus going in, but they'll let you out at your street on the way back out. Damn screwed-up deal, but that's the way it is. Good luck, bud, and stay in school, ya hear?"

I started walking, turning often to stick out my thumb. I got picked up twice. I found the right bus and got off at the street with the name Zummy had given me. It was dark now, and it was hard to read the numbers on the houses. The house I was looking for had my number on the right side and another number on the left side. I climbed up the narrow and very steep stairs to reach the door, with a dim light just above it. I reached up and knocked several times. When there was no answer, I sat on the top step, put my suitcase on my lap, and folded my arms over it. I dropped off to sleep immediately.

I was awakened by a loud voice. "Wheeler! Wake up and piss, the world's on fire." I was too groggy to appreciate Zummy's humor. He and Fred expressed their disbelief that I really took them up on their invitation. But they were glad, and they made me feel welcome to their "humble abode," which, I quickly discovered, was less than humble when I saw cockroaches on one of the walls. I had the feeling I would prefer sleeping in my clothes but decided that would sound like I didn't appreciate their hospitality. If the cockroaches didn't bother them, they didn't bother me. They told me where to go to apply for a job and, for good measure, wrote the address down.

I found it the next morning, after sleeping until ten o'clock. Budd Wheel Corporation took up a whole city block, it looked like, and the tiny no-frills office building on the corner seemed totally out of proportion. It looked like an enlarged phone booth. But the attendant and the friendly nurse were totally efficient. I signed a paper and filled out my address. The nurse took a blood sample. The man told me to show up for work the next morning. I was amazed.

My first job was a simple one-man punch operation, and within a week I found myself on the assembly line. I had to

install a section of felt into a slot and pull down an overhead
rivet gun that blasted the rivet into the felt of the window's
runway. I placed the felt into place with my left hand and at
the same time reached up for the rivet gun with my right, all in
one synchronized motion. In a short time, my hand found the
rivet gun without my having to look up. Any disruption of the
rhythm and the assembly line would stop. The foreman would
be unhappy and tell me so in a voice loud enough for all to hear.
The workers to my left and right razzed me good-naturedly.
But they rooted for me too, their young hillbilly greenhorn. Of
course, there were a lot of hillbillies at Budd Wheel. And the real
Yankees would "y'all" us all to death.

After a few weeks, my coworkers started playing jokes on me,
a sign that I was being accepted. One of the worst tricks was
applying glue to my rivet gun. When I automatically reached
up for the gun, I couldn't let go. The line would come to a halt.
The foreman would cuss me out, knowing it wasn't my fault. But
I never blamed anyone but myself. In time, in many ways, they
let me know they liked me. And just like some of the people
who gave me rides en route to Detroit, they encouraged me to
stay in school. They all had excuses for dropping out of school
themselves, but I never pressed them to tell me why.

I had left Zummy and Fred after a week on the job and found
a room upstairs owned by two old ladies who had a strict set of
rules. No alcohol, no sleepover ladies. No playing the radio loud,
as if I had a radio. No cooking, as if I had a stove or hot plate. I
had one friend, Ricardo, with whom I played pool sometimes or
went to the movies. And I rarely saw Zummy or Fred.

After four weeks at Budd, I got a letter from Aunt Louise,
saying General Motors Truck and Coach Division was hiring
in Pontiac, and I was welcome to come and stay with them at,
I think, Cooley Lake. There were so many lakes in the area I
got them mixed up. I was thrilled to get her letter. She and Ben

always made me feel welcome, and the boys did too, treating me like a brother.

My job at General Motors Truck and Coach Division was unloading big trucks. Very boring when there were no trucks to unload. One day, to keep busy, I picked up a broom and started sweeping. When the boss of the dock saw me, he rushed toward me. I thought he was going to praise me for taking the initiative to spiff up the place. He jerked the broom away from me and said, "What in the hell you doing, Wheeler? You're a truck unloader, not a sweeper. The union guys see you sweeping, it's my ass they'll chew out, not yours." I wondered what Mr. Hudson would have thought about that. It was contrary to everything I learned from him.

I was having a great time, working and fishing with Uncle Ben, when Aunt Louise got a letter from her little sister, my old playmate, Shirley Faye. She was at Warren Wilson. Uncle Babe had paid her tuition and put her on the bus, and she was wondering where I was. School had started two weeks ago. When Aunt Louise told me that, I was dumbfounded. "Shirley Faye's at Warren Wilson? I don't believe it." Louise said, "It's right here in the letter, honey. I guess you lost track of time. Whatche gonna do?"

I said I didn't know. I had saved about fifty dollars, thanks to her free meals, but that was not enough for tuition. I wrote a letter to Dr. Jensen, asking him what I should do. Join the army? Keep working until I earned enough money to come back to school? Dr. Jensen wrote back immediately, in longhand, and told me to come on back to WWC, and he would give me a scholarship. My heart leaped up and sang for joy. I already owed Dr. Jensen so much for the inspiration he had given me, and I had done nothing about it. Now, right then, I started making a silent vow that I *would* do something about it. I didn't know what, but something.

Chapter Six

LOVE TO MY LOVE

Tell me little darling do you like it when I sing
And will you wait for me until I come back in the spring
And will you think of me as I will think of you
And sing a song of our true love as we have sung before, we two
I love you like a chicken loves a barnyard full of corn
I love you like the evening loves to hear the beetle's horn
I love you like a chimney loves a chimney swift to rest
In its smoky bosom nice and warm upon its nest

As you might guess from that lyric, I was starting to write folk-flavored songs, some of them as simple as expanded nursery rhymes. And it started the first week I got back to Warren Wilson and moved into my room and shook hands with my roommate, George Gazmararian. But before I even got unpacked, Roland Pettry walked in and said he had something for me from his sister, Nancy, who wasn't coming back that year. It was a portable record player and an LP recording of folk songs by Burl Ives. I'd never heard of him, but I loved his voice from the first minute I heard it. He was singing a song called "Goober Peas." The only folk song I'd ever heard was "Froggy Went a-Courting," back in Eskdale, with Carl West singing it. Now I was feasting on a cornucopia of them

59

as sung by a consummate artist with perfect timing, plus perfect accompaniment by an acoustic guitar. What a great introduction to the world of folk music! I was so lost in this discovery I skipped supper, as if under a spell I didn't want to break. George said, "Ole Lady, you must eat. You cannot live on music alone. Come, let's go." ("Ole Lady" was what we called our roommates, and I was surprised that George had used it so naturally.) I said, "Oh yes, my Armenian Ole Lady, I can live on this music. You go on. I'm OK. I'm better than OK."

I listened to Burl Ives sing "Blue Tail Fly," "Waly Waly (aka: The Water Is Wide)," "The Fox," "Black Jack Davy," "Big Rock Candy Mountain," and some other songs not in the folk tradition. But the way he sang them, they fit the album perfectly. Because I heard him first, he set the standard for me as the best all-around folk voice ever. This places him, as sacrilegious as it may sound, above Woody Guthrie, Pete Seeger, and other giants of the folk world. Of course, Burl Ives was an interpreter, and those great guys were creators.

There are moments in life you may not be ready for. I was ready for this moment. It was the kick start I had been waiting for. I started learning the songs from that album, skipping all other activities except baseball practice.

By Christmastime I had memorized all the folk tunes, and my guitar playing had improved enough for me to think about singing in front of people, like Dr. Jenson. Guys started coming into my room to listen to me practice, including Omar Zayas, who played along with me sometimes, using his acoustic guitar that was much better than mine. George put up with it most of the time. But when he was studying for a test or an exam, he was frustrated. He was too polite to run the guys out, but he let me know with his eyes and subtle grimaces he'd had enough.

Two things happened during Christmas break that amazed me. Ray Darnell, who had come back to school after being in the army, had an electric shaver he could cut hair with. One night he said, "Hey Wheeler, let's cut each other's hair."

I said, "Sure, why not? I put a towel around my neck, and he lit into my head with bold strokes. My hair went flying away like crazy. I told him to stop.

I said, "Ray, are you a real barber?" He said no, he just gave guys close shaves until they looked like skin heads. New recruits. I said, "I don't want to look like a baldy. How's about trying to taper it up, instead of taking it all off?" He said he'd try. When he finished, I looked in the mirror and was not pleased at what I saw. My hair was uneven with several gaps showing. I said to myself, *OK, buddy, now it's my turn.*

I clicked on the clippers and started making bold strokes, as Ray had done, but without cutting very close to the skin all the way up. I was tapering it up. After five minutes of this, I stopped and looked closely at what I had done. I thought it looked great. I decided I would try to make it look like a barber had done it, instead of getting even with Ray.

When I was almost finished, Bob Cole, the history professor who had a suite at the end of the hallway, came by. He stopped for a look-see and said, "Why, Mr. Wheeler, I didn't know you could cut hair."

I said, "Oh yes, Mr. Cole, I'm not a professional, but yes, I do cut hair."

He said, "Would you give me a haircut?" I nodded. He said, "How much do you charge?" I said fifty cents. He said that was fine. And just like that, I was in the barbering business. When word got out that I had cut a faculty member's hair, I started making lots of spending money when everyone came back from Christmas break.

Before that happened, though, I finished a poem I had been working on for a long time. I read it over and over, satisfied it was as good as I could make it. Then I got an idea that was more than bold. It was brazenly, audaciously stupid. I decided to take it to Dr. Jensen's house, just beyond Bryson gym. It was at least two hours after supper when I trudged through a foot of new-fallen snow and climbed the rock steps to his porch. The light was still on. With an almost shaking hand (partly because it was freezing), I knocked on the door. When Dr. Jensen opened it, holding a cigarette in his left hand, he looked very surprised. He didn't ask me what I wanted; he waited for me to tell him. Holding up the sheet of paper, I said, "Uh, Dr. Jensen, I've been working on a poem, and I, uh, wondered if you might take a look at it, if it's not too late. And I apologize for just …" He cut me off with a smile and said, "Come on in."

He pointed to an easy chair, put his cigarette out, and sat down. He brought my hand-written paper close to his nervous eyes and took his time reading. I can't remember his saying anything. Surely he did, but I was so dazzled, it didn't sink in. He put the poem down and walked upstairs. As I waited, I looked at the fire burning in the fireplace, and how its flames danced on a dimpled copper piece hanging on the wall, something that might have been used for making muffins. There were Danish paintings and small sculpture-like figurines of pure white glass, with blue accents, here and there, also reflecting the flames. I thought, *What a living room! Art museums must look like this.*

Dr. Jensen descended the stairs with a book and some poems of his own that he read. Needless to say, it made me feel more than special. Honored is a better word. And hearing his poetry told me I had a long way to go as a wanna-be poet. He lit another cigarette and offered me one. I told him I didn't smoke but thanked him for offering. Actually, I was amazed at the gesture and took it as a compliment, but considered the moment "off the record" and assumed things would be back to normal tomorrow.

How was I to know the best was yet to come? Dr. Jensen opened the book he had brought down and started reading poems called "Mending Wall," "Stopping by Woods on a Snowy

Evening," "Birches," and "The Road Not Taken." I had never heard of this New England poet named Robert Frost. But his words put the cap on a magical evening. To hear a poem in which the poet used ordinary words that somehow transcended the ordinary and became poetry of the highest order was something I couldn't easily understand. I didn't sleep a wink that night. I was on a literary high, with images of everything I had seen and heard that evening dancing in my head. It was high-octane stuff. It would take me days to come down out of the clouds.

A variety show was scheduled on a Saturday night early in 1952, and the log chapel was packed with students, faculty and staff. I thought almost all of the performers were really good, which made me feel nervous about getting on a stage for the second time in my life.

Omar Zayas sang a Cuban song in English, "Rancho Grande," and then sang a short number in Spanish. He said, in broken English, "My fren, Beelie Eduardo, will please to come here now and say what I have jus' sing for you." I thanked him and we shook hands as he was coming off. As the applause ended, I spoke. "Omar's song said, if I come to Cuba I'll be a big star, because I am so good looking." There was an outburst of cat calls, laughter, and classmates waving hands that meant, "You're full of it. Get out of here." I loved this reaction. I went on. "He also said I would love the hot tamales, and because I am the greatest folk singer he's ever heard, they would be free." The response was almost as loud as their first howling razzing. I said, "Actually, I am the greatest folk singer he's ever heard, because I'm the only one he's ever heard." As the mild laughter and scattered applause died out, I started singing "The Fox." I hammed it up, quaking for the goose, and got a nice applause.

After singing the second song, "Goober Peas," I ventured into unknown territory—I told a joke. "You know, folk songs

come from regular people, and oftentimes you pick up folktales
from them, or a joke that helps tell you about their way of life.
Like…this mountain man was sitting on his porch one day
when a tourist stopped and asked him how to get to Burlington.
He said, "I don't really know." The tourist then asked him how
to get to Kitty Hawk, and he said, "Beats me. Don't know." After
getting the same answer three times, the tourist said, "Mister,
you don't know much, do you?" The man said, "Well, I ain't
lost."

It got a big hand, and I was tickled to death. I said, "We can
thank Mr. Davidson for that. As most of you know, he's the
boss at the woodworking shop where I work. He was born and
raised in these mountains, and he has a great sense of humor.
I asked him why he'd never married. He said, "Well, the older
I get, the more particular I am and the less desirable." That
got a good laugh. I sang one more song, "Big Rock Candy
Mountain," said "Thank y'all," and unstrapped my guitar.

I was on a high for several days. I wanted to tell Mr.
Davidson how well I went over, but he beat me to the punch.
As soon as he put his violin down, he looked at me sort of
sideways and said, "You're making me famous, and I'm not sure
I like it." I squinted at him, puzzled. He said, "Telling everyone
I'm a humorist. And now the dean wants me to talk at a chapel
sometime. They're always on the lookout for speakers, as
you'll find out. Every club and organization will want you to
entertain them while they have tea and crumpets. Especially if
it's free."

Miss Schafer convinced the president he should take me to
his next Civitan Club luncheon, and soon, there I was, sitting
in the front seat of his car, and he was giving me the lowdown.
"Talk, but not too long. These business men and other
professionals are on a strict schedule." He said, "Can you write
me a short poem as an opening speech by way of introducing
you?" He handed me a tablet and a pencil. Twenty minutes

later I handed the tablet to him as he parked the car. The piece I wrote, that I wouldn't call poetry, went something like this:

What's a Civitan, some kind of a clan?
Is it a woman or a pretty rich man?
And what do they do, these Civitans,
Give stuff away, if so what's the plan
For making a dummy a smart business man?
Why, it's as easy as just waving a fan.
So let's ask Mister Wheeler, he's a good ham
At making up stuff you can't understand
Like cock-a-doodle don't, or cock-a-doodle do
He does what the pres-i-dent tells him to

Dr. Bannerman spoke like a real gentleman, giving the audience a brief update on what was going on at Warren Wilson. He closed by saying the Presbyterian Church (USA) had given him notice that during the next three years their financial support would be phased out. He and his board of trustees would have to start building an endowment in order to make the college self-sufficient. It was a huge challenge, but he was confident it could be done, especially if members of the Civitan Club, who were able, could donate to the cause. The club president stood up and said, "Arthur, Dr. Bannerman, I am sure you can count on us to pitch in. Warren Wilson College must not wither and die on the vine. Its mission is too important. Thank you, and good luck, sir. And Sonny, thank you for singing for us. Meeting adjourned."

About a week later, Miss Schafer gave me a book Dr. Bannerman had asked her to buy at the Folk Art Center. It was called *Jack Tales*, by Richard Chase. She said it might give me material to use in my "act." Two weeks later, a man came to the woodworking shop and asked Mr. Davidson if he knew where I was. Mr. Davidson told him I was putting hinges on a cabinet in the Administration Building, but would be back soon. When I got back to the shop, the man put down the copy of *Punch* he was holding, got up, and said, "My name's Jack Priedeman. A friend of mine caught your act at Civitan, and I might have a job for you." Hearing the word "act" again, I thought it must mean I'm in show business.

We shook hands and he went on. "I own Smoky Mountain Tours Company, and I feed my customers supper twice a week at a place less than a half-mile east from this campus. It's just thirty yards or so up the hill from the road. I was wondering if you'd come out there and sing for us?" I didn't say it, but I thought, "*For free, right?*" He must have read my mind. "I can't pay you anything, but we'll pass the hat when you're done. Most of these groups are good tippers. Hell, sometimes when I'm driving, they even tip me. Whatta you say?"

I said yes, and Friday at five o'clock my right hand was holding one end of a large cooler full of Cokes on ice, and Mr. Priedeman was holding the other end. As Mr. Priedeman huffed and puffed up the path, he said in a low voice, "Give 'em a Coke first thing. The more they drink, the less they'll eat. Don't sing anything religious. Smile a lot. Turn on the charm. Make 'em like you and they'll fill up your hat. Except it'll be a cigar box or something."

I was a little nervous at first, but the group was so receptive I relaxed and did OK. The lost tourist joke went over well, and Mr. Davidson's remark about why he'd never married seemed to hit home with a lot of the older ones. After the box was passed there were a couple of bills, and the rest was change. But it filled my pants pocket half full. When I was let off at the main gate, I couldn't wait to get to my room and count it. It was heavy and jingled a little, bouncing off my thigh as I walked. George watched as I dropped the coins noisily onto my desk and started sorting it out. He laughed at my excitement. "Ole Lady, you are going to be rich." I told him no, it was only about eleven dollars.

"But that is a fortune," he said, "when you have nothing. Is that not so?"

In April, Dr. Jensen summoned all boys to the lounge of Sunderland Hall, right after supper. Bob Cole walked in too, and Nathan Sharp quickly jumped up and offered him his chair. Mr. Cole thanked him with a nod, and Sharpie sat on the floor with me. This meeting was a first. Something was up, but none of us had a clue that we were about to make history.

Dr. Jensen placed some cards on the ping-pong table and turned to address us. "Gentlemen," he began, with words to this effect: "For several years Dr. Bannerman and I, along with a unanimous staff and the board of trustees, have dreamed of Warren Wilson's becoming more inclusive. More diverse. Well, with your approval, this can happen. We have received an application for admission from a man from right here in Swannanoa. His name is Alma Shippy, a person of color. In other words, he's a Negro."

This created quite a buzz, and I thought I heard someone say, just barely audibly, "A nigger?" Dr. Jensen continued. "As I said, this cannot happen without your approval. Mr. Shippy will live among you, share all facilities equally, eat with you, and attend classes with you. I truly believe that this is an act of courage on this man's part. He will need all of our support. If you have questions, let's discus them, openly and honestly."

After a lively but brief discussion, Dr. Jensen handed out index cards and some pencils. It was a secret ballot vote, no signatures required, just a simple yes or no. Bob Cole collected the cards and handed them to Dr. Jensen. The two of them stood at the far end of the ping-pong table and counted the votes. Nobody left the room. I had no idea how it would go, but I told Sharpie it was a black man who saved my Uncle Vincent's life when he lost his leg in the coal mines. The slate fall had pinned him down, and the foreman would not let anyone rush in to help. He said there was always a second fall, worse than the first. It was too dangerous to chance it. But the black man pushed the foreman aside, went in, managed to lift the slab of slate off of Vincent's leg, and walk him out. I voted yes, and Sharpie did too.

Dr. Jensen announced that the vote was fifty-four yeas, and one nay. There were no cheers, but a lot of smiles, positive nods, and some handshaking, especially by the foreign students. A few days later I was walking down the stairs to the dining hall beside Miss Schafer. She said, "You know we're having a colored man come to school here as a full-time student. According to Dr. Bannerman, this is the first time this has happened this far south. His name is Alma Shippy. Would you be willing to room with him?" I said, "Yes, ma'am. I voted for him. He'd be welcome to move in with me." As it turned out, there was an empty room next to mine, and Alma roomed there.

I started writing a diary about Alma's presence on campus, and how it subtly changed the atmosphere. I sensed I could feel it. Alma was such a gentle soul and so humble, he took every chance he could to express his thanks for our welcoming him to the campus. I really believed that all students, male and female, were proud to have him among us, not just because we were involved in making history but because we were part of doing something good the Warren Wilson way. But we *were* making history. This was before Brown vs. the Board of Education.

Dr. Bannerman met with the editors of the *Asheville Citizen* often, asking them to play down Alma's presence. No front-page stories, please. Asheville and the Swannanoa Valley were not ready, as a whole, to open their arms and minds to equal rights. My creative endeavors continued to expand. In addition to learning the Jack tales, I started painting a self-portrait that took months. Just trial and error.

The self-portrait, "Fun at Harvest," showed me standing behind the corner of a bin full of ears of corn, holding a dark

brown corn silk moustache between my nose and upper lip. One
of my eyes was squinting, as the other widened dramatically, as if
I were imitating Baron von Shinglehoffer. I was immensely proud
of it. I gave it to Dr. and Mrs. Jensen, and after he died, she wrote
on the back, "At my death, this should be returned to Billy Edd."
And so it was. I have entered it in many of my shows and could
have sold it at every one, except for the NFS posted below it.
Eventually, galleries started accepting paintings for sale only. One
of my art critics, John Koegel, who was a creative force at Warren
Wilson as an artist, teacher, and play director, told me it was one
of my best paintings ever.

Uncle Babe had sent me a letter containing fifty dollars,
inviting me to spend the summer months with him, Louise, and
Mama Nan. Or Ma Nan. Uncle Babe still had his West Virginia
twang. And he had a keen eye for the places that served the best
hot dogs.

Uncle Babe was proud of his service station in Crestview.
He let me start pumping gas and waiting on customers, cleaning
windshields, and sometimes vacuuming the floorboards. One
standard anecdote was supposed to be true but sounded like a
joke to me. A lady pulled up to the gas pump and asked if they
had a restroom. Junior, the guy waiting on her, thought she said,
"Do you have a whisk broom?" He said, "No, ma'am, but if you'll
pull on up a little, I'll blow it out for you." She thought he was
crazy and quickly drove away. Another lady asked Babe to put
fresh air into all four of her tires. He did as she asked, or at least
went through the motions.

According to Junior, a longtime employee, Babe's service
station was the most popular in Crestview. Some of his customers
would not let anyone touch their car but him. One very rich
man owned a big luxury boat, and Babe could use it any time he
wanted to go fishing or just driving around.

Uncle Babe worked long hours, and Aunt Louise had a
prestigious job as the girl Friday to the commanding officer at

Eglin Air Force base at Valparaiso, Florida. On weekends, after supper, we spread a blanket on the floor of the living room, had drinks, and listened to records of a Cajun comedian named Justin Wilson, from New Orleans. He told dumb stories, but told them with his personality and unique Cajun vocabulary. Babe, like Uncle Vincent, was extremely generous. But he was rich, compared to Vincent. When it came time for me to go back to Warren Wilson, Babe took me to a men's clothing store and bought me a nice sports coat, my first ever, and a matching pair of pants. He also gave me several hundred dollars for working in the service station. I used it to pay my tuition for 1952–53 and had a lot left over.

Being back at Warren Wilson felt like coming home. After all, I was starting my fifth year, and my head was full of good memories. But this time I had the feeling that the new memories I would be making were going to be special. My creative juices were pumping. Remembering the Justin Wilson song, "Sure Cure for a Sick Mule," made me think of writing one about a Kentucky mule. The verses were hopping in my head like Mexican jumping beans.

> *I want to go to heaven when I die*
> *But I don't want to go if I can't fly*
> *Cause if I have ride it'll be my luck*
> *To get a stubborn mule from ole Kaintuck*
> *Get up mule, get u, you orn'ry thing you*

Obviously, the song is not a jewel. Probably a throwaway, I confess. But I wrote it down, so as not to make the song-writing muse mad. I had to take what she gave me. Two more came to me in a rush, "The Wasp," and "Along the Trail," an overly sentimental wanna-be western. I wrote them down anyway, honoring the muse. Then another one came quickly, in the same folksy genre, but this time I felt right off that it might be a keeper.

SASSAFRAS

Well, way down yonder in the tall grass
Lived a little woman named Sassafras
Had wiggle in her walk and a giggle in her talk
And a pony tail putting on the class
They say white lightning that's in a jar
Clear like water but it's hot as fire
Well it may be true but let me tell you
Glass won't hold Sassafras
So tell all the neighborhood, boys
I'm the one making all the noise
For I let a cup o' tea make a fool outta me
And that cup o' tea was Sassafras

My initial opinion was, maybe it's too cutesy, or corny. But
I liked it, and thanked the muse profusely. Eventually, it made it
onto my first album, and The Modern Folk Quartet put it on
their first album. And then, Van Dyke Parks "gussied it up a little"
(his phrase) and made it into a fifteen-minute symphonic piece,
playing all the instruments and singing it himself. What a thrill for
an old folk singer.

Actually, I didn't know who Van Dyke was until Janis Ian spent
a few days with Mary and me. "What's happening," she asked.

I said, "Nothing much. But this guy left word on my phone
that he was going to use my song 'Sassafras' someday, with my
permission. Man named Van Dyke Parks."

Janis stopped in her tracks and stared at me. She said, "*The*
Van Dyke Parks?" I said I had no idea. "Billy Edd, he's one of
America's greatest arrangers."

But all this was yet to come. At the time, those
simple-sounding songs were the best I could do. I didn't sing
many of them in public, sticking instead to the folk songs, and
started trying my hand at telling a few of the Jack Tales. Hotels
like the Grove Park Inn and the Sheraton, in Asheville, would

invite folk dancers, cloggers, and tale-tellers to entertain their guests with a taste of local color. I performed with them several times, earning twenty bucks or so each rime.

My last year at Warren Wilson found me playing soccer for the first time, a game I'd never heard of, and I got to play shortstop on the baseball team. Fortunately for me, plant manager Julio Guissasola was big into folk dancing and was taking a group of Warren Wilson dancers to Berea College for a spring festival. While there, he went by the admission director's office to inquire about the application status of several Warren Wilson students. One of them was mine. He told Julio he was afraid he could not accept me, because my stepfather made too much money. Five thousand dollars a year. When Julio explained that I didn't receive financial help from home, he responded, "Well, in that case, we can accept Mr. Wheeler."

After graduating from Warren Wilson Jr. College, I was allowed to stay in the dorm for the summer by working wherever I was needed—on the farm, the dairy, or spreading fertilizer in various pastures, using old Duchess, the horse, to pull the spreader. I also worked after hours for and with Dr. Jensen, doing landscaping around his house, and I continued to sing twice a week for Smoky Mountain Tours. By the time Uncle Vincent and his wife, June, came to pick me up and take me to Berea, I had saved quite a bit of money. I had also written about ten more songs.

Leaving Warren Wilson filled me with a deep sadness, as if I could feel the atmosphere of leaving in my blood and see a montage of images that called up precious memories that tumbled in my mind like clothes in a dryer. I would miss the high, blue mountains where white mists rising out of coves had strangely reminded me of places I had never seen. I had learned so much more than book knowledge there, thanks to the most caring teachers, staff, and work supervisors imaginable. I wrote

the following poem of thanks, knowing I owed Warren Wilson
more than I could ever repay.

> *The hills are friendly here. Valley loam stretches wide.*
> *Cutting thistles in the school's dairy pasture with my hoe*
> *In bright yellow early summer sun light I knew I had found home,*
> *A soil to sow the anxious seeds of my longing, spaces*
> *Between high mountains for mind to glide or climb to*
> *The limits of its wings, then tumble back on itself*
> *Free-falling feather over tail like birds mating in air.*

Vincent insisted on taking me to Highcoal on the way to
Berea. "Your mother wants to see you, and so does your brother.
It's OK with Arthur." I didn't try to talk him out of it. In fact, I
wanted to see Highcoal again, but as we got closer and closer,
I was experiencing a mixture of anxiety and nostalgia. But
when I walked through the gate at their new house next to the
poolroom and saw Sister, whose eyes were close to tears, I got
teary myself. Arthur had always stifled my ability to show love or
affection to her. But now, as she and I hugged, he smiled a smile
that looked genuine. Not forced or edged with sarcasm. He held
out a hand to Vincent. As they shook, he nodded to June and said,
"Y'all come on in." As if June didn't want to leave Bobby out, she
smothered him with her big fleshy arms, calling him honey and
bragging on how big he'd got since the last time she saw him. I
took my turn with Bobby, hitting him softly on the shoulder. I
said, "Are you gettin' used to indoor plumbing, or do you miss
that ole house out back?"

Bobby assured me he didn't miss the outhouse. Sister said to
Vincent, "I'm sorry we don't have a guest room for y'all." Vincent
said he and June would get a room at the boardinghouse. Bobby
said proudly, "Billy Edd, we have a shower now, too. No more
bathing in number two washtubs."

Vincent made a comment to Arthur to the effect that he had
to have a lot of pull to get a house like this. Arthur nodded and
smiled broadly. Vincent had a natural and easy way of bragging
on people, and they loved him for it. After a wonderful dinner,
complete with pineapple upside-down cake for dessert, Bobby
and I walked all over Highcoal, talking about his final year
coming up at Whitesville Jr. High. He'd be going to Sherman
High School at Seth and hoped to make the basketball team,
even though he was a freshman. He was full of questions about
what I'd been doing, and my going to Berea College. He didn't
say it in so many words, but he was proud of me for standing up
to Arthur and having the nerve to leave home. He loved his dad,
but he also understood the trouble I'd had with him. Bobby was
a good-looking sixteen-year-old and had a modest and confident
manner about him. I was proud of him.

Me and my mother in Elk
Run, West Virginia, 1933

Me and my uncle,
Vincent Wheeler, in 1942

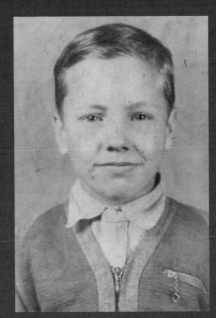

An early school photo

My baseball days!

Sitting at the feet of my greatest inspiration, Dr. Henry W. Jensen, Dean of
Warren Wilson College, who played guitar left-handed and upside-down

One of my early publicity photos

Me and Mary on our
wedding day, 1963

With Bobbie Gentry and John Hartford at a Nashville
Songwriters Association International banquet

With Merle Travis, BB King, Jean Ritchie, and Tom Paxton
filming an episode of the *American Odyssey* TV series

Entertaining at one of the annual DJ Conventions in Nashville

Attending the Country Music Association
Awards after "Jackson" became a hit

Finalizing the formation of Family of Man Music
with Johnny Cash and our attorneys

Filming the *Country Suite* TV series with guests
(L-R): Danny Rowland, Don McLean, and John Darnal

At work in my home studio in Swannanoa

The Wheeler Family: my wife Mary, our son Travis, and our daughter Lucy at Pipe Stem State Park in West Virginia

Me with Chet Atkins, Garrison Keillor, Les Paul, and Duane Eddy taping the *Nashville Now* TV show

Playing with Chet Atkins at the Great Outhouse
Blowout in Gravel Switch, Kentucky, 1992

Me and my trusty guitar – always courting the muse for a song idea!

Chapter Seven

FAREWELL BROTHER

So fare you well then, my good people
Whoever you are, whatever you do
Wherever you come from, wherever you're traveling
I know your name
I have seen you in my travels, north and south
East and west, you love freedom, man and woman
And I know your name, I know your name
And this I know:
God hath made of one blood all the nations of mankind
To live as brothers and sisters on the earth
So fare you well then, farewell brother, farewell sister
Farewell father and mother, fare you well

A boy named Phillip, from West Virginia, told me he was my roommate. Another boy introduced himself as Charles Counts but said I could call him Peedie. A third introduced himself as Dick Ramsay. I liked Gilbert, just an ordinary-looking old house with a small front porch facing Scaffold Cane Road, just a few feet away. To me it was much better than living in a big dorm. There were eight of us sharing two bathrooms, one on the first floor and the other on the second floor. There was a piano in the small living room.

After registering in the main Administration Building, I went to the labor office and found that I would be working in the pottery lab, on the top floor of the Art Building. The dean of labor introduced himself as Wilson Evans. He asked if I'd be interested in playing tennis. I said, "Yes, but I'm a beginner." He assured me it didn't matter. I should come and give it a shot anyway. I told him I would think seriously about it. I loved baseball, but I had done that at Warren Wilson. He gave me a time card to fill out after every work session, and said I would be paid twenty-two cents an hour. This was a surprise. I was getting free tuition and also being paid. What a great deal!

My initial feeling about the Berea College campus was that it was big, really big, compared to Warren Wilson.

I was soon to learn that getting to classes on time required a lot of walking. Right off, my favorite classes were Greek and Roman history, and art appreciation. My least favorite was Charlotte Ludlum's French class. She would ask different ones to read passages, in French, and finally would say, "All right, Mr. Wheeler, let's see how bad it can get. You read for us." I think she picked on me to show she had a sense of humor. But nothing about her voice, her looks, or her demeanor was funny. Still, a few in the class would giggle when she insulted me. A couple of times, I could have read certain lines fairly well, but because they were simple I used them as a vehicle to ham it up. Instead of pronouncing Pinot Noir correctly, for example, I would say, in my best hillbilly voice, "pine knot no-ear." The class would howl, while Miss Ludlum glared.

Because of its size, I was not taking to Berea College as I had to Warren Wilson. But then, it took a while for me to start liking Warren Wilson also, until I heard about the dignity of labor from so many teachers and work bosses. It seems funny, looking back, how that one idea lit a spark in me. Those people knew where I came from, how poor I was and how naïve. But they treated me as an equal. They challenged me. Would Berea do the same?

I would keep an open mind. After all, I was going to be working in a pottery lab. I had seen photos of potters turning wet clay into beautiful vases and bowls. Was it going to be as much fun as writing a song or painting a picture?

I started at the bottom, literally. My first job was to carry clay from the basement up three floors to the lab. I had to clean up after skilled pottery "throwers"—a strange word for creating a thing of beauty out of clay. I learned by just listening to the potters' conversations, as they worked, that Charles Counts was exceptionally talented, not just at throwing pots but decorating them with great designs and colors. I started looking for chances to talk to him at Gilbert. The head of the lab was Jim Bobbitt, a very pleasant man. When he introduced himself and we shook hands, I smelled cigarette smoke on his breath. I smiled inside. I had heard that members of the faculty were not supposed to smoke or drink. The drinking part applied to students, too, but we were allowed to smoke in certain specified areas.

As the weeks became months, I found myself busier than I had ever been at Warren Wilson. I joined Twenty Writers Club and signed up for singing lessons with an older lady named Gladys Jameson. She had the reputation of being the expert goddess of folk music and its interpretation. I couldn't wait to sing her some of my folksy songs. But it didn't work out that way. She was a perfectionist. I spent weeks just learning how to enunciate simple words and phrases to her satisfaction. Her favorite was: "I shot an arrow into the air. It fell to earth I know not where. For so swiftly it flew, the eye could not follow it in its flight." This had to be done in a one note monotone. No matter how hard I tried, I could not sing it to her approval. One day, I tried to break the monotony. I told her I was a songwriter and would like to sing her a couple of my songs that had a folk flavor but were original. She scoffed and told me to keep on with the voice lessons. After a while, I quit. I didn't want to be a vocalist and sing folk songs exactly the way she insisted they be sung.

At the pottery lab I started getting instructions from Mr. Bobbitt on how to throw pots. There was a wooden lever you had to peddle with your foot to make the flat wheel above turn. With wet hands you'd take a ball of clay and center it on that wheel. The size of the ball was determined by how big the vase or bowl was you wanted to make. After weeks of practice, I settled on making tumblers that were six inches high and three inches wide. After firing them in the kiln, I colored them with a mottled blue glaze. The ones that met Mr. Bobbitt's approval were taken to the Boone Tavern gift shop and sold. It made me feel good to know I was giving something back to the college.

On the bottom floor, next to where the clay was mixed and dried, I discovered a collection of photographs that were so beautiful I couldn't believe it. They were not like any black-and-white photographs I had ever seen. I can't describe the color, but it was rich, sepia-like. The subjects were, by and large, poor-looking people in their log homes, making quilts or using looms to weave. Some were in gardens or barns doing chores, tending to horses, chickens, and other animals. Sometimes they would be dressed in their best clothes or photographed in simple garments, women wearing aprons, slouchy dresses, bonnets, and all sorts of hats while doing ordinary chores. But in most cases, regardless of their clothing, they exuded a quiet dignity and proud contentment.

This went on for weeks until I had looked at almost all the files. When I mentioned it to Mr. Bobbitt, he stared at me. He said, "That sounds like…it has to be the Doris Ulmann collection. It's famous and extremely valuable. She's famous. I can't believe you had easy access to it. Oh my god, you didn't touch any of them, did you?"

"No sir. Something told me they were extra special. There's no fingerprints on them." He was pleased to hear that. He said he would see to it that the room was locked. He said, "That collection should be in the library, in a special room with controlled temperature and air quality." I would learn more about Miss Ulmann and her travel companions in due time.

As summer approached, there was talk that Paul Green, a famous playwright from the University of North Carolina at Chapel Hill, was being commissioned to write a play to celebrate Berea College's centennial in 1955, the year I would graduate. Also, the producers of *Horn in the West*, an outdoor drama at Boone, North Carolina, were looking for actors to be Indian dancers. I thought it would be nice to see what an outdoor drama was. I was hired for thirty dollars a week. I was told by Bill, the choreographer, where I could find a room with a couple of other dancers. It was at the home of a retired lady who used to be a state home economics agent. We became "her boys," and she was our mother hen. She charged each of us five bucks a week because, she said, we were sleeping in crowded conditions, and she loved having us around.

Mother Hen introduced me to a good-looking local girl, and on off-nights the girl would drive me around in a nice Buick. We'd have a milkshake or burger, her treat, before parking at a favorite spot high on the mountainside, with a good view of the valley below. In between necking sessions, we'd watch for glimpses of what was known as the "Brown Mountain Lights." It was in a swampy area where mists often made it impossible to see the lights. I heard explanations that the lights were caused by swamp gas, phosphorus, or some other phenomenon. Some locals said the eerie lights were from lanterns being carried by faithful old slaves come back from the grave, searching for their lost masters.

The following year at Berea, I wrote and directed a one-act play at the old ramshackle playhouse on campus, called the Tab, short for Tabernacle. The name of my play was *Eyes of the Devil's Horses*. There was no major in playwriting, but the Tab was quite active. It seemed that at least every other week a short play was produced. Some staff and students, plus Berea locals, would remain after the show and participate in a critique. These sessions were always positive, with no harsh criticism. Fred Parrot, a member of the English department who taught theater, led the discussions. He directed at least three major productions a year, one of which was usually Shakespeare.

At Berea, I learned that Paul Green called his plays symphonic dramas, a form of epic theater that involves all the arts to present the story of a particular person or event. *Wilderness Road* would be about Berea College's history. It would feature an idealistic teacher named John Freeman, who wanted to teach in an interracial school. His brother Davy was pro-southern, as was most of the community. They would become enemies with the outbreak of the Civil War.

This theme was in keeping with the history of Berea College, as I came to hear more and more about it. Cassius Clay, a prominent man in Kentucky politics, donated the land on which the college was founded. He was the son of Green Clay, a very wealthy planter and slave owner. While Cassius was at Yale College, he heard a speech by an abolitionist named William Lloyd Garrison that inspired him to join the antislavery movement. He became a target of the proslavery crowd that several times tried to assassinate him. In 1843 a hired gunman, Sam Brown, shot him in the chest and cut him with a knife, but Cassius used his Bowie knife to seriously wound Brown and then threw him over an embankment. In 1849, six Turner brothers, and Cyrus Turner, stabbed him, beat him, and tried to shoot him. But he fought off all six and killed Cyrus Turner with his Bowie knife.

In 1853 Cassius donated ten acres to abolitionist John G. Fee, who, in 1855, founded the town of Berea and Berea College, modeled on Oberlin College. So long as Cassius, who had released his own slaves, supported the college, the anti-abolitionists left the faculty alone, for the most part. But at least twice they had to flee from town to escape being hanged.

When school started again, Ted Cronk, on behalf of Paul
Green, set up an office across from Little Mama's on Short Street.
He requested that I come to work for him, saying he had some
plans for me to help promote *Wilderness Road*. I helped write
press releases, when class schedules permitted, and sometimes
Mr. Cronk would take me with him when he was speaking at
important meetings in the capitol city of Frankfort. He sang
the praises of Paul Green, who had won a Pulitzer Prize for his
Broadway play *In Abraham's Bosom*. Mr. Cronk said Paul Green's
principles were in perfect harmony with Berea College's. In
earlier years, Paul had stood alone as a white southern man of
letters preaching equality of the races, the richness of southern
tradition, and the perfectibility of every human being. That took
courage.

Mr. Cronk came off at first as a hotshot promoter, full of
nervous energy and always in a hurry. At that time, he didn't
bother to be polite. He wanted to get things done. Right now.
But there was one big obstacle keeping it from happening: a lady
in the president's office whose name was, as I remember, Betty
Edinger. She insisted on proofreading his press releases before
they went out. It was driving him crazy. Sometimes it took her
days to get them back to him. He wanted them back in hours. I
asked him why he didn't have Paul Green intervene. He vetoed
the idea, preferring to handle it himself, and he didn't want to
bother the playwright while he was writing. This impatient Ted
Cronk didn't bother me at all. I was humbled and grateful to be
working for him. We were together so much he told me to call
him Ted. In public, I could use "Mister" to avoid seeming brash or
impertinent.

Dylan Thomas was really big at Berea in those days, and
my other favorite teacher, Louise Scrivner, who taught oral
interpretation, had us read his *Under Milk Wood* out loud in class.
It was a portrait of the town where he grew up in Wales. "Mama
Scrivner," as she was called by many of her students, challenged

me to write a play for voices about the coal mining town where
I grew up. I accepted her challenge and started writing *Slatefall*.
But my portrait of Highcoal was nothing like Dylan Thomas'
town, nor was my cast of characters. It goes without saying I
was not as gifted as Thomas. But I worked hard on *Slatefall* and
was extremely gratified when Mama Scrivner said she loved it.
Imagine the boost to my ego when it was announced that our
class was going to stage a reading of *Slatefall*, and everyone was
invited, staff and students alike. Our performance went well. Ted
didn't attend, but he slapped me on the back for the kudos I was
getting. He said it reaffirmed his decision to invite me to work
for him. He was cooking up some big promotion plans.

I was taking a creative writing class with Emily Ann Smith,
who had also seen our *Slatefall* performance. She said she thought
it was a good start, but needed more characters to paint a portrait
of a town as fully as Dylan Thomas had. She said, "I thought
Louise's staging was creative and very effective." Emily Ann did
not hand out compliments easily. With most of the prose and
poetry of mine, she thought I used too many words. I had a
tendency to say things twice and thrice, by forecasting something,
saying it, and then saying it again in summation. She suggested
I read *River of Earth*, by Kentucky author James Still. I asked her
why. Did she like his writing? She said, "Never mind. I want you
to write a review of it. A critique. Tell me if you like it, and why.
If you don't like it, tell me why. Your grade will depend on that
paper."

I went to the library and asked the librarian if she had *River of
Earth*. She found the book immediately, and as I signed the card
I told her Emily Ann Smith wanted me to read it. I said, "It must
be a really good book, huh?" She asked if I was in Miss Smith's
class. I said yes. She smiled. "Was this, like, an assignment?" I
nodded. "Then maybe Miss Smith wants to know your opinion,
not mine." I thought, *This librarian and Miss Smith must be in
collusion*. Except I didn't know that word then.

Charles "Chad" Drake, a teacher in Berea's Foundation
School, had also heard about *Slatefall* and liked what he heard. He
cornered me one day in the dining hall and said he wanted me
to go to Viper, Kentucky, and take photos of the Ritchie family's
annual reunion. He asked if I'd ever taken photographs, and did I
have a camera? I said no. He said, "Now you do," and handed me
a small camera. "I'll show you how to use it, with the idea of you
taking over my job as editor of *Mountain Life and Work* magazine.
I'm getting involved in the War on Poverty as a consultant in
Washington, DC." I said I'd think about it. He said, "I hope you
will, seriously. And please call me Chad."

Within a week, before I had made up my mind, he took me
and my guitar to Washington with him and managed to get the
government to give me two hundred dollars. I think he passed
me off as his helper, a researcher, secretary, or something. I had to
be photographed, fingerprinted, and confirm my social security
number. He had me entertain at a gathering of thirty or so
people, who gave me a perfunctory glance, then were engaged in
noisy conversation. I had no idea what the theme or purpose of
the meeting was, but they were definitely not interested in folk
music, or at least not the way I sang it. I managed a brave, two-
hundred-dollar smile and tried to consider it a good chance to
practice in public. As the meeting broke up, a few of them told
me they really enjoyed my music. *Liars,* I thought, *practicing for
politics.*

Back at the college, he did teach me how to take pictures and
how to develop the negatives and make prints. The darkroom
was in the basement of Ben Welsh. Other than booking flights
for Bereans who traveled a lot, I never knew what "gentle" Ben
did. But I thought there must be more to him than met the eye,
because he was married to a very nice-looking woman and had
at least thirty years on her.

I received three more checks from DC's War on Poverty
division and was dropped from their roster. I opened an account

at Berea Bank & Trust. My plan was to save enough money to
buy a used car by the end of my senior year. That was a good
start.

As Christmas approached, the majority of students went home.
But I had been hearing about Christmas Country Dance School
and was asked to participate by singing folk songs and telling Jack
tales. Many folks came from New York and other places and loved
to be introduced to local color. It was expensive for them, having
to pay for rooms and meals, but if I agreed, I would get a free ride.

I didn't know quite what to expect, but I had a wonderful
time. It surprised me that the New Yorkers and other city folks
were really good dancers and loved it. Many of them, I learned,
belonged to dance clubs in New York, Ohio, West Virginia, and
also Kentucky. These people were the most gregarious strangers
I'd ever met, and they didn't remain strangers for long. What
a contrast to the DC crowd. They gave rapt attention to story
tellers and were constantly thanking them and the musicians who
played for dances. I sang several folk songs: "The Fox," "Black Jack
Davy," "Big Rock Candy Mountain," and an original humorous
song, "The Wasp." In addition to folk tales, I talked about being at
Warren Wilson and meeting characters like Hardy Davidson. His
quote about why he'd never married got a big laugh, especially
from the older folks.

After my last performance, a well-dressed middle-aged man
caught up with me and said he liked my coal camp song. I
thanked him and started walking on, but he caught up with me
again and said, "I've written a song and I was going to play it, but
I lost my nerve, because I wrote it with a dulcimer, and…well,
I'm not very good." His attitude was so self-deprecating, I felt
sorry for him.

I said, "Do you want to play it for me?" His eyes brightened. I
said, "Come on. You in the dorm?"

He shook his head and said, almost apologetically, "I'm
staying in Boone Tavern." I told him there was nothing wrong

with that. "But I don't want them to think I feel I'm better than, uh, anybody."

I told him to put that out of his mind. We went to his nice room and he played me a song that wandered all over the place so much, I didn't know what it was about. And his dulcimer playing seemed to never change chords. He laid it aside and said, "It's just not my instrument. You want it? Give me five dollars and it's yours. It would make a nice wall decoration, if you don't want to play it."

I said, "I'll be. My guitar cost my parents fourteen dollars. This sets a new record. I'll take it. If you're sure." He was sure. I said, "If you don't mind, I'd like you to show me where to put my fingers to play the chords you were using, so I can practice on my own." He sat on the couch, with the dulcimer on his lap, and I pulled a chair up close. "You just need three to get started," he said. "In fact, that's all I used in my song, as you may have noticed." He would make the chord, strum it with a flat pick, and hand it to me. He adjusted my fingers patiently, and I would strum. Then hand the dulcimer back to him.

After about twenty minutes, I had the finger positions memorized. I think it boosted his ego to be helping me. He lost his hang-dog attitude. He smiled. He was the teacher, and I was the student. I said, "I feel like I should give the five bucks back to you." He shook his head, said "Absolutely not," and wished me good luck. He also gave me the flat pick he had used, plus two more in different sizes. He looked so pleased with himself, I felt I had done my good deed for the day.

Chapter Eight

STEP LIGHTLY ON THE EARTH

A dewdrop on a blade of grass
Shimmers as the moments pass
Waiting for the sun to come and love it to death
Then the trees light up so bright, I swear
Like Morning's combing out her hair
In colors so beautiful, oh, it takes your breath
Step lightly brother on the earth
Walk softly sister, oh we won't know its worth
Till it's not around, hey what's that sound
In the trees and flowers
Step lightly on this earth of ours

Toward the end of my junior year at Berea College, I finished reading *River of Earth* and worked really hard on my "critique." I wrote it like a letter to Emily Ann Smith. I started by saying Mr. Still's novel was so good I didn't have words strong enough to tell how deeply I was touched by it. It seemed to me he invented a new-old language to describe his characters and how they spoke. Their sentences were condensed, lots of words left out—not many the's or and's, using nouns as verbs, with unique and sometimes funny words. But it all rang dead-on true. If I had to label it, I'd call it pure folk poetry. Robert Frost's poems portrayed his New England characters perfectly. But James Still's Appalachian characters required a language with crackling salt in it, the smell of rooty earth, the sloshing-bounce of creeks full of mountain brine, salt pork, and tobacco straight from one of his "Devil's snuff-boxes." He created words like, "rifle-gun, sun balls, parrot-birds, squat lamps, fly-bugs, crane-birds, and a man-person who was mean-mad. I loved this verse of a song he included:

> Ol' gray goose went to the river
> If'n I'd been a gander
> I'd a went thar with her
> Holler-ding, baby, holler-ding

River of Earth moved me. I'll just say, I think it's a masterpiece. Well, that's my critique, Miss Smith, and now I have a bone to pick with you. In a poem of mine, I wrote, *Only the gentle snow could flatter the dark, coal-dusted ground.* You told me that humans can be gentle, but physical objects cannot. Well, James Still wrote that when Mother's clothesline broke, "the clean garments now lay miserably in the dirt." Can clothes be miserable?

When classes ended, Miss Smith gave me an A. Then answered my question by writing: "Your snow was an inanimate object lying on a similar object. The clothes were human objects that belonged to a woman who cared about them, and was distraught to see them lying, to her, miserably in the dirt. The word helps explain her emotion." Emily Ann Smith was a great teacher. I accepted her explanation wholeheartedly.

> The earth brings forth so many things
> Some on feet and some on wings
> They all got a right to drink from the river and lake
> But man is so busy walking tall
> Pretending like we own it all
> We don't hear their voices call
> Hey, give us a break

Chad Drake loaned me his car to drive to Viper, Kentucky, to attend the Ritchie family reunion. I met Mom and Dad, daughters Jean, Edna, and the oldest, May, with other family, relatives and friends. I took pictures like crazy, even when everybody held hands while grace was spoken and heads were bowed. Jean sang folk songs after dinner, and her voice knocked me out, perfect pitch, and a sincerity in her whole demeanor, accompanying herself with a dulcimer. What a perfect combination. I had never heard anyone play the dulcimer. The man who sold me his dulcimer didn't count.

I was able to stay in Gilbert for a few days but had no idea where I was going to board for the summer. Then one day a lady walked into Mr. Cronk's office and said she had written an oratorio called *Children of God*, and wondered if he could help her find a composer. Her name was Clara Chassel Cooper, a teacher of psychology at Berea. She also had a room for rent, with some board involved, if necessary. Would he post it on his wall, in case some actors were coming in early to try out for *Wilderness Road*? He said, sure, but she was a little early. The play wouldn't premier until next summer. But he said he knew some music staff at the University of North Carolina and would ask around about a possible composer. She was elated and thanked him profusely. When she walked out, I followed and stopped her. I told her I was looking for a room. Fortunately, she had heard of me and said she'd be glad to show it to me.

I walked with her a long way down Centre Street, amazed at how fast she was on her feet, especially for a woman as heavyset as she was, carrying a briefcase and an armload of books and papers to boot. Her house was old and offered up some musty smells, but my room on the second floor had a small back porch and stairs leading up to it from outside. She would give me a key. She said she would charge me five dollars a week, and I could enjoy meals sometimes with her and her son, Olin, who also cooked now and then. When she introduced me to him, he looked at me with squinted eyes that seemed to be laughing at me. I had the feeling she was charging me such low rent because Olin had scared previous renters away, and she might be hoping I could be his friend.

I edited *Mountain Life and Work* for the first time, leading into summer. The main article was the Ritchie family reunion. It took time to read articles sent in and decide in what order to use them, along with announcements of fairs, folk festivals, book reviews, poetry, and photos. But Chad was right. With volunteer help, it was not a gigantic chore. But it did take time, and as summer wore on, sometimes time was scarce. Ted kept me busy going places with him. As we traveled, he talked about his promotion ideas. His special knack was getting free publicity. When Ted talked to editors, TV, and radio people, he emphasized any public service angle that came to mind, the good it could do by letting audiences hear about it. The fact that Berea College charged no tuition helped tremendously in their fundraising. He could make it work for *Wilderness Road*, too. One or two minutes on a news show, he said, was better than an hour on some other format. He asked how much I charged for singing for service clubs, garden clubs, and so on. I said, "Seven dollars. But I hate it when I have to sing during dessert, with spoons and cups rattling and people talking."

He said, "Charge more and you won't have to." I countered, "But I'm a nobody. What if I price myself too high? I'm outta business." He told me I was somebody, and I was worth what I thought I was. I let that sink in.

I said, "When I was a student, I sang for you as part of my college job. I got twenty-two cents an hour. I'm not a student now, and I've been working for you for three weeks already, without even making twenty-two cents an hour. So how much you gonna pay me for those three weeks and to continue singing and working in the office?"

He laughed. "You're a crafty bastard, aren't you?

"You set it up, sir. So how 'bout it?"

He laughed, heartily this time, and said, "I see a lot of me in you. Let me look at my budget. I'll make sure you get a good wage. You can take time to sing for whomever and keep what they pay you. Deal?"

I said, "Yeah. But can't you just give me a hint what it might
be?" He said it would be at least fifty. I nodded, happy as all
get-out. I was liking Ted more and more.

For almost a month Ted recruited shifts of students to sit at the
main stoplight in town and write down the names of the states
on the license plates of each car that passed. Ohio outnumbered
all the others put together. His big idea big idea was to have
Dr. Norris Woodie, the alumni director, and his staff, including
student workers, set up a tour for me in Ohio. I would entertain
service clubs, garden clubs, sewing circles, schools, colleges—any
group wanting free entertainment, provided they would let me
set up a screen and show slides about *Wilderness Road*.

My trip would begin in the fall and last into winter. If my host
could schedule radio or TV interviews, all the better. Ted persuaded
Dr. Woodie to get out a mailing to all alumni in Ohio, ASAP. The
tour would be based on these contacts. It was a simple plan, but a
massive undertaking. Dr. Woodie realized this and started enlisting
local retired alumni as volunteers, mostly older ladies. Soon his
office was swarming with activity. He and I would take breaks
together, usually at the soda shop. He'd have tea and I'd have a
milkshake. On our second or third break, he rubbed his bald head
and told me, in confidence, he preferred teaching philosophy and
religion to alumni affairs He said he had heard I sang folk songs,
but did I also write songs? I told him yes, and I hoped to have
enough for an album, an LP record someday. He said, "I wrote a
song. Would you like to hear it?" Of course, I said yes. He sang:

I'm so humble, humble, humble
I don't grumble, grumble, grumble
When I stumble, stumble, stumble and fall.

He sang it straight-faced and rubbed his head almost as if in
apology. I chuckled and told him I liked it. He grinned and sipped
tea. His nonresponse made me think maybe he was waiting for

more. I said, "I can see you have a sense of humor. And you're a low-key person, seems to me. I bet you never get flustered. In a way, your song describes you." He told me I was astute, and said yes, the song did describe him. He nodded. "It's like the saying I've heard from country people: 'Never stand when you can sit, and never sit when you can lie.' I don't like to waste energy. Every time I get the notion to exercise, I take a nap until it blows over."

Ted and I were looking over a rough draft of a press release when a man named Bernard Davidson came to the office and asked if I'd sing for a meeting of the Berea Lions Club at Boone Tavern. And how much would I charge? I said, "Ten bucks."

He looked taken aback and said, "I heard you only charged five. You'd just be singing twenty or twenty-five minutes, if they like you."

I said, "Yes sir, that's right. But I'm more in demand now and have less free time. And it doesn't matter to me if I sing twenty minutes or half an hour. It's ten bucks." He said he'd have to get back to me.

Two days later, he came to the office and hired me. Ted Cronk heard him, and when he left, Ted said, "What did I tell you? I think you owe me a commission."

I said, "Book a nice date for me and I'll give you ten percent." He said twenty. I said fifteen. And we both laughed.

At about this time, Ted told my landlady, Mrs. Cooper, that a well-known composer, Norman Della Joio, liked her oratorio, and when it was finished, it might be recorded by the Cincinnati Symphony. She was so thrilled her walking pace kicked into another gear.

Ted told me I would start my tour in late summer or early fall, if the ladies had it set up by then. So I thought I'd better start practicing on the dulcimer. It would make me appear more like a bona fide folk singer, especially to folks outside of Appalachia. I was also thinking about the next issue of *Mountain Life and Work*. I needed to have it ready before I hit the road for Ohio. So I decided to go see James Still. He lived on a small farm between Wolfpen

Creek and Dead Mare Branch in Knott County. Ted told me he
could spare me for a couple of days. I had to stop and ask directions
a few times and profited from local knowledge. I also heard
statements like, "You mean that quare feller what makes up tales
and sells 'em?" Or, "He's crazy-like, but mebbe crazy like a fox."

Mr. Still seemed very normal to me. He welcomed me to his
ancient log house and, after listening to me praise him and tell
him how honored I was to meet him, he picked some leafy things
from his garden and cooked lunch for us. He autographed my
book, and even read some passages for me. I sat on the hardwood
floor at the feet of the master and felt a bit intoxicated as he read.
He said I could stay all night if I didn't mind sleeping on the floor.

After we got talked out, I got my sleeping bag, unrolled it, and
had no problem going to sleep. Mr. Still had told me he was an
early riser and had some errands to run, so he was gone when I
woke up. I stopped at a store on the way back to Berea, bought a
pint of milk and some donuts. I was still high from the time spent
with a great mountain host, who just happened to be one of
America's greatest authors. And I now had my lead story for the
fall issue of *Mountain Life and Work.*

During those summer weeks I had sung, on my own, for five
different Lions clubs, plus two Kiwanis clubs, and a Rotary club,
earning seventy dollars. I didn't keep track of the places where I
sang, but I got free meals, and while accompanying Ted, he picked
up the bills. For all those weeks, plus working in Ted's office, I made
$450. Dr. Cooper only charged me forty bucks, but I now had
$370 more to add to my account at Berea Bank & Trust, making
the total 1,440 smackeroos. Yippee! There was a new Ford Sunliner
convertible at Glenn Pennington Autos, with a beautiful blue body
and a white top. Looking at it for the first time gave my heart a rush.
But it cost $2230. I had a long way to go to get even a used one.

Ted provided me with a very used Jeep wagon-type car, with
plenty of room in the back for my guitar, dulcimer, and slide
show equipment. Because classes had started, this touring job was

partly in fulfillment of my student labor obligation of ten hours a week. Because of that, Ted said he would give me a $100 per week, as usual. I would be given travel money for meals and gas. He figured I would get my main meal from the groups I was entertaining, mostly at lunch but often at dinner, too.

The volunteers at the alumni office did a superb job, providing me with complete information about my alumni hosts who, in turn, would brief me on those I would be singing for. I was given phone numbers and maps in abundance. Ted also gave me his home number, in case of emergencies after business hours. I can't say I was perfectly at ease with this upcoming tour. But I liked the idea of being on my own and having a car, even though it was an old one.

I had gone over all of this with Ted, and at the end of the workday one afternoon, he said, "Well, what do you think? You don't look too fired up."

I said, partly playacting, "I've been looking at what these ladies have scheduled for me, and, I don't know…I think I'm gonna need some Hadacol to keep me going."

He said, "That stuff's eighty percent alcohol." I nodded, still putting on the sad act.

I said, "I know. But most days they got me singing twice a day, and now and then, I'm singing, talking, and putting that screen up for breakfast, lunch, and supper. Every week I'm doing at least twelve shows. You know I get ten bucks a show, singing for service clubs, for just twenty or thirty minutes. These shows take an hour."

He said, "I've never heard you whine like this. What are you getting at?"

I said, "I think I need something stronger than Hadacol, 'cause ten times twelve is 120 bucks. Could we meet half way and say 60?"

His laugh was like an explosion. "Damn, you must be my son! So a raise would pep you up?" I nodded, with a hopeful look. He exhaled, looked at me and shook his head. He said, "Sounds reasonable."

My first stop was Cincinnati, where I sang for two meetings. There were photographers from different newspapers, and I sang

"The Fox," learned from Burl Ives' album, plus "Groundhog," two of my own songs, "Wind Spiritual" and "Lonesome Gal." I had learned to play "Barbara Allen," and my "Kentucky Mule" on the dulcimer. I sang "Goober Peas," the song from the Civil War era, that helped get me into my pitch for *Wilderness Road.*

After doing a presentation in the town of Jackson, I went to Marietta and checked into a motel, one I kept while doing a program in nearby Washington. Then I went to Yellow Springs, where I had two programs scheduled, lunch and dinner, but took time to check out Antioch College, where I was performing the next day. The president of the student body and a man from the theatre department showed me where I would set up my slide projector and screen and sing for the students. This made me wonder why the ladies had booked me to sing for students. They were not apt to travel to Berea to see the play. On the other hand, I thought, there might be a couple of drama students who'd want to try out for a role or check out the outdoor drama scene. And my visit might get some publicity in academic circles, newsletters, and newspapers. Ted would know.

When I called in, he said he had received some wonderful press. He said, "Son, your trip is paying off, just like I hoped it would. I'm delighted." I said, "Do I get a raise?" He laughed louder than before and said, "Yes, by god, you do."

Toward the middle of October, it was time for me to return to Berea. I was feeling road weary and more than ready for a break. I had a great reunion with Ted in his office, along with some of the ladies who had set up the tour. They also had received great reports from their alumni contacts. I thanked them all, and Ted put a stack of newspapers on his desk. He patted it with his hand said, "This means we're going to have a hell of a premiere for *Wilderness Road.* Ohioans are the travelingest people in the world." For the fifteen weeks, Ted wrote me a check for $1125, which I promptly deposited into my Berea Bank & Trust account.

The next evening, I went to Mama Scrivner's and saw someone I'd never seen. She was wearing a slouchy shirt, but it didn't detract from her beauty: high cheekbones, sultry eyes, and dark hair. Not a student, I was sure, too mature and poised, in a nonchalant manner. "Billy Edd," Mama said, "This is my daughter, Joan." I said hi, feeling nervous for some reason. And when she spoke I heard a deep, musical voice.

"Mom's been telling me about you. I won't tell you what she's said; don't want to give you the big head, but…"

Mama Scrivner interrupted, saying, "Joan!" Her one word meant Joan should knock it off.

Joan shot back: "I was about to say, but I wish you'd brought your guitar." Mama said, "Oh."

"I'll bring it next time," I said. "From your voice, I bet you're a singer. I'd like to sing you some of my songs." I was nervous before. Now I was on a nervous high. Not that I thought I had a chance with Joan, or would even think of trying to date her. She was mature. I was naïve. Before we had a chance to get engaged in conversation, Joan stood up and said, "Goodbye, Mom. Goodbye you," looking at me with a smile. And she was gone.

I said to Mama Scrivner, "She is a singer, right?"

Mama took her time answering. "Yes. A very good one. She's also a mother with three boys and in the middle of a divorce."

I didn't push for more information, and before she could ask me about my tour, I started talking about it.

She surprised me by saying, "I'm going to try out for a role in *Wilderness Road*. I'm sure you'll try for a role too, huh?" I said I hadn't thought about it, which was true. The few roles I'd done at Warren Wilson didn't convince me I was an actor.

She said, "I have an idea Joan will also get a chance to sing in the play, if she wants to. When she sings 'Jesus Walked That Lonesome Valley' you feel chills all over your body."

Chapter Nine

SASSAFRAS

Well, way down yonder in the tall grass
Lived a little woman named Sassafras
Had a wiggle in her walk and a giggle in her talk
A pony tail puttin' on the class
So tell all the neighborhood boys
I'm the one making all the noise
For I let a cup o' tea melt the heart outta me
And that cup o' tea was Sassafras

Too soon, I was back on the Ohio tour that would take me into mid-December. One pretty day as I was strolling along in Canton, a man came abreast of me and asked where I was from. When I told him, he asked what I was doing in town. When I told him about my presentations, he acted really interested and wanted to know more. So I followed him for a very short distance off the main street to a bench on the edge of a park. We chit-chatted a while.

Then he directed my attention to a particular set of windows on the corner of a large apartment building, saying it was where he lived. He said, "We're having a party there tonight, and would love to have you join us." I said, "Lots of girls?" He said. "No, it's an all-men get together. We talk about hunting and fishing, poker—you know, men stuff."

I was beginning to feel uneasy. I said, "What's a party without girls?"

He said, "You can have a lot of fun without girls," and gave my thigh a little pat.

I stood up and said, "I'm busy tonight. Thanks but no thanks. You guys have fun." I walked away without looking back, feeling a little sorry for him. I thought, *What's life without a girl or woman in it?* Later in life, I came to like, and love, several gay friends, good friends, in whose company I never felt the least bit uneasy. Certainly I didn't feel sorry for them.

The people, towns, meals, and presentations fuse together in my memory, except for two. In Springfield, my host was Bradley Kincaid, a nice-looking man about sixty years of age. I'd been told he had attended Berea Academy and was a singer of country music. Not much else. He picked me up at my motel and took me to my first appointment, a garden club. After a nice lunch, I set up my screen and slide projector, gave my speech, and sang a few songs, including "Barbara Allen."

Then he took me to his music store where we had glasses of sweet tea and talked. He said, "I hope you won't take offense if I offer a few suggestions." I said, "Of course not."

He began in a pleasant tone of voice, but not apologetically. "You're rushing through your songs. You didn't appear nervous, but I think you were. Hopefully not because I was there." I shook my head.

He said, "Maybe not. There may be some other reasons. But no matter, the point I'm getting to is, you've got to pause between songs and give your audience a chance to clap. Maybe you're afraid they won't clap, and you're not taking any chances, so you rush into your next number. But believe me, they will clap. They want to. Is this making any sense?" He took his time to take a big swig of tea as I said, "Yes. Were you nervous when you started singing?"

He chuckled loudly. "Tell you the truth, Billy, I can't remember. It was a long time ago. But I was with pros, and I was learning from them. I take it you've always been a solo act."

I nodded and took a drink of tea. "Well, Billy, er, do you prefer Billy Edd?" I told him Billy Edd. "OK, Billy Edd, back to the clapping business. I like your voice and your phrasing. It has a natural, folksy quality. So your audiences *will* clap. Just give them a chance. How's about I stop gabbing and give you a tour of Springfield, and then maybe catch a bite of supper. If you don't have plans."

We ate at a very nice steak house, of which he was part owner, and I told him it was his turn—would he please tell me more about himself. He said, "That song you sang, 'Barbara Allen,' I sang it at the National Barn Dance on WLS-AM in Chicago, and no country audience had ever heard it. It made my career. One writer said 'Barbara Allen' made me a star overnight. Another one claimed I was a bridge from folk music to commercial country. All this because of a traditional folk song. As for the star business, I never felt like a star or tried to act like one. I was just a country boy having a good time doing what I liked to do. 'Course, I'm not a boy anymore. I'm retired, having fun with my radio station and my music store."

"You're very humble about your success," I said. "Which one were you, folk or country?"

He said, "I've always considered myself a folk singer. I studied it, researched it, knew hundreds of folk songs. But most of the radio stations I was on were country."

He laughed loud, as if having just remembered something. "I was on an early morning show in Boston, station WBZ-FM, and this guy, Marshall Jones, was always fussy and crabby. So I called him Grandpa Jones, and the name stuck. He used it all his life from then on."

> They say white lightning that's in a jar
> Clear like water but it's hot as fire
> Well it may be true, but let me tell you
> Glass won't hold Sassafras

REFRAIN
So tell all the neighbor boys
I'm the one making all the noise
For I let a cup o' tea melt the heart outta me
And that cup o' tea was Sassafras

One other program, and what it led to, stands out in my mind.
I sang for a church group in Richmond, Indiana, and the food
fixings were very sparse. So my hosts, Rose and Paul, invited me
to their home for some real food. As Rose was warming it up, I
looked at photographs, mostly portraits, on the walls and small
tables and was immediately struck by the unusual tones of blacks,
whites, and grays, and the artful highlights. They reminded me of
the Doris Ulmann photos. A lot of them were of their daughter, a
beautiful girl the photographer made to look like a movie star.

I commented on it to Rose, and she said, casually, "Oh yes,
those are by our local photographer, Roy Hirshburg. He's a
professional and quite famous."

I said, "I'd like to meet him, but it's probably too late." She
assured me it wasn't, because he worked at night. After the late
dinner, I followed my hosts to his studio on Main Street. We walked
upstairs, me carrying my dulcimer, and entered without knocking.

A loud voice exclaimed, "Hey Rose, Paul, glad to see you!
Who you got tagging along there?" I was introduced to Roy
Hirshburg, and my hosts excused themselves.

Roy noticed my dulcimer, grabbed it out of my hands, and said,
"My god, how beautiful. Shaped like a curvaceous woman's body.
I gotta photograph it." He ran to a phone, dialed, and practically
yelled, "Baby, get your ass over here. I've got a prop like you've
never seen. The two of you are gonna be glorious together." When
she arrived, he said, "Excuse me, Billy. Got work to do." He placed
the girl's face in the curve in the middle of the dulcimer, arranging
her hair this way and that, and shot pictures like crazy. After half an
hour, he let her go, poured himself some tea, and offered me a glass.

He took several shots of me, mostly close-ups, and then asked me to tell him about my tour. He seemed very interested in the upcoming drama by Paul Green. In his darkroom he showed me prints of a famous British singer, whose name I can't recall. She was not as famous as the German-American, Marlene Dietrich, but just as beautiful. He had portraits of Robert Frost, prompting me to tell how I was introduced to Frost's poetry and how much I loved it. "Ah," he said, "I love it, too. I write poetry myself, almost every day." He showed me several shots of Admiral Richard E. Byrd. "A tough old bastard," he said. Roy showed me photos and talked for several hours. He was the most physically active, creative man I'd ever met.

Ted welcomed me back and wanted a list of all the places where I sang and showed slides. I had been keeping a list, and he was dazzled when I reported the following:

- Twenty-six programs at twenty different colleges and universities.
- Twenty-eight church groups.
- Seventeen miscellaneous groups, including Daughters of the American Revolution, Daughters of the Confederacy, Ohio historical societies, chambers of commerce, folk festivals and dances, etc.
- Berea alumni groups in eight cities.
- Eight programs at elementary schools, six at junior high schools, twenty-four at high schools.
- Towns and cities visited in Ohio and Indiana: fifty-four.

"Damn, Hillbilly Billy, that makes me tired just reading it," Ted said. You worked your buns off, and I'm sure it's going to pay off at the box office. Here, you earned it." It was a check for $955.00. When I deposited it, I took out $100 to get me through Christmas. If I was careful, I would end the year with around $3500, more than enough for the car of my dreams. But when school was out I would have to pay for food and rent until I found out if I'd have a job in *Wilderness Road*.

As if I didn't have enough to do, I was approached by
Professor Rolf Hovey, who directed the Berea College Choir, and
asked if I would sing some folk songs on an album he was doing
with the choir. He convinced me it would not take much of my
time, but his budget didn't allow him to pay anyone for singing.
It would be a labor of love and could be good publicity for the
college. I told him it would be an honor to be on the album. It
was being recorded in the Music Building, and sure enough, I put
down six songs in one afternoon, all traditional folk songs.

The final production at the Tab, directed by Fred Parrot, was
Our Town, by Thornton Wilder. I loved the play. And just like
Robert Frost, Wilder made magic out of just plain people in
small-town USA. When it was announced, weeks before the
opening, that the playwright himself was coming and would meet
with students interested in writing plays, I signed up. He would
meet us individually, fifteen minutes each, at Boone Tavern.

When it was my turn, I entered the room where I had
performed for the Lions Club. He sat at a card table and pointed
at the straight-backed chair opposite. He smiled cordially, asking
my name and what kind of writing I did.

I said, "I write folk-flavored songs, poetry, and, so far, only one
short play." He asked for the title. I said, "*Eyes of the Devil's Horses*,"
and told him about the Brown Mountain lights and the black
slaves searching for their lost masters.

He said, "Interesting. A natural phenomenon, and a folk
legend. But unless you have interesting, real people, you may have
problems. The spooky stuff won't carry it alone."

I said, "I agree. I don't plan to rewrite it."

He asked if I had a drama school in mind. I shook my
head. He said, "If you ever do, I recommend Yale." I was totally
surprised, and wide-eyed, and said, "Wow." As if reading my
thoughts, he said, "They give scholarships. Berea students are
known for their work ethic." I didn't follow up on that. After a
lull, he said, "If you're going to write, take time to ponder. Good

luck." That was my cue. Time was up. I rose and started thanking him profusely, but he waved me off, and I skedaddled.

At the end of the year, when all the grades were in, I graduated in the lower third of my class. But one bright spot that made me proud was our commencement speaker, Dr. Bannerman, who received an honorary PhD. He was presented by Dr. Ross, who called him a "downright upright man." One other honorary doctorate was given earlier to a speaker whose main topic was about the ending of World War II. He talked about Hitler being killed in a bunker along with his paramour. When he ate with us in the dining hall, one country boy said to him, "I can see why they'd kill Hitler, but why'd they have to go and destroy a good power mower?" The student was serious, but didn't seem to mind when everybody laughed.

I was no longer on Ted's payroll but still worked the required ten hours a week, and more, in his office with two staffers, one of whom was photographer Bob Connor that Ted hired on my recommendation.

School would close soon, so I found a room available in Dr. Henderson's house on Frost Court, on campus, just behind Union Church. I remembered Dr. Henderson as one of the doctors who helped give physical exams to new students. He was trying out for *Wilderness Road,* too.

When tryouts began at India Fort Theatre, beautiful and perfectly blended in with nature, it became a long and boring process. Because I was a dancer, Dr. Sam Selden gave me the role of Squire Martin Sims' oldest son, Henry, known to be a hard bargainer as well as being a tightwad. Mama Scrivner landed a big role as the mother of John Freeman, the play's leading character.

Ted Cronk said, "I think damn near eighty percent of our cast and crew are Berea teachers and students. Everybody's willing to pitch in and help."

Bob Elkins, Martin Ambrose, and I took advantage of these boring days by singing a lot of my songs. We got good enough to think we needed a name, so we became The Berea Three. Martin had the use of his mom's car, so he took me to Glenn Pennington Autos, where I had seen that beautiful 1953 Ford convertible.

On the way, Martin said, "Glenn Pennington is married to Lily May, a member of the famous group called The Coon Creek Girls. They performed for the Queen of England at the White House a few years ago. She plays fiddle and sings."

I said, "You sure know a lot about 'em."

He glanced over at me like I was crazy. "Well, I ought to. I've lived here all my life."

Mr. Pennington came out to join us as we strolled down the lines of cars. I greeted him with, "No Ford convertibles?" He said no, but he did have a great, slightly used black Thunderbird. I shook my head. "Do you sell new cars too?" He shook his head. I told him I wanted a new Ford Fairlane convertible, adding, "Couldn't you take me to a dealer in Richmond or Lexington and get a commission for bringing them a customer?"

He chuckled. "You're in a big hurry. You'll never get a good deal like that."

I raised my eyebrows. "You giving me tricks of the trade?"

He nodded. "I know pretty quick which car a customer's got his eye on. He'll pretend to be looking at others, but he's already sold."

I said, "Wow. An honest car salesman." I gave him the Henderson's phone number.

The stage was always busy with rehearsals, and behind the stage it was even busier. Sets were being constructed and painted, though several small scenes were acted in natural outdoor settings, enhanced by creative lighting. The activity and the noise of construction were exciting, as was the anticipation of opening night. A couple of sightings of Paul Green, accompanied by Ted Cronk and Sam Selden, were exciting in a different way. He was a legendary celebrity, right there, in person in Berea.

The most moving scene in *Wilderness Road* was when the Cherokee Indians were being force-marched from Cherokee, North Carolina, to Oklahoma. Families of women and children

were seen moving across the stage, many of them falling by the
wayside, exhausted, bandaged, crippled and dying. The most
brutal scene was seeing John Freeman's schoolhouse being
ransacked, John being beaten, books put in a pile and burned.
Berea College's story was portrayed just as it happened, and how
it survived brutality and prejudice, to become an educational
beacon of tolerance and learning, proclaiming to the world that
"God has made of one blood all the people of the earth."

After the show closed in mid-August, it was proclaimed a
hit, having entertained 75,000 theatergoers. Ted was jubilant. He
said, "We've got a successful show on our hands, but we've got
to work hard to make sure it's a success next year also. But now
we've got a lot of fodder to work with, PR- and publicity-wise,
thanks to you and me."

I said, "Aren't you tooting our horns a little too loud?"

His reply to my playful jab was, "Hell no. You can have
a wonderful product, but if the world out there doesn't hear
about it, it'll fail. The local audience alone couldn't support it.
Promotion, son, promotion."

I said, "OK, when you put it like that, I'll accept a few boo-kays."

He said, "This was Kentucky's first outdoor drama, and also
the first ever to be sponsored by a college. You can be proud of
what we did." I told him I loved having him as my boss, and
thanked him for giving me a chance to learn things from him.
Not to mention the money I made.

I earned $360 from the show, part of which I put in the bank.
Chad managed to give me $150 for the previous issues I had
done, and for continuing to edit *Mountain Life and Work*. I had
two more issues to do during the fall and winter. I still went on
trips with Ted now and then, at no charge, and found time to
write more songs, plus rewrite those I had already written.

One evening I had a phone call from Glenn Pennington
Autos. He said, "I've got your car. Used, but not a scratch on it,
and very low mileage."

I told him I couldn't wait to see it, but I didn't have a ride. "Can you take it for a test drive and swing by here?" When he arrived, I leaped off the porch, shook his hand, opened the door, and looked inside. It seemed to sparkle. I asked, "How's it drive?"

He answered, continuing to smile, "Smooth as a rat running through cotton."

I ran into the house, got my checkbook, jumped in, and asked as he drove, "How much you asking…in case I decide I can afford it." He looked sideways at me and just smiled, as if to say, "Yeah, right." I said, "Of course, I'm being funny. Even an idiot salesman would know I want this car bad, and you're no idiot. I remember all your tips of the trade, and you know what? I think you'll give me the best deal you can. Right?" He nodded. I went on. "I know this Fairlane costs $2,250 new. Soooo, how much?"

He said, "I got it for $1700. You can have it for $1900."

"I can't believe you're just making two hundred bucks," I responded. "How come?"

He shrugged. "I'm not greedy, and I know you pick and sing. My kind of people, and I want your business."

I said, "You're my kind of people, too. I know you and your wife are way ahead of me, but I'd like to sit in with you sometime. Will you do an insurance policy for me, too, and add it to my bill?" He said he would.

I said, "By the way, how much is a gallon of gas?" He told me, thirty-one cents. I said, "That's a hamburger and a half at the Carlton. I'm wondering about one more thing. Who in the world would let go of a car like this with such low mileage on it?"

He chuckled and said, "Somebody whose wife got wind that he was bragging and calling it his love buggy. That's what he called it at large. To his buddies he called it his pussy wagon. At least that's what the dealer told me."

I said, "Dumb bastard. I'm sure glad he got caught."

It's hard for me to describe how much that car meant to me. Somehow I felt as if I had finally realized my birthright…what

every American boy dreams of, rich or poor. I enjoyed that Ford
Fairlane convertible during autumn days and winter wonders, the
Christmas Country Dance School, and traveling to get interviews
for *Mountain Life and Work* articles.

In July I got a letter from Uncle Sam telling me I was going
to be drafted. I met with a naval officer in Dr. Woodie's office
who told me about the AOC program, aviation officer candidate.
He asked if I knew what made a plane fly, and would I like to
find out? I answered no, and yes. The good news was, if accepted,
I would begin my military service in Pensacola, Florida, just fifty
miles from Uncle Joe and Louise in Crestview.

On July 13, I got on a bus in Berea that took me and a group
of guys to a naval aviation facility in Ohio. A navy pilot took
me aloft and did all sorts of maneuvers to see if I liked it or got
sick…loops, dives, upside down periods where ashes from the ash
trays fell into my face and headgear. I hated the ashes but loved
the flying. I wondered who was allowed to smoke while flying or
just sitting in the plane on the ground, but never got the chance
to ask.

Back in Berea, I said goodbye to my friends and drove to
Pensacola. The Mickey Mouse stuff started at once that night as
I stood in front of a desk being checked in. "Stand at attention,
college boy," the sergeant barked. I was directed to a room in a
barrack where I introduced myself to a New York guy named
Winston Bridge. I showered, went to bed, and woke up after
what seemed like a half-hour's sleep. Bridge showed me how to
make up a bunk expertly, as required, before I followed him to
the chow hall. Breakfast included orange juice, coffee, scrambled
eggs, and some kind of gravy over a biscuit, called "shit on a
shingle." It was OK but not as good as Grandmother's or Sister's.

As I stood in line for a uniform, a sergeant noticed my belt
buckle and asked in a rough voice, "Soldier, are you a communist?"

I said, "No sir, that stands for Berea College."

In a softer tone, he said, "I know. Fine school."

Bridge told me he was referring to Beria, the Russian head of the KGB." I said, "Oh, right. I think I heard that on the radio back in the hills."

He laughed a mocking laugh. "Don't bullshit me, Smiley. You're no dumb hillbilly."

I said, "Then why'd you have to tell me?" He said, "Touché." His nickname for me stuck. Pretty soon everybody called me Smiley.

Our first big test as an AOC was to run the obstacle course. We were timed individually as we climbed ropes and ladder-like obstacles, jumped over water slots, and crawled through large drain pipes and under barbed wire. Already fatigued, we ran through sand to the finish line. I loved it. The time keeper told me, "Congratulations, Wheeler. You almost tied the record."

Bridge was standing close enough to hear. He said, "Way to go, Smiley. All that tree climbing and creek jumping paid off."

I answered with, "Yep, us hillbillies are quick-footed and slow-brained." As we left the O course, he was singing something to himself, but loud enough for me to hear: "Ain't misbehavin' I'm savin' my love for you." It sounded like sophisticated pop stuff. My guess was he'd never heard folk or country music, and would think poorly of it if he did.

But not so for the base at large. A sort of open-mic show was put on, and once again I found that everybody was looking for free entertainment. And these new recruits were hard-up for it. After about thirty minutes of whistlers, joke tellers, and a guy who sang a short opera piece without accompaniment, I walked on with my guitar and dulcimer. I sat and sang "Goober Peas" and "Big Rock Candy Mountain," getting a big hand. Then I put the dulcimer on my lap and sang "Ground Hog" and "Barbara Allen." To my surprise it got the biggest applause.

The officer who produced the show bragged on me to high heaven, telling me he'd love for me to do future shows, and also to be a guest on the base radio show. It was mostly talking, and my music would perk it up.

Bridge waited his turn and told me, "Damn, Smiley, you didn't tell me you're a professional."

I said, "Cut the comedy, J. Winston Bridge. You're misbehavin' and savin' the bullcrap for last."

He was adamant. "No, no, I loved that shit. Never heard anything like it."

Before classes started, we had two days off, so Bridge and some other guys invited me to play golf with them. I told them I'd never played and didn't have any golf clubs. They said I could get them on loan for free at the pro shop. All three of them told what their handicaps were, and I found out that first day that all three were liars. My baseball swing helped me break a hundred. It was almost like a good golf swing, with a few adjustments. Little did I realize then how meaningful golf would become in my life, professionally and otherwise.

In late March of 1957 I received a news item from Richmond, Indiana, that famed photographer Roy Hirshburg was shot and killed by a thirty-year-old divorcée named Ethel Wise. The murder stemmed from Miss Wise's jealousy over Hirshburg's attentions to Miss Anne McFarland. Miss McFarland had been a receptionist in Hirshburg's studio for three months. Miss Wise gave the couple a ride downtown and parked in front of the studio. She grabbed a .22 rifle, and as Anne McFarland stood by screaming, she shot Hirshburg once near the heart and twice in the head. Hirshburg had won many national and international awards.

In spite of the terrible news, it seemed to me it was the perfect way for Roy to go out. I could not imagine him growing old and withering on the vine.

Classes started with a full week of engines study, and I failed the big test. I was sent back a week to another class. Then I failed navigation and got sent back again. Then it was instruments, which I managed to muddle through. Finally, I got to start learning how to fly, and on the ninth hop we landed in a farmer's field. The instructor got out and said, "Take her for a spin."

Excited as all get-out, I made my first solo hop. Then all the class learning was put to practical use, as I was cursed, screamed at, and called the "dumbest son of a bitch he'd ever seen," by my Marine instructors. They try to break you down. They also play tricks to see if you're really listening to their airborne lectures. In the middle of one they'll say, "And see that bird on the wing?" Like a drone you'll say uh-huh, and his shouting response will be something you'd never want your mother or father to hear. It would cast aspersions on how they raised you to become so nitwitted, idiotic, ignorant, and just plain fucking dumb.

On November 3 I was commissioned as an ensign and got to start living in officers' quarters, eating at officers' mess, and drawing an officer's flight pay. I was introduced to Tuborg beer at the officer's club, though I didn't particularly like beer at all. But hey, it was imported from Denmark. It had to be a cut above, right? I was assigned to Whiting Field, at Milton, Florida, where I started learning to fly a T-28, a big tri-prop plane. When you cranked it up, it sounded like shotguns going off in a well. It was so powerful, on my first time up the instructor told me, "Do not spin this plane more than one and a half times. More than that and you're up shit creek. You can't get out of the spin, and you'll make a hell of a greasy spot when you hit the ground."

I went through instrument training, the hardest thing I ever tried to master, especially the ox yoke pattern, under the hood, nothing in front of you but instruments. It took me three hops to get a thumbs-up. In night flying you had to learn to deal with vertigo and the lights from moving vehicles below.

My next assignment was carrier landings, something I was not looking forward to. All our landing patterns were simulated carrier landings. You flew downwind past the target, turned left, and then left again into the wind as you descended. To give us a feel for the real thing, we were shuttled out to a carrier, climbed aboard, and were placed just on the edge of the flight deck. The thunderous noise, the action, and being that close to the landing aircraft made you feel like you were hearing it with your whole body, not just your ears. An awesome experience. I had a hard time picturing myself in that cockpit when it hit the deck, coming to a screeching stop. We were given a tour of the different levels of the carrier, where officers and non-coms slept and ate, bowled, shopped, saw movies, and got haircuts. It was a floating city.

That night I had nightmares about landing on that carrier. It was a mixture of excitement and dangerous adventure. What a rush, even though I was dreaming. But it was also a reality check, making me confront my fears. Could I do it? Did I *want* to do it? I woke up sweating, twice. I could DOR, drop on request, and serve out my four years somewhere else. But that was considered cowardly, disgraceful. I would not DOR, even if I might get killed. West Virginia boys were not cowards. Well, even if they were, in such a fix, they would not show it. They'd do it and see what happens.

My anxieties were all for naught. Lady Luck smiled upon me. Two days later, we AOCs were called together for an important statement by the base commander: "Gentlemen, I've called you together to discuss something that concerns your future and the US Navy's. You signed up for four years, and it takes a hell of a lot of money to teach you how to fly, the navy way, in two years. Then, after just two years of real service to our country, you're eligible for discharge. That's not a good return on our investment. So here's the deal: sign up for four more years, right now, or save us money and get out."

I looked to the guy next to me. "Did I hear him say we're free to go, if we don't sign for more time?" He said, "Yeah, four years."

I put the tips of my fingers together and held them under my chin, as if in prayer. I looked heavenward and said to myself, *Thank you, God. I'm getting out alive!*

Chapter Ten

ROCK BOLL WEEVIL

Well, the boll weevil am a little black bug
Come from Mexico, then what
Come all the way from Texas looking for a place to rock
He had to rock boll weevil, rock boll weevil,
Rock boll weevil, had to rock
Lost my cotton crop, lost my cotton crop
Cause that weevil had to rock

There I was in Pensacola, Florida, suddenly out of a job. I had two weeks to clear out while they worked up my discharge papers. I sat down and wrote a letter to Dr. Woodie, told him of my situation, and asked if he might have a job for me in the alumni office. If not, did he have any ideas where I might start looking? I also wrote to the Hendersons to see if my old room was available, and to Sister and Arthur. I played some golf and ended up buying a set of clubs from the pro. They were well used, but he had seen me many times and seemed glad to be able to encourage me to keep on playing. He let me have them for fifty bucks, and threw in a sleeve of golf balls as a bonus.

During the hiatus, I started working on a new song about a boll weevil. My idea was to dress up the traditional boll weevil and have him create a dance inspired by the twist. The cast of characters might include beetles, grasshoppers, snake doctors, June bugs, lovebugs, wooly worms, and glowworms. I wrote down all the words I could think of that rhymed with twist: list, cyst, and fist—plus a lot of off-rhymes like risk. None of them suggested a song, so I put the yellow pad away.

After six days I received a letter from Dr. Woodie, saying he had no job. But he had an idea, so come on to Berea. I was mustered out of active service on October 31, but with release papers instead of an honorable discharge. The top sergeant explained that I was now on stand-by status, and for a period of three or four years, I could be recalled if necessary. In the meantime, it was my duty to keep them informed of where I could be contacted at all times. He saluted me, shook my hand, and thanked me for my service. I awkwardly returned his salute. Off the record, he said it was unlikely I would be recalled. Essentially, I was free as a bird.

On a whim, driving back north, I decided to visit Warren Wilson College to look at the mountains and see who I could see without notice. Dr. Jensen was not in the office, nor was Julio Guissasola, so I drove to the Bannerman house and knocked on the door. The girl who opened it had a gorgeous shade of red hair. I'd never seen her before, but she was beautiful and sharply dressed, a full-figured woman. I was speechless. She filled the lull with, "Hello, I'm Mary. Have you come to see Mom and Dad?"

I told her who I was, and with my wits collected, I said, "Wow, you've grown up some since the last time I saw you. You were, I think, nine years old. I'd been out with your mother, watching her paint."

She smiled. "Oh yes, I've heard Mom and Dad talk about you. Want to come in?" I went inside and was received cordially. I told them my story, and, as I talked, I tried to look at Mary without staring. I think it's fair to say I was smitten. After I left, I got in the car and drove away. But instead of hitting the road for Berea, I went to the nearest phone booth I could find and looked up the number for Bannerman. There was only one listing. When Mary answered, I told her who I was, and she said, "Do you want to talk to Dad?"

I said, "No, I want to talk to you. Would you like to play some golf?"

She said she had played a little golf in one of her phys ed classes, but insisted she wasn't very good. I told her it didn't matter. I just wanted to get to know her a little better, since she had changed a lot since the first time I saw her. She finally agreed to meet me the next afternoon at the municipal golf course in Asheville.

She arrived right on time…with her dad. She played two holes and said, "I told you I wasn't very good. You'll have more fun finishing the round with Dad." She drove away in his car without giving me a goodbye hug, which I'd hoped for. Dr. Bannerman and I had a really good time finishing the round, despite my disappointment. He weighed about a hundred and thirty pounds, but he hit the ball straight down the middle with his left-handed swing. He loved golf more than anyone I knew, but he made it a point to ask about what I'd been doing since leaving Warren Wilson. We talked about the times I'd gone with him to this club and that, our trip to Gatlinburg, and his speech at Berea's Centennial Commencement. After I drove him home, I left thinking what a truly great gentleman he was. And what a beautiful daughter he had! I thought about her all the way to Berea.

My brother, Bob, was now at Berea, and I found out he was living at Bingham Dorm. I paid him a visit, and after we swapped hugs, he introduced me to Richard Bellando, who played the guitar and said he was interested in learning some traditional Appalachian folk songs. Knowing how close Arthur was with his money, I gave Bob a few bucks, with the promise of more if he needed it.

I had a great reunion with the Hendersons but made it as short as possible, since I was eager to hear what Dr. Woodie's idea

was. He told me he wanted to take me see President Hutchins
and try to convince him to hire me, at least part time, because
he wanted to eventually return to teaching philosophy and
religion. Dr. Hutchins was in a good mood, asking me about
my commission as an officer, how I liked flying, and how in the
world did I get out in less than two years. He listened closely, but
I could tell his mind was busy. At last, he said, "Well, Mr. Wheeler,
Billy, you know we ask our faculty not to smoke or drink. Is that
going to cramp your style?"

Thinking he was still in a good mood, I said, "Dr. Hutchins,
since you're going to hire me part time, I hope, I'll only smoke or
drink part time."

He laughed loud, as he pushed his glasses back up high on his
nose with his forefinger, and said, "Very well."

I was elated. On our way to the alumni office, I said, "You
know, the president has the reputation of being stuck up, the way
he walks with his head held so high. You know what I think? I
think it's because of his glasses. He has a good sense of humor."

Norris said, "That's a great observation. I think I agree with
you."

As we entered the building, a nice-looking man got up from
his chair and presented Norris with some papers, saying, "Here is
the biographical information you requested."

Norris thanked him and introduced me, saying "Fuad Abu
Zyad, from Jordan, this is Billy Edd Wheeler, from West Virginia.
My new assistant." He had a very firm handshake and sported a
perfectly trimmed moustache, as dark as his hair.

"Actually," he said, "my name is *Doctor* Abu Zyad." Norris
smiled and pointed to a line in Fuad's bio as I walked out the
door. I hadn't gone far before Fuad caught up with me.

"If you would permit me," he said, "I would like to walk with
you. There are not a lot of faculty our age. Lots of old fuddy-duddies,
as you say here in America." He was starting to say more, but
interrupted himself. "Billy, tell me who is that beautiful woman?"

I looked to see Lila Davis coming out of the post office. I told him her name and said, "I hear she was runner-up to Miss Tennessee back home."

He quickly said, "You must introduce me."

I yelled loud enough to catch her attention, and when she approached, I said, "Lila, this is Fuad Abu Zyad." Lila shook his hand and said she was glad to meet him, but she was late for class and had to scoot.

He watched her walk away, then turned to me. "Listen, my friend, in the future you must introduce me as *Doctor* Abu Zyad."

I couldn't believe it. I said, "You pompous son of a camel salesman. I thought you wanted to meet her, thinking you might want to ask for a date, or something."

I shook my head as he placed a hand on my shoulder and said, "All the same. You must not let the students become too familiar."

I said, "**Doctor** Fuad, I roomed with a Jordanian at Warren Wilson College. He was humble and polite, but you...you take the cake. If you're going to be friends with me, you'll have to cut the bullshit."

He let out a booming laugh, slapped me on the chest, and said, "Ah-ha! I knew we were going to be friends."

I said, "Maybe so. But I don't think she'd accept, even if you asked her. She hangs out with my brother's first roommate, Richard Bellando, a lot, and his buddy, Sonny Osborne. I think they're pretty tight."

Fuad smiled broadly and said, "I don't mind a little competition. In fact, I welcome it. Is she married?" I said I didn't think so. "Well, there you are, my friend."

I got to know Lila and her friends gradually, meeting them so many times in different places it was hard to remember any one incident that made me realize how much I liked them.

For some reason, getting into November, I was more fired up about writing songs than I'd ever been. I finished the boll weevil song, without that outlandish cast of characters I'd considered. And without them it was simple. I just put the word *rock* into every traditional verse, plus the ones I wrote, finishing it in just two sittings. I asked two friends who loved music, Larry Blondell and Phil Ogle, to practice with me, offering to pay them. They said they were honored just to be considered and thought it would be fun, adding that if I ever put the songs out as a record, I had to put their names on it.

I went to Mama Scrivner's house just to say hello and found that Joan was staying with her for a while. I told her about the album I was doing and asked if she would sing with me on it, plus do some songs of her own choosing, hopefully folk or other songs in the public domain. "But you haven't even heard me sing," she protested. I said, "I don't need to. Mama says you're good, better than good, so that's good enough for me. But…if you want to, sing something, like the one she told me about, 'Jesus Walked.'"

Joan picked up the guitar, saying she wasn't very good, but could fake it. She played and started singing: "Jesus walked this lonesome valley, he had to walk it by himself, oh, nobody else could walk it for him, he had to walk it by himself." I was in awe, completely blown away. I'd never heard such a rich tone come out of any woman's mouth. There was nobody like her.

I said, "Mama was right, of course. You're…well, I don't belittle your voice by trying to describe it. It's so great, I'm afraid you're going to think a lot of my songs are trivial and beneath you."

She said, "I can do trivial. Let's start learning your songs."

> Captain said to the Missus, now whatta you think o' that
> Boll Weevil done rock and rolled in my best Sunday hat
> He had to rock Boll Weevil, had to rock
> Boll Weevil said to the farmer, you better leave me alone
> I done rocked in your cotton, gonna roll in y our sweet corn
> He had to rock Boll Weevil, had to rock

By the middle of November, we were ready to record fifteen songs for my album, plus "Rock Boll Weevil" on a second reel.

A Cincinnati man recommended by Dr. Hovey came down with his wire recorder and charged me just $200 for the two-day session in the basement of the art building. I loved the acoustics there. Joan and I did duets on "Wind Spiritual," "The Tailor and the Maid," "Just So He Come," and "Ain't Going Home Soon."

I had learned how to play her song, "Jesus Walked This Lonesome Valley," on the guitar, and the way she sang it gave me chill bumps. I had no idea what I would do with these tracks. I had no contacts with a recording company. But I didn't worry about it. It was a milestone, even if it never got commercially released. I was busy working for Norris, and I still did solo shows for service clubs and other special groups. But I upped my fee to fifteen dollars. I accepted invites to sing at small student functions or get-togethers and charged nothing for those.

In mid-December, I thought about going to Highcoal for Christmas but ended up just letting Bob take home a nice Churchill Weavers scarf for Sister and a tie for Arthur. I had decided to register for Christmas Country Dance School. It was getting close to the time of year when most students would be going home. I thought it would be fun to be a participant and not a performer, freeing me to pick and choose the dances without having to schedule them around my singing chores. It also entitled me to dine with everybody at the college dining hall.

Norris invited me to have dinner with him, his wife, Hilda, and family of two girls and a boy. A friend of theirs was also present. I was introduced to a West Virginia girl named Judy Hayes. She was very good looking, with dark hair, and spoke with a voice that sounded somewhat West Virginian, but with a vocabulary more sophisticated than any girl I'd ever met in those hills of home. She had to leave early, but I hoped I'd see her again.

During Christmas Country Dance School, I enjoyed being free to dance without worrying about when I was going to be asked to perform. There was one older couple who seemed to be part of the New York group, and after one of the English dances,

I saw the man talking to Bunn McClain. After some conversation, Bunn pointed at me, and the white-haired man walked over. His smile showed a row of perfect white teeth.

He said, "I was hoping you would be singing tonight. I wanted to hear you in person." I looked questioningly at him. He went on: "I have listened to you sing folk songs on the Berea College Choir album." I had totally forgotten about that album and was surprised he had a copy. "You have a way of phrasing that reminds me of Theo Bikel, though your repertoire is different."

My look told him I'd never heard of Theo Bikel. "He's a well-known New York folk singer and actor. Have you ever been on other albums?" I shook my head. "I like your singing and wondered if you might like to do an album of your own?" I told him, of course I would.

He said, "I publish music, a lot of it folk music."

I was getting interested but not yet excited. I said, "By *publish*, you mean you produce albums?"

He shook his head. "No, I publish songs in collections and folios. But I have some connections with record labels. If you'd like, I'll see what I can do." Now I was excited.

Mr. Newman said it was a pleasure meeting me. We shook hands, and he turned away to rejoin his lady, who'd been watching from a distance. I dashed after him. He stopped. I said, "By the way, I've written sixteen new songs, very folksy-like, and just recorded them on wire tape, or whatever you call it. I was wondering if you might like to have a listen." His eyes brightened and he smiled, showing that row of beautiful teeth again.

He invited me to join them for dinner at Boone Tavern, where I gave him two reels, telling him "Rock Boll Weevil" was on a reel by itself. I said it was my opinion that, because it sounded so commercial, it didn't fit well with all the other folksy songs, and I hoped he'd agree. But, of course, it was his decision. He was quick to tell me my opinion mattered a lot to him, and if I was not happy, he would not be either. What a gentleman. He reminded me of Dr. Bannerman.

He introduced his lady, whose last name was different from his. I think he was courting her. He had that air of slightly nervous excitement about him, wanting to please her in every way. I think he was also trying to impress her by the way he was making a deal with me, thoughtful and gently aggressive. He gave me his card, telling me I would be hearing from him. Mr. Newman told me about publishing folios of folk songs from around the world, plus jazz and classical music.

He was also the importer of Kyung recorders from Switzerland. I had no idea what they were, but as he educated me, I saw he was passionate about them, describing the wood used in making them, the beautiful tones they produced, and how thrilling it was to hear them played in concert by skilled musicians. He played one too, but was not gifted, just barely competent. He said recorders were mentioned in Shakespeare's *Hamlet*, and he had started a memoir entitled *The House That Hamlet Built*.

I had never heard of any music publisher coming to Christmas Country Dance School before. And now I had met the first one, from New York City, no less, who just happened to pick up the Berea College Choir album, listen to it, and look me up. What a coincidence. What a Christmas present!

In 1958, Norris went back into teaching and I took over his job as alumni director. Actually, the title back then was alumni secretary. But director sounds more prestigious. I was in charge of editing the quarterly *Berea Alumnus*. I already had an idea for a future issue: our sister college, Warren Wilson. I would ask Tom Fern to design the cover showing an owl in flight. A senior citizen named Charles Morgan, recommended by the president, was helping me plan a fund-raising visitation in Cincinnati for the summer.

When the days started warming, Bernard Davidson came to my office. When I first saw him I figured he wanted me to sing again, and I anticipated it would become another haggling session over my fee increase, just like our previous meeting. But no, he had come on behalf of a Berea golf course committee.

They were looking to increase membership. I listened to his pitch, and when he told me yearly dues were forty dollars a year, I said, "I'll give you thirty." He laughed, knowing I was kidding. He said Betty and Tom Fern were members, and Coach Wyatt, too. I said, "When do you want to tee it up? I'm a beginner, so I want strokes." He seemed pleased I was such an easy sell. But he refused to offer strokes, saying he'd have to check out my game first. Besides, he didn't bet but three dollars per round. So we set a date for Saturday afternoon.

When I got out of my car and walked up toward the club house and pro shop, Bernard was waiting on the porch. When he saw my clubs and bag, he said, "Where in the world'd you get those, at a garage sale?"

I said, "Hey, I paid twenty-five bucks for these down at Whiting Field in Florida."

He said, "For forty, our pro can get you a brand-new set. Come on."

I paid forty bucks to the pro and asked him to order me some new clubs. He wanted to know what brand I wanted. I told him I didn't know. "Just get me what you'd recommend," I said. "I'm a beginner, but I hope not for long. How's about the kind you play with?" He said OK, but that would cost me fifty. I agreed.

We teed off, and I triple bogeyed the first hole, a par four with a dogleg left. The second hole was a par three, just beyond a small pond. My drive plunked right into it, so, with a stroke penalty, I hit across the green in three, hit back onto the green in four, and two putted. Another triple bogey. Bernard was good company, very patient with me, and, on the fourth tee, he pulled a bottle of vodka from his bag and took a swig. He offered the bottle to me. I declined, telling him I was not into the strong stuff yet. Afraid I might like it. Standing close to me, he said, "Always drink vodka. They can't smell it on your breath." I thought it was funny. His breath still made me back away, but I didn't say anything.

As we played, he asked if I knew Red Foley. I shook my head, but said, of course I knew *of* him. He said, "He lives right here in Berea. How's about Pat Boone?"

I said, "Oh, yeah. I heard 'Love Letters in the Sand' on the radio day and night for weeks when I was in the service down in Florida in 1957. And, later that year, 'April Love' came along, too. The DJ said they both went to number one."

He grinned at me like the cat that swallowed the canary and said, "He's Red Foley's son-in-law. Married Shirley." I looked at him with wide eyes, causing him to ask, "What?"

I told him about my recording session. "I might have a song for Pat, if I could get it to him."

He jumped right in, telling me Shirley's sister, Betty, might just do it. He'd introduce me, if I wanted him to.

I said, "Do, and I'll buy you a bottle of vodka."

Two days later, my secretary, Betty Lamb, said a Bernard Davidson was on the phone. I said, "Great, tell him I'll be right there."

I took the phone and Bernard said, "I've got Betty and her husband, Bentley Cummins, here in the office. I'm in the east end of town on the right. You'll see my sign." I dropped everything and drove to his place where the sign proclaimed: *Davidson Foods, Inc.* Two large refrigerated trucks had the same writing on them. I had driven by his company many times but failed to connect it with the man who hired me to sing for his Lions Club.

Bernard seemed to enjoy playing host, as did his brother, Harold, a little taller and definitely more slender than he. Betty Foley Cummins was also showing some excitement for being the center of attention. Bentley gave me his card. He was a used-car salesman, just like Glenn Pennington, but on the opposite end of town. Betty was talkative, telling about the times she had spent with sister, Shirley, and brother-in-law, Pat, and their kids. And she was proud of her dad, the *best country singer in the world, and definitely the best entertainer.*

She promised to get my reel in the mail to Pat's manager, Jack Spina, on Monday. Special delivery. Bernard suggested we have a drink to celebrate the occasion, and Betty agreed, despite the frowns of her husband, who declined. I said I had to get back to the office but thanked them all profusely. I shook hands with Bentley and offered my hand to Betty, but she swept it away and gave me a very warm hug.

That night after supper I did a little office work until I tired of it and picked up my guitar. At midnight, a sliver of moonlight shined across the floor, and for some reason, it made me think of Highcoal and how I used to look up at the sky, watching birds fly over the mountaintops. I remembered wishing I could fly up and out of the coal camp like one of those birds. I was not a good guitar player, but I pretended I was and started banging those strings like a jazz artist. I didn't have a pad and pencil handy, I just started singing:

> *There's a high flyin' bird up in the sky*
> *And I wonder if that bird looks down as he flies on by*
> *Riding on the air so easy in the sky*
> *Sun comes along.... Lights up the day*
> *And when he gets tired he slides on over the way*
> *East to the west he gets gone every day*
> *But Lord look at me here, tired as can be here*
> *I got the sit down, can't fly, oh lord I'm gonna die blues*

Years later, when I was rehearsing the song and Jerry Leiber walked by and heard me sing, "But Lord look at me here, tired as can be here," he stopped, said, "rooted like a tree here," and walked on by. I thought, *Wow, what a perfect line. It's a better song now, like, ten times better now.* And Jerry didn't ask for part of the song.

Chapter Eleven

THE CHAIN GANG OF LOVE

There is iron in the touch of your tender fingertips
Your soft smile is strong as any steel
There's a chain holding me, one that I can't see
A chain of love that only hearts can feel
And I'm working on the chain gang of love
I'm your prisoner when you turn out the light
Yes I'm working, working on the chain gang of love
Come lock me in your loving arms tonight
(cowritten with Roger Bowling)

The God of coincidences was still blessing me. I came back down to earth when I heard through the grapevine on campus that some faculty members had bought some cheap houses from the military facility near Richmond and had them moved to Berea. One of the faculty members was Emily Ann Smith. I caught up with her after one of her classes and asked if her house was for rent. She said, "My, my, news travels fast. I've just had mine painted pink to cover that god-awful military gray. The paint's barely dry, and here you are. Could you live with pink?"

She drove me down Scaffold Cane Road and turned left just past a store there. Fifty yards up a short ridge, another left, and there it was in the middle of a sparse pine forest: the little house with the worst shade of pink I'd ever seen. And I loved it. It was a mess inside. The shelves had spilled honey in them, topped off with mouse droppings. Fuad would have nothing to do with the shelves. He said, "In my country this sort of work is done by servants. This is dirty work." Bob cleaned the shelves and lined them with material he brought from Boone Tavern, one of his perks as a hotel management major working there.

The floors were uneven from one side to the other. On the right was the kitchen area. On the other side of the divider wall was the small toilet, an old couch, a single bed, and a propane heater. I could see daylight through some of the cracks in the walls. But it was home. It was mine. I said I knew we were going to have fun there. Fuad agreed. "Yes, my friend, we shall party most seriously in Billy Edd's Pink Palace." I told him he was right, but because he hardly broke a sweat and didn't want to dirty his hands, his only drink would be a can of warm beer.

My first issue of the *Berea Alumnus* was a success. Tom Fern's painting of the owl in flight carrying a spade with his claws was a beauty. Dr. Hutchins complimented me on it, which was reassuring. If the boss was happy, I was happy. I was working on the next quarterly featuring the Berea student. The fourth season of *Wilderness Road* was coming up in a few months and was already on people's minds. The talk was it would probably be its last season. The college was in a slump financially, and by the way, Sam Selden was wondering if I could coach the square dancers. Frank Smith would not be available. I said yes, but I would not be trying out for a role. Too much work to do in the alumni office. He still hired me to appear in crowd scenes so I could make some money.

I received a packet from Harold Newman that contained song contracts and an advance check for $100. He said he was putting together a folio containing all the songs on reel number one, and he was calling it: *Honey in the Horn: A Collection of Songs*

with Arrangements, Guitar Chords, Words and Music by Billy Edd
Wheeler, published by Hargail Music Press, 157 West 57th Street,
New York, NY. I was thrilled. I was in showbiz! And there was
the proof in black and white. I drew a sketch of a man working
in a field with mountains in the background, titled "Mountain
Spring," and autographed it from me to him on the cover. When
I got a copy of it, I was pleased and honored to read a foreword
by John Jacob Niles.

The Pink House was becoming more and more popular. Guys
loved to bring their dates there where they could court more
freely and often be entertained with music at the same time.
John Payne became a regular, always bringing moonshine and
inventing ways to fondle the girls by calling them model material.
He became known as the dirty old man from Disputanta. After a
round of golf with Glenn Pennington, I invited him to bring Lily
May sometime.

When we had set a date, I ran into Judy Hayes again and said,
"I know you really like classical music, but if you don't mind
slumming, how's about coming out to hear Lily May Pennington
play the fiddle? She's a member of the famous Coon Creek Girls
and has performed at the White House."

She got her back up. "Yes, I love classical music, but I'm a West
Virginia girl, remember? It's about time you invited me. I think
you like Fuad more than me." I loved seeing her get a little feisty.

When the date came around, Glenn and Lily May arrived
with a banjo player named Shorty Van Winkle. It came out during
the evening that he was not supposed to be playing the banjo
again, especially on a Sunday, by order of his wife and his church's
preacher. It was a double no-no, and Shorty joked that maybe
one would cancel out the other. Judy remarked that the same
thing happened in churches in West Virginia. They were good
people, just narrow minded.

The picking was lusty and stirring. Shorty was red hot, and
Lily May fiddled so joyously, I swear, it looked like tiny beads of

sunshine sprouted out of her cheeks above her mile-wide smile. Glenn played upright bass and smiled more than I'd ever seen. He played like it was all business, just like he played golf. But he was good-hearted and had sold me the car of my dreams. I owed him. Driving Judy home, I didn't have to worry about trying for a kiss. She made it easy for me and I loved it.

In May of 1959 Bentley Cummins showed up at the alumni building and asked if we could talk. I led him into my office and closed the door. He had trouble telling me exactly why he was there. I figured it had to be about "Rock Boll Weevil," and after some unrelated chit-chat, he finally said he'd talked with manager Jack Spina, who was having difficulty convincing Pat to record it. I said, "Bentley, that's out of our hands. There's nothing we can do about it, so why worry? We don't know what goes into their decisions." He had no response to that. But after another half hour of seemingly irrelevant conversation, with his mention of Betty a few times, in one context or another, I was sure he had the idea that there *was* something we could do about it. But he was not able to come right out and say it.

I said, "If you think Jack and Pat are close to making a decision, but they need a little family input, what might that be? Does it have to do with Betty?"

He perked up one hundredth of a percent, as if surprised, and said, "Well, uh, maybe, uh, yeah, I guess so."

Now I was sure I knew, but I wanted it to look like I was just guessing. I said, "Do you suppose if we made Betty cowriter of the song, it would do the trick?" After pretending to ponder the question, he nodded.

I said, "Bentley, I wrote the song. I don't think I can, in good faith, say she wrote it with me. Can you understand that?" He nodded.

I went on. "However, if they cut it, and I make some money, I'll be glad to give her a finder's fee. How 'bout that?" He jumped all over it, hiding his disappointment, and said yeah, that would be great.

On June 13, Harold Newman invited me to fly to New York at his expense. He didn't say why, so I assumed it was about the folio. But he told me Randy Wood, owner of Dot Records, which was Pat Boone's label, was in town. He was staying at a fancy hotel on Central Park West. Harold had tried to call him, but the hotel operator wouldn't put it through. I asked what this was all about. Harold said, "I know they've recorded 'Rock Boll Weevil' because I was notified they had applied for a license."

I was suddenly very, very excited by this great news, and after I had calmed down, I said, "You want me to give it a try?" He dialed the number and handed me the phone. I took some deep breaths to overcome my nervousness. When the main desk answered I put on my best hillbilly voice and said, "Ma'am, my buddy Randy told me he'd be mighty ticked off if I didn't call while I was here, so put him on and I'll give him a holler." She asked if I was talking about Mr. Wood, Randy Wood. I said, "Yep, the one and only, from Nashville." She said just a minute.

I heard the ring, and when he picked up, I told him who I was. He seemed so surprised he didn't know what to say for a moment. I said, "Mr. Newman and I would love to hear the record, if you'd be kind enough to play it for us."

He hemmed and hawed, said he was too busy, had lots of stuff to get done while he was here, and didn't have a moment to spare.

I said, "I realize you're a very busy man, but Pat singing one of my song's the best thing that ever happened to me. I sure would appreciate getting to hear it."

There were a few seconds of silence before he said, "Oh, what the hell. Come on up."

When we arrived at his suite, a nicely dressed man opened the door and asked us to come in and make ourselves comfortable. He picked up the pad and pen he'd laid down, and rushed into an adjacent room's open door. He followed Mr. Wood as he left that room and entered another, taking notes as the boss dictated.

It looked like a show he was putting on for us, to prove he really was busy, but it may have been for real.

Harold and I sat on a couch until Mr. Wood came in and introduced himself. The man, the first male secretary I'd ever seen—if that's what he was—put a small black acetate record on a player, and I was startled at the loud intro to the song. It sounded like a whole bunch of saxophones playing a bouncy riff of eight or ten seconds. Then Pat's voice. What a thrill, to hear him sing it so well. When asked how we liked it, Harold and I praised it to high heaven. And then Mr. Wood patted Harold on the thigh and said, "You will give us a rate, right?"

Harold looked to me. I had no idea what he was talking about, but I said, "Sure, if you say so."

And in those few seconds we agreed to receive a penny and a half, instead of the two cents per record sold that was the customary statutory rate (*Song Publishing 101*).

Harold took me to the Russian Tea Room for a late lunch, and I had my first ever Bloody Mary, New York style, to celebrate the occasion. I also had borscht soup and a meat sandwich baked inside a shell-like pastry, about the size of a thin hamburger. I can't remember what it was called, but it was delicious.

On June 15, I was back in Berea when Betty Lamb entered my office and said a DJ in Richmond was on the phone, and he sounded excited. I picked up, and yes, he was excited and talking a mile a minute. He told me he was getting ready to play the song I'd written for Pat Boone, and I should get to a radio if I wanted to hear it. And would I please call him back afterwards? I hurried to the car and, within minutes, I was listening to "Rock Boll Weevil." Even though I'd heard it once, it was more exciting to hear it on the radio for some reason. Maybe because I knew a whole lot of other people would be listening, too. Well, that was an understatement. The DJ begged me to come right away so he could interview me on the air. When I got to Richmond, I went to a liquor store and said I wanted to buy the most expensive vodka they had. It was Russian, Stoli something or other, and it was pricey.

The DJ's interview turned out to be more about him than me. He told me how he knew Red Foley and family, and Pat's connection to Berea. And wasn't it great that I was associated with such a renowned musical family? When he asked how I came to write the song, he only half-listened, as if he had a really important question to ask. When we were off microphone, he spoke in a tone of voice that was almost hushed, "Tell me, Bill, besides the Foleys, have you met any stars?" So much for the creative process.

When I told Bernard Davidson I was keeping my promise, and I would bring the vodka to his office, he said he had a better idea. He told me to bring it to Berea Country Club, and he and Harold would have their secretary invite Bentley and Betty, plus Glenn Pennington, Teaberry Coffee, and my college golfer friends, the Ferns and Coach Wyatt. It was a jovial affair. Normally, I was told, members could not bring bottles of booze to the bar. But because I was an overnight celebrity, it would be permitted. The bartender said this vodka could ruin his business, because he could not afford this premium stuff by the drink. Toasts were given to Betty for making it all happen, and I was toasted too, but managed to nurse a vodka and tonic for an hour before making my getaway, saying I had a lot of work to catch up on since returning from New York.

Chapter Twelve

THE REVEREND MR. BLACK

He rode easy in the saddle, he was tall and lean
And at first you thought nothing but a streak of mean
Could make a man look so downright strong
But one look in his eyes and you knew you 'as wrong
He was a mountain man and I want you to know
He could preach hot hell or freezing snow
He carried a Bible in a canvas sack
And folks just called him the Reverend Mr. Black
He was poor as a beggar but he rode like a king
And sometimes in the evening I'd hear him sing:
I got to walk that lonesome valley, I got to walk it by myself,
Oh, nobody else can walk it for me, I got to walk it by myself

I received a box from Harold Newman. I hadn't heard from him in several months, so I didn't tear into it, as I would have done had I known what was inside. But I was curious about what it might be. My guess was a shipment of folios. I was totally surprised to see a stack of LP records, with the title: *Billy Edd USA / Monitor presents Billy Edd Wheeler and Joan Sommer.* A Warren Brunner photograph of me was on the cover. I've never been accused of being good looking, but to me this cover was beautiful. Joan and I had our first record. Even my first review, which panned my record, didn't dampen my excitement. The *Little Sandy Review* said I didn't sound like a folk singer. I sounded more like Curley in the musical *Oklahoma*, which I took as a compliment. It referred to those songs I made up while cutting weeds in West Virginia and let loose into the air, saying, "Hopefully they will never be recovered."

Lots of parties ensued at the Pink House with different groups, several of which had never been there. I gave a copy of the album to Judy and to Rich Bellando, who would share it with Lila and Sonny. And of course copies went to the Woodies, the Wyatts, the Drukkers, Emily Ann Smith, Bernard Davidson, and Betty and Bentley Cummins. I autographed copies to my band members, Larry Blondell and Phil Ogle.

I gave a copy of the album to Joseph Firszt, and soon he picked out the song he wanted to arrange for the Lexington Symphony: "Sassafras." He liked the bouncy, stop-and-starts of the verses, and the chorus that featured a frisky mountain girl, the singer's cup of tea, who could make a body of water dry up with just one kiss. Outrageously far-fetched, but fun. I was very nervous singing with an orchestra in front of an audience full of "long-haired music lovers," as I kiddingly called Judy. But other performers had told me, "Don't let 'em see you sweat," I think I succeeded, but barely. I was definitely out of my element. But I thanked Mr. Firszt profusely for trying to help further my career in music. He had given me a jewel to add to my short resume.

Berea College had been beyond good to me, but I was starting to feel like it was time to get on with my dream career in music and writing. Ever since my brief meeting with Thornton Wilder, I had kept the idea of studying at Yale's drama school tucked away in the back of my mind. I applied and was accepted for the fall semester of 1961. I couldn't believe they let me in! The best I could figure was that they needed to fill the "token hillbilly" slot in their new class of incoming students.

I cashed my last paycheck from Berea College and put most of the money in the bank. I got another checkbook for paying the bills at Yale. The Drukkers let me store my golf clubs, papers, books, and other things in their basement. After settling up with Miss Smith for the Pink House, I started saying my goodbyes to special friends in Berea. The list included all those to whom I'd given a copy of my album, plus the Hendersons, and finally my brother Bob, who was beginning his fifth and last year at Berea College. Saying goodbye to Berea made me feel as melancholy as Warren Wilson had, but there was an added poignancy this time because the music was more diverse, and (there was promise in the sadness I felt. An ending and a beginning.)

This was not to say I was full of confidence. I had never lived near or studied on a big campus like Yale. I was prepared to feel intimidated. But with my guitar and some clothes stashed in my car, plus a bunch of yellow pads, some half-filled with lyrics and song ideas, I headed north at 7 a.m.

When I got to New Haven, I found a room for rent in a dentist's office at 1157 Chapel Street, in easy walking distance to Yale Drama. I would be sharing a bathroom with an older couple living in the back rooms. When the dentist showed me the room and gave me a key, he said, "Paul Newman rented this room, and look what he did. I'm expecting big things from you, young man. Good luck." I had about a week before my work assignment kicked in, so I wandered around the main campus of Yale University, paying particular attention to the dorms. I imagined students in rooms with private baths, nice furniture, and other amenities. The architecture looked English to me, but I had nothing to base it on, and ultimately I didn't envy the students at all. They couldn't help it if their parents were rich, or at least well-off.

I decided to use this free week writing a gunfighter ballad, because there were so many TV shows with western themes. How much more commercial could you get? My hero would be a badass gunfighter, good hearted at the core, but someone you didn't mess with. His counterpart would be country music's Big Bad John, Jimmy Dean's hero in his song of the same name:

My hero had about the same physical dimensions as Big John, and my first verse described him pretty well. But the further I got into the lyric, the more I realized I didn't know a roan from a gelding, a palomino from a stallion, or anything else about western lore. Big John's territory, yes, but my gunfighter's territory? No. So I laid it aside.

When classes started, Professor Ed Wilson introduced himself, telling us that Dr. John Gassner, head of the department, was on semisabbatical, so we were stuck with him in between Dr. Gassner's lectures. He had a southern accent, and his casual attitude made me like him at once.

He said he had gotten hold of a script to Edward Albee's show on Broadway, *Who's Afraid of Virginia Woolf*, and held it up in class, asking who wanted to read it first. I stuck my hand up and was told to read it quickly, then pass it on so we could discuss it while it was in production. He also encouraged us to go see it, if possible. I read it one night and reread it the second night. I was amazed at how vicious the married couple was toward each other. He was a college professor, and she was the president's daughter. I couldn't get the play out of my mind, and couldn't wait to discuss it in class.

My work supervisor was Dr. Alois Nagler, professor of theater history, and my job was to print photos of Greek and Roman theatres from negatives. He was curator of the Yale Rockefeller collection of theater memorabilia. I was taught how to prepare trays of developing fluid and how to dry the wet photographs. It was the same procedure Chad had taught me in Ben Welch's basement.

After a while it became boring. But the very large room where the small darkroom was located was totally bare of furniture, except for two chairs. I loved the acoustics that made my modest voice sound louder and more impressive. I could write songs and sing on Yale's time, while prints were developing or drying. When Dr. Nagler checked my progress from time to time, his remark was often, "Mr. Veeler, no outpoot!" The more I learned about him, the more impressed I was. He was known as the founder and godfather of theater historical studies. The book he had written on the subject was, for many years, considered a classic.

Ed Wilson and I became friends. We even tried to cowrite a cowboy song about a horse, "Palomino Bill," but it was never recorded. Too sappy, I guess, but it was fun trying.

I was pleased that some of my classmates had heard of "Rock Boll Weevil," including Gladden Schrock, from Indiana, and Walter Reed, a student actor from Kentucky, whose stage name was Walter Rhodes. He said he got tired of hearing people say, "Oh, Reed, like the hospital, yeah?" Walter's scholarship job was the same as mine, and Dr. Nagler had used the same "No outpoot" line on him. Gladden told me he played some guitar and would like to get together with me and swap songs.

Harold Newman invited me to bring my guitar down to New York, and he took me to some restaurants, where I sang for the owners. But not a single place felt right to me, and I didn't knock any of them out with my folksy material. I wasn't ready for New York, and it wasn't ready for me.

In class, our first major discussion was about *A Streetcar Named Desire*, by Tennessee Williams, analyzing it scene by scene. Even the shortest scene would be discussed. How important was it? Would the play work without it? We did the same exercise with *On the Waterfront*, by Budd Shulberg. The film versions of both were directed by Elia Kazan, and each starred Marlon Brando. *Who's Afraid of Virginia Woolf* was not yet discussed, but I kept thinking about it. And as absurd and implausible as it seemed, something about it made me think it might be an idea for a song.

As unpleasant as my first try was at getting a possible singing job in the city, I thought I'd give it another shot, this time by approaching the talent manager Ed Wilson told me about. Harold Leventhal, he said, booked Pete Seeger and the Weavers, plus lots of other folk singers and actors. So my guitar and I got on the train again and, from Grand Central Station, made our way to Mr. Leventhal's office in mid-Manhattan. I got off the elevator on the second floor to find a really large room full of ladies typing and working the phones. The door to Mr. Leventhal's office was closed.

I stood to the side with my guitar and waited for twenty minutes or so until a man came out. He started for the elevator, but glanced aside and, seeing me, he walked over and held out his hand. "Hi, I'm Norman Gimbel." He had a warm smile that put me at ease. I told him my name and was absolutely floored when he said, "You're Billy Edd Wheeler? My wife's in love with you. Well, not exactly, but she likes your Monitor album." I was too flabbergasted to comment. "Yes, she's a model, and, on her way to work a few weeks ago she passed by Monitor and saw your album in their window. She bought it and gave it to me." I just shook my head in amazement, and probably muttered something. I can't remember.

Norman went on. "Billy, you're a natural songwriter. You write songs like people breathe, but ..." He paused, as if thinking how to proceed, and of course I kept my mouth shut. "...well, unfortunately, you'll never make any money at it."

Finally gaining a voice, I said, "Well, Norman, if I'm so 'natural,' how come I can't make any money?"

He pondered the question for a while, then said, "Look, I can't explain the creative process, but I have a couple of friends who can. Jerry Leiber and Mike Stoller. They've made a lot of money writing and publishing music. Maybe I can set up a meeting with them. We're old friends. Where you staying?"

I told Norman about studying at Yale but said I could get away almost any time. He gave me his number and told me to stay in touch. When I told Gladden and Walter about meeting

Norman, and what he had told me, they just shook their heads in amazement.

Gladden said, "You lucky bastard. Talk about coincidences."

I told them, "Norman Gimbel's a world-class lyricist. 'Canadian Sunset,' for instance. And Leiber and Stoller? Ever hear of a song called 'Hound Dog?'" They nodded. "They wrote it and produced it. They own Broadway."

Gladden said, "And you're gonna meet 'em in person?" I said, "Yeah, I guess."

Norman took me to Leiber and Stoller's office in the famous Brill Building above Jack Dempsey's bar on 49th and Broadway. Yes, I was nervous, despite Norman's calm demeanor. It was impressed upon me that producers and publishers don't usually like to meet writers face-to-face. They prefer a recording so they don't have to deal with personalities. These guys had made an exception, thanks to their friend Norman. Not knowing what to expect from New York guys, I found them to be very friendly.

They listened to me sing parts of three songs, stopping me after just a verse and chorus each time. They told me my songs were too folksy, and they couldn't use them. I asked how I could get better. Jerry spoke first: "Listen to songs more critically. What's the idea? There should be only one idea in a song. One main theme. Once you decide what the song's about, write a verse to introduce it and get to the hook, or payoff, as quick as possible." Mike said the melody should be singable and not too complex. Jerry said, "Norman tells me you're coming to the city after your year at Yale. If you get an idea you think is commercial, give us a call. If we like it, you can bring it in. Good luck."

Norman and I talked about the meeting over a cup of coffee. He said, "Something to think about. Harold Newman has publishing rights to all the songs on your album, right?" I said yes. "Well then, even if Jerry and Mike liked them, they wouldn't be interested unless they could publish. Does Mr. Newman have an exclusive contract with you?" I said I didn't know. He asked if Harold paid me advances. I said yes, sometimes. He said, "But nothing in writing, like so much a week, or month?" I shook my head. "Well then, Billy, I'll tell you what my attorney told me. He said, 'Abraham Lincoln freed the slaves a long time ago.' So, you're free to leave Mr. Newman. All you have to do is say, 'I'm not writing for you anymore.' I know that sounds heartless. But it's business." I told him I thought it would break Harold's heart if I did that. His nod was sympathetic. "As I said earlier, it's something to think about." I thanked him and rode back to Yale with my tail between my legs. I had bombed. But—and it was a big but— Jerry had held out a carrot.

The winter in New Haven was wet and dreary. I had trouble staying warm. And my money was running out. But I got a photo in the mail that was merry and bright. One of my teachers at Warren Wilson was Birdina Bishop. For some reason she decided to send me a picture of John C. Campbell, the man who founded the folk school named after him at Brasstown, North Carolina. Sitting on a beautiful horse, he wore boots that reached his knees. The letter said he was also a minister who went out into communities that had no regular preacher. He would preach, marry, bury, and baptize people. He made me think of a line in the song, "Mule Train," that went, "There's a Bible in the sack for the Reverend Mister Black." The photograph and the phrase made me think, instantly, *There's my hero for the western song I couldn't finish.* My hero is not a gunfighter; he's a preacher, a man among men. And remembering how in mountain towns the pecking order is quickly established as to who can whip whom, my preacher's faith would be challenged, one way or another. There was possible conflict. And "Thank you, Mrs. Bishop," there was the song. All I had to do was write it down.

The room I lived in was usually depressing. It was too small, and the smells that wafted forth from the darkness where the older couple lived were sometimes beyond unpleasant. But the letter I got from Birdina, and the resulting song idea, buoyed my spirits.

I set about writing lyrics and creating music to help tell the story, with spoken verses and sung choruses. I couldn't wait to smoke it by Jerry, once I got it good enough to show him. And miraculously, it seemed, I was getting ideas on how to use *Who's Afraid of Virginia Woolf.* It was the arguing between husband and wife. That was the key, I thought, but didn't know yet what it would unlock.

As winter was waning and spring wasn't too far away, I wrote to Martin Ambrose at his apartment on East 83rd Street in Manhattan, asking if I could stay with him for a while when I left Yale. He said yes. As the weather warmed, I spent a lot of time at Walter's trailer park, getting to know him and his wife, Marylyn, better. Gladden was often there as well. He, Walter, and I were bonding as a threesome.

My old convertible was showing its age badly, making me think I should park it on the street and walk away. I wouldn't need it in New York where parking was always a problem. But when I voiced the idea, two of Walter's neighbors looked at me like I was crazy.

One of the guys said, "Put an ad in the paper and sell it."

I said, "But there's a knock in the engine, and the top won't go down by itself. You have to manually help it, plus a laundry list of other stuff."

The guy said, "But it's a convertible and it looks great. Some dad's young daughter would drool over it. And it's only seven years old, for chrissake. Forget the mileage deal."

Walter, Gladden, and Marylyn agreed. So I did buy an ad, using Walter's address and phone number, and wrote that interested buyers should call on the weekend.

The first Saturday, a man came and looked it over. I priced it at $250. He said he'd think about it. Later, a man came and I told him I'd priced it to the first guy at $250, but I'd decided it was worth $300. Same story. He'd have to think about it. But when the third man came and I took him for a drive, he didn't have to tell me. Just as Glenn Pennington had said, I knew this man wanted the car badly. He said he would give me $375, cash. My conscience made me tell him about everything wrong with it. He didn't care. His

daughter was going to love him for it. I bought some beer, and the
two guys who made me place the ad drank their share of it.

Dr. Nagler invited Walter and me to his home for drinks and
conversation, and we thanked him graciously for our scholarships.
He said he was glad we were taking his and Dr. Gassner's advice:
if you're not going to teach, get out of Yale and start writing and
acting. The only way to become a good writer, or a good actor,
is to write, write, write, and act, act, act. He was a warm and
gracious host, and he had good taste in liquor, according to Walter,
a bourbon drinker. As mixed drinks go, I couldn't tell much
difference. And I really couldn't afford any booze at all anyway.

Gladden was hooking up with a fellow picker named Asaad
Kelada who came the same year as we did, and they would call
themselves The Kinsmen. Gladden said Asaad had come from Cairo,
where he'd already established himself in a band and was known in
Egypt as *Little Elvis*. Gladden also told me that in his first year, Asaad
roomed with Jim Burrows, who himself later became the Grand
Pooh-Bah of all TV directors...*Cheers*...right on through dozens of
other hits. Asaad used Jim's semiacoustic guitar for the Kinsmen gigs,
as he had not brought his own guitar over from Egypt.

Martin Ambrose's pad at East 83rd Street was on the fifth floor,
quite a climb for me, my guitar, and my sports bag that passed
for a suitcase. With its several zippered compartments, it held my
shaving stuff and toothbrush, tennis shoes for walking and jogging,
pens and papers, an address book, an all-purpose Swiss Army knife,
and a few tools like a screwdriver, pliers, and scissors.

I knocked on the door opposite Martin's number, and a lady
who looked to be in her late twenties or early thirties opened it. I
said, "Are you Sarah?"

She smiled broadly and replied, "Yes, and you must be Billy
Edd. I love that name. You're the song writer. How exciting.
I'll cook for you some time, if you'll sing for me." She gave me
Martin's apartment key and told me to be sure and let her know
if I needed anything.

I said, "Maybe you could tell me where to buy groceries. I'm sure you know Martin's been on the road for weeks. I bet the frig is bare."

And sure enough it was. But I saw a jar of peanut butter and part of a loaf of bread. I would make a list and go shopping, but first I wanted to call Norman and Harold Newman. I brought Norman up to date on my ideas for the Rev. Black, telling him I thought it was good enough to show Jerry. While he agreed, without actually hearing the lyrics, I hesitated for three days because he asked what I was going to do about Harold. I knew what I needed to do, but I couldn't make myself do it. So I took time to explore the neighborhood. I found it took me only twenty minutes to discover a really nice art museum. It was the Metropolitan Museum of Art, and I was blown away by what I saw. Artists from all over the world had paintings there. I could stand for hours and soak it in.

Finally, I asked Harold if I could come by for a talk. I think he knew what was up, but I hemmed and hawed until I finally said, "Harold, I can never repay you for taking me under your wing, and publishing my songs, and getting me the deal with Monitor. And in many ways you've become the father I never had." I thought he would cut to the chase and ask what was on my mind. But he didn't, so I went on. "Norman Gimbel took me to meet Jerry Leiber and Mike Stoller, and I played a few of our songs for them. They weren't interested, but Jerry told me to call if I thought I had a more commercial type of song. I think I have one. But I don't think it would interest him if he couldn't publish it. So I'm asking you to let me go. I feel I'm at a new stage in my song writing, and…"

I saw Harold's hands trembling, and my heart sank. I was going to tell him I would stay with him, but he said, "I know. I can't… won't hold you back. But I value your friendship."

He was going to say more but, relieved, I said, "We met on the dance floor, folk dancing. Let's do some more of it, okay?"

I called the Leiber and Stoller office. A lady named Faith Whitehill answered, and after about ten minutes, Jerry was on the line. I told him about "The Reverend Mr. Black." He told me to let him hear what I had, so I started reciting the lyrics, and after what seemed an eternity, he started snapping his fingers, saying, "Yeah, baby, yeah, baby." And when I got to the chorus, he said, "Bring that one in." He gave me back to Faith Whitehill, who set up a time for me to come in and wait my turn.

When I took my guitar and the lyrics to "Rev. Black" to 49th and Broadway, Faith showed me where to sit and wait for Jerry and Mike to come and discuss the song. They took me back to their private quarters, and I played the entire song to them. Mike had picked up the chorus melody and was writing it down after playing it on his piano. Jerry's first comment was, "This is about an eight-minute song, so we've got to edit it down to three minutes. Three-and-a-half at most. So they both chipped in and started working on the song, which totally surprised me. I thought, yes, the chorus melody was public domain, but it was still my version of it. There was nothing Mike could contribute.

But I was wrong. These two guys were pros, and I didn't argue with them. As we all three whittled away at the song, I realized how lucky I was. When we finished, Jerry said we would demo it in the studio, with me singing. He also said, "Mike and I will take fifty percent of the writer's share. Before we dug in, you had one hundred percent of nothing. Or, at least one hundred percent of a song that didn't work. Now you have fifty percent of a song that does." I told him that made sense to me.

Jerry told me that as soon as we made a studio demo of the song, he was sending it with his songplugger to LA, where the Kingston Trio was recording. In the meantime, he said, he and Mike had written a country song and needed help with it. The name of the song was, "The Man Who Robbed the Bank at Santa Fe and Got Away." It was the longest song title I'd ever heard. When they played it for me, I said, "It's not working because there's no woman in it.

What does a bunch of gold mean to a man if he has no woman to spend it on?" Jerry's smile and nod said, *Why didn't I think of that?* He and I rewrote it, with the new story line and title "The Girl Who Loved the Man Who Robbed the Bank at Santa Fe and Got Away." We demo'ed the song, with me doing the vocal.

Faith booked me a flight to Nashville and set up an appointment with Chet Atkins, head of RCA, on the famous Music Row. I couldn't believe my good luck. First, I was flattered that the great writing team of Leiber and Stoller had asked me to collaborate with them. And now I was going to meet the man Andreas Segovia said was America's greatest guitarist. I heard him say that when he gave a concert at Berea College.

After seeing New York City, I was not blown away by Nashville. But it was big enough, in its own way, to make me feel the special aura of Music Row, home to legions of legends like Hank Williams, Minnie Pearl, Eddy Arnold, Red Foley, West Virginia's Little Jimmy Dickens, and the great Patsy Cline, to name just a few. My plane got in two hours before my appointment with Chet, so I walked down to the Grand Ole Opry House, remembering how Mommy and my aunts and uncles had gathered around the radio every Saturday night back in Whitesville.

Later at the RCA building, I got off the elevator and walked to the desk of Mary Lynch. Without having to wait too long, she showed me into her boss's office. Chet was on the phone, so she told me to have a seat. I heard Chet say "Bobby" several times, and when he hung up the phone, he said, "That was Bobby Bare. His 'Detroit City' is doing pretty well." That was my first clue as to Chet's nature, how he understated things in his soft-spoken way. "Detroit City" was burning up *Billboard*'s charts and getting tons of airplay. It was doing a zillion times better than "pretty well."

As Chet listened to the four acetate recordings I'd given him, three by Jerry and Mike and one by Jerry and me, I looked around his office. There where guitars everywhere, two very close to his chair, and the rest leaning against walls or lying on a black leather couch. I saw framed album covers and single records on the walls, and what looked like a photo of Chet and the president.

Chet handed me three recordings back and said he was keeping the one about the bank robber to show to Hank Snow. He asked me where I was from, and I told him about being raised by my grandmother in West Virginia. He said, "Grandmothers are great, aren't they?" He told me about a restaurant named Jimmy Kelly's, in case I liked steaks. He said, "Lots of hillbilly pickers and singers eat there. Producers, too. The fried cornbread is pretty good too. They allow brown bagging, if you want a drink with dinner." I'd never heard the term. He said, "You can't buy liquor by the drink in Nashville. So you take your own bottle and they provide the mixers. I'd go with you tonight, but I'm busy. Maybe next time. Come on back and bring me some more songs."

Since he said the fried cornbread was "pretty good," I figured it was delicious. Jimmy Kelly's was obviously the "in" place to go, so I went. And yes, the fried cornbread was dammed good, and the steaks were the best I'd ever eaten. I hoped Jerry would send me back soon.

Walter had moved to the city with Marylyn, and he came to Martin's place to visit me. As if reading my mind, he told me about a great place to live, if I decided it was time to leave Martin's pad. Brooklyn Heights. Marylyn had landed a job as a server at a posh restaurant and was making great tips. When she dressed for work, she was a knockout brunette. Walter said, in addition to tips, guys were offering her their hotel room keys at least once or twice a week. He went with me to Brooklyn Heights, the first stop on the subway from lower Manhattan.

The boardwalk overlooking where the two rivers came together was enough to sell me on the area. So we went to a realty company, and soon I had found a ground floor apartment on Remsen Street I really liked. I say "apartment," but really it was only one room with a long hallway, and the rent was $120 a month. I put a payment down for the first month, and went back to East 83rd Street to tell Martin and Sarah goodbye. I had enjoyed his apartment and the neighborhood they called Yorktown. And I had enjoyed the walks to the Met and Central Park from there. I thanked Martin for being so hospitable and Sarah for being such a good neighbor.

My new home at 51 Remsen Street was totally bare. No blinds, nothing on the walls or in the small kitchen except the small refrigerator, but there was half a roll of toilet paper in the phone booth-sized bathroom.

For some reason I started writing songs like crazy in my new environment. There were no distractions. Well, there was one pleasant distraction when the phone rang. I picked it up and the voice on the other end said, "Billy Edd, how in the world are you?" It was a woman's sultry voice that rang a distant bell, but I couldn't place it.

Before I could admit that, she went on, "It's Margaret Sanders. My friend Judy Drukker gave me your number. Honey, you've got to come and meet me at the Guggenheim. There's a sculpture exhibit on. You didn't know I was a sculptress, did you?"

I said, "No. I thought you were too busy chasing retired colonels. By the way, how is your Christian Scientist husband? Is he with you?"

She said, "Heavens no, honey. I got rid of him. Now I've got me a twenty-two-year-old piano player."

I asked, "Is he a good lover?"

She said, "Oh my, honey, oh my, yes."

I said, "So you're a closet sculptress. What a surprise."

She said, "Oh no, darlin', I'm well known in Kentucky. I did one of my father, and a great one of Governor Happy Chandler. Come on, and I'll take you to lunch after the show."

As we made our way up the spiraled walkway, she had a comment about every sculpture. In one case, a sculpture of a man's buttocks, she said, "Come and touch, honey. You have to feel this one to appreciate it." She was stroking the contours of his rear end as if it were precious gold. I glanced at it as I passed her and walked on up the ramp. Later at lunch, I studied her face.

It was somewhat wrinkled, as was her upper chest. It reminded me of elephant skin. But that didn't keep her from looking very attractive. Her hair, her eyes, and her smile exuded an aura that was definitely sexy. Her charm and her lust for life made her look ageless.

She asked if I'd seen any Broadway plays yet. I told her I couldn't afford it.

She said, "Well, there's a wonderful show off Broadway, *The Fantasticks*, you've got to see, and it's not that expensive."

I asked, "Have you seen it?" She said, "No, darling, but a friend of mine who's in the know told me it was a masterpiece, with fabulous music. She's never praised anything that much." She handed me a twenty-dollar bill, making me promise I'd go see it. So I did, and her friend was right. I thought it was magical, great plot, minimal set, and very small cast. One song, "Try to Remember," stuck in my head for weeks.

On one of those first days as I sat reading a back issue of Jim Comstock's "weakly" newspaper, *The West Virginia Hillbilly*, I saw something written in a box separate from the rest of the page's copy. It was titled "Desert Pete." In one paragraph, I read the story of a man who built a pump, with a big handle, on the edge of a desert. It looked out of place standing there by itself, with no building close by. In a hole next to it, covered by a piece of plywood with a rock on top, there was a jar of water and a note that cautioned the reader not to drink the water, but use it to prime the pump. Then after you'd drunk your fill, Pete said to be sure and leave the jar full of water so the next person could have a drink. There were details like the new sucker washer he put in the pump, and then he philosophized, saying you had to give water to get water back. Just like you had to give to others before you were worthy to receive. I thought, good God, it's a great story with a built-in sermon. All I had to do was create some details of my own, make them rhyme, and I had a song.

I started writing as soon as I finished reading, and by midnight I had the song, words and music:

Desert Pete

I was traveling west to buckskin on my way to a cattle run
Across the Little Cactus desert under a hard bargaining sun
Thirsty down to my toenails I stopped to rest me on a stump
But I tell you I just couldn't believe it when I saw that water pump
I took it to be a mirage at first, it'll fool a thirsty man
Then I saw a note stuck in a baking powder can
This pump is old, the note began, but she works so give her a try
I put a new sucker washer in 'er and you may find the leather dry
You've got to prime the pump, you must have faith and believe
And you must give of yourself before you're worthy to receive
Drink all the water you can hold, wash your face, cool your feet
But leave the bottle full for others, thank ye kindly, Desert Pete

The next day I called Norman and recited the lyrics to "our" new song (I didn't know what his deal was with Leiber and Stoller, but I figured it had to be more than a finder's fee). He loved the song and said he was amazed I had written it so quickly. I told him I, too, was amazed, but the song idea was delivered to me on a platter, the main dish plus a delicious dessert. It was then, and has remained, the quickest I've ever written a song. I had two more song ideas to work on, but I decided to make myself a bed to sleep on. I was getting tired of sleeping on the floor. I found a big lumber yard that had discarded hollow doors without doorknobs, and stray cinder blocks lying around, so I bought a door and four cinder blocks for two dollars. It took me three trips to carry it all home.

But it was noisy sleeping on the door, mounted on the four blocks, so I went looking for a fabric place the next day and found one several blocks into Brooklyn, away from Brooklyn Heights. I paid three bucks for a roll of bedding material, and now had me a nice bed. It creaked when I sat on it, but it was softer than Harold's magazine table. Sitting on this bed, over a period of two weeks or so, I wrote three songs. Jerry and Mike— the Boys, as Norman and I started calling them—liked them well enough to set up a session at Capitol Studios for July 22, 1962. On that date, I noted in my diary:

> Today I slept late, saving my energy for my first pop recording session. To pass the time I went to see Birdman of Alcatraz, starring Burt Lancaster, at the Trans-Lux, 85th & Madison. A great movie. At the Session I recorded "Not Me," "Bunkum Town," and "Truck Stop Romance." The Boys produced. On July 31, Norman called to say The Boys played the tapes for Art Talmadge, VP or something at United Artists, and he flipped over them. Encouraging.

By the end of 1962, I was almost finished writing three more songs. One was "Coal Tattoo," which Joan loved, so I finished it and we started rehearsing it. The other two were the result of my trip to the house of Lucia Rosmini, a place famous for putting up folk singers like Tom Paxton. It was a big house on Jayne Street, near Greenwich Village, with a bathtub in the kitchen and a toilet in the hall. A welcoming, friendly place. I had participated in a guitar pull and was about to leave when Lucia's son, Dick, came in. He looked exhausted, having just ended a tour as Bobby Daren's guitarist. He said he hadn't slept for three days. I noticed little flakes of dandruff hanging from the lids of his bloodshot eyes. Lucia told him to go on to bed, but he wanted to meet everybody first.

When somebody told him I'd written a song with Jerry Leiber for the Kingston Trio, he insisted on staying up to hear me sing. When he heard "The Reverend Mister Black," he quickly proclaimed it would be a hit. I told him I'd just finished a new one they might like, but nobody had heard it yet. I didn't even have a demo. He had to hear it, he said, so I played a rough version of "Desert Pete." He shook his head in amazement, saying it, too, would be a hit, no matter who did it. He took his guitar out of its case and played me a song that absolutely knocked me out. I don't remember what it was, but I would never forget his playing. He sounded like two or three guitarists at the same time, the way he hammered on and pulled off the strings, all the while never losing the beat. It blew me away. When I got back to Remsen Street, I was so inspired I wrote two songs, or at least had them solidly in progress: "Blistered" and "Ann."

Lucia spent a lot of time in the Village, and she proclaimed that a black stand-up comedian named Bill Cosby was going to be a star, so we should go and check him out. She also said that Mississippi John Hurt was playing at the Gaslight where Tom Paxton was a mainstay. I didn't catch Cosby, but I did go and see Mississippi. He had been discovered by a prominent folklorist, and I thoroughly enjoyed him. He was incredibly humble and natural. It was a really small venue, but all the better for seeing performers up close and personal. He was not amplified and had his own unique style of fingerpicking. Folk blues and Deep South–sounding, not that I'm a musicologist.

Joan took me back to the Village to see a good friend named Sloan, whose guest was Harvey Schmidt. He wrote the music to *The Fantasticks*, so I felt privileged to be there. We all lay on the floor, drank wine, and talked, with candles and incense burning. Joan said Sloan was a superb actor who had played the main character in *The Mad Woman of Chaillot* by Jean Giraudoux many times. I had never heard of it. Joan told me later it was about an eccentric woman in Paris who struggled against the straitlaced authority figures in her life. I told Harvey how much I loved his music, and how long "Try to Remember" had stayed in my mind. He was easy to be around, with no put-on about him. Sloan was the same. But I expected nothing else, she being Joan's friend.

Jerry Leiber started inviting me to come to his house on Central Park West, after hours, to write with him. It amazed me. He was an active guy, interacting with Mike and other writers, famous singers, and their managers, all day at the office. Yet he never seemed tired. He always asked if I was hungry, and I always was. He would treat me to leftover dinner food. Sometimes, while I ate, he would share lines from a song he was working on. I remember one in particular, "Some Cats Know," with a line about the "Old prospector's nose for gold…some cats just know." Years later, when I heard the song sung by Peggy Lee, that line was not in it. When I wrote with Jerry, I had a yellow pad and pen handy, but every time I said, "That's it, that line's perfect, I'll write it down," he wouldn't let me. Later, we came up with a better line, or a line that suited the song better after he had rewritten it, all in his head. Then, only then, would he let me write it down. To me, he was a genius, with a mind that reminded me of heat lightning, flashing with brilliance. I was flattered that he would ask me to write with him.

One of our songs was "After Taxes." When we demo'ed it, a member of The Coasters was hanging around the office, so Mike asked him to come and sit in on the session. He did more than that. With his beautiful bass voice, he named off all the taxes one at a time, to which I replied. Like: "Mmmm, Federal tax. There goes that new fence for my farm. Mmmm, State income tax. There goes that bracelet for her arm," and so on. The Boys produced the Coasters and the Drifters, one of their greatest songs being "On Broadway." I recorded "After Taxes" on my first album with Joan, produced by The Boys. Johnny Cash recorded it as a single late in his career, and I was sure it would be a hit. But it fizzled instead of soaring. I was proud, just the same. Nobody could do for a song what Johnny could do for a song.

Chapter Thirteen

JACKSON

I thought you'd be a big spender
I thought you'd reach the top
But let me tell you something, baby
You're just a great big flop

I finally got around to working on the song inspired by *Who's Afraid of Virginia Woolf*. After I decided on the name "Jackson," I had some crazy verses like those above.

When I played it for Jerry, the verses were better than that, but it didn't matter. He said, "Throw all those verses away and start the song with your better ones: 'We got married in a fever,' and so on."

I said, "Jerry, that verse is the climax. I can't start the song with the climax."

He said, "Oh yes, you can. Just write some better verses. And end the song with that same first verse. It's your chorus." And that's what I did, writing it as a duet.

We got married in a fever hotter than a pepper sprout
We been talking 'bout Jackson ever since the fire went out
I'm going to Jackson, gonna mess around
Yeah, I'm going to Jackson, look out Jackson town
Well, go on down to Jackson, go ahead and wreck your health
Play you hand like a lover man, make a big fool of yourself
Yeah, yeah go to Jackson, but comb your hair
Honey, I'm gonna snowball Jackson
See if I care

For that editorial contribution, Jerry took 25% of the writer's share of the song and was listed as cowriter. At first, I thought that should have been his contribution as the publisher. But, in retrospect, I realize his input made the song work. So he deserved it. The Kingston Trio was the first to record it, but it took the great Johnny Cash to make it a hit, with June Carter, and they won a Grammy for it.

One day, Jerry called and asked if I had seen the movie *A Face in the Crowd*. I said I had and loved it. He said, "Since the main character is a southern guy…"

"Yeah. Andy Griffith," I said.

"Right, that's why I called," Jerry went on, as if I hadn't interrupted. "The director was Elia Kazan, and he's coming here tomorrow. He wants to write and produce a Broadway version of it, with us doing the music. You interested?"

Taken aback, I made some inane remark, like "Does an accordion player wear rings?" I was giddy inside and let Jerry know it.

He said, "Okay, I want you in on the meeting. I can't speak for Mr. Kazan, but I think you'd be a good fit, helping with southern dialect, writing songs, whatever. By the way, did you know he went to Yale Drama School?" I said no, even though in class we had discussed every line and scene in *A Streetcar*

Named Desire. Jerry said, "Well, tomorrow you'll be in the presence of one of the most influential directors in Broadway and Hollywood history."

When we met the next day, I was in awe of the man and felt honored just to be in the same room listening to him and Jerry. He was all business. No Yale chit-chat. But I was inspired. I started writing like crazy—songs, dialogue, making up stories for Lonesome Rhodes, the name of both the star and the show. After almost two months, Jerry called and told me the project was canceled. It was over. I was deeply dejected, but managed somehow to put it in the category of win-some, lose-some, and get on with life.

The days that ended 1962 and began 1963 were exciting times for me. So much unbelievably good stuff was happening, career-wise. But the most exciting thing of all was about to happen. It would change my life forever and ever. I learned that Mary Mitchell Bannerman had come to New York and was staying with her sister, Janet. The memory of seeing her on my way to Berea, after getting out of the navy, excited me. I called Martin Ambrose and asked if he could come to a get-together with the Bannerman girls at my place, and if so, would he pay a lot of attention to Janet so I could try to impress Mary?

He agreed, saying he had actually thought of calling Janet himself, but just never got around to it. So big sister Janet and little sister Mary came. I thought Mary looked prettier now than back at the golf course in Asheville. Martin and I sang for them (for too long, according to my diary). So I turned on the radio and some twist music was playing. Here's my diary account:

I said, "Mary, let's twist." She got up. She twisted. I flipped. She is the goddess of motion. She moved, she really moved without much inhibition, but not in a vulgar way. She was sexy and at the same time wholesome, or cute, as they describe Ann-Margaret's appeal. I was extremely moved and excited by her, and probably made a fool of myself, showing off with dance steps, but I didn't care. I asked Mary to go to a country dance meeting with me the next Saturday in Manhattan, and she agreed. Happy me! We slow danced, and on the last couple of dances I pressed just slightly closer than usual, and I believe she responded, just as slightly. It may have been my imagination. But ......from that moment I was in love.

On Saturday, Mary and I went to the folk dance where she was a smash hit. A man named Libert, about sixty-five, kept chasing her to talk to her, and we had to escape him to go to a party given by Mel Shestack, a would-be writer and producer. His house was on West 28th Street, or thereabouts, and was packed with artists and the largest selection of Village bohemia I'd ever witnessed. Shocking women, wearing all kinds of leotard costumes, some aggressive, some reticent. One with wild, multicolored hair made a pass at Mary. I met an actress named Nancy Pinkerton, and *Life* entertainment editor. Then I met Izzy, the man who runs the folklore center. He was just cutting out to do a radio show on WBAI and asked me to come by. I said I would. It gave me an excuse to leave the party. I didn't want to stay there and fight all the young bastards off Mary. The radio show was badly managed, but Izzy did a fairly good job. He played some of the songs from my and Joan's album, and I talked. The engineer came in frantically to beg me to stay and talk some more, and he would give me some more plugs. He said a lot of calls had come in. But I said I had to get Mary home.

After several more dates with Mary, I posted this in the diary:

Why do I love Mary?

She is physically appealing to me. I like her personality. She is open and friendly, without overdoing it. She is not an actress. I feel no professional competition in her. She is humorous and she laughs easily, but is also serious and thoughtful. She is young and energetic. We'll have fun times, golfing, dancing, swimming, etc. I love her family. I loved them before I even thought of her.

Finally, I am not sure she is as attracted to me as I am to her. I am not sure if she considers me, at thirty, to be too old for her, at twenty-one. Tomorrow night she and I will eat with Walter and Marylyn Reed, and then play cards with them.

March 1

Our schedules were beginning to get crowded, sending all of us in different directions. Mary and Janet were going out of town to see someone, I didn't know who, and I was invited to come to Gatlinburg to sing at a fair put on by the Southern Highlands Crafts Guild. On my return, Joan and I sang on WBAI. Our rehearsals for the album proposed by The Boys were becoming more frequent. When Walter and Marylyn had moved into their Manhattan apartment, they brought their TV with them from the trailer park and gave me the one left there by the previous renters. It was a small portable black-and-white TV with adjustable rabbit ears.

I started putting it to good use by inviting Mary to come and watch westerns with me in the evenings. This was when *Gunsmoke, The Virginian; Rifleman*; and *Have Gun, Will Travel*, starring Richard Boone, were popular. But my favorite was *Bonanza*, featuring Hoss Cartwright, simple-minded, but with a heart of gold, and his younger brother, dashing Little Joe. Hoss was so strong he could knock a horse down with one punch to the forehead. He did the same thing to the bad guys. But what I liked best about all of it were the commercials. That's when Mary and I did some spirited necking, making the hollow door we sat on creak and screech.

After a month or two of sitting on the bed, I reaped a bonanza from Norman. He was getting married to a lady named Elinor who would be moving from her apartment into his. I was invited to take a look at the furnishings in her apartment and choose the things I wanted. He said she was quitting her job as an airline stewardess. When Martin and I went to take a look, I thought, wow, airline stewardesses must make good money. I chose a large wrap-around couch that would fit nicely into a corner, a king-size bed, a color TV, and some bar chairs. We loaded it all into the U-Haul I'd rented and took it to Brooklyn Heights.

One afternoon while I was using a pair of pliers to bend coat hangers, intending to make a flat, three-foot-wide sculpture to hang on the wall, I heard a knock on the door.

Two guys stood there, and one said, "Billy Edd Wheeler?" I said, "Yes." He said, "I'm Russ Moneyham, and this is my apartment mate, Rod. We heard you on WBAI Radio. You said you lived in Brooklyn Heights, so I contacted Doug Massey, alumni director at Berea College, and he gave me your address. He was class of 54, a year behind you, I believe. I just wanted to come by and say hello. Rod and I are your neighbors around on Hicks Street."

They gave me the address and phone number, and I promised to have a drink with them soon.

During this time, I also spent hours late at night talking on the phone with Norman. He would share lines with me of a lyric in progress, like "Killing me softly with his song." I'd never heard that phrase before, so I believe Norman invented it especially for the song that became one of the most listened to in the world. He had a Rolodex filled with song titles, filed alphabetically. One night, when he got to the B's, he read, "Blue Roses." I said, "I like that one." He told me to take it. It was mine. So I started a song with that title, and when I had what I thought might be the opening verse, I started trying to come up with a melody for it. The first one sounded too folksy, so I tried another with a country flavor, and it sounded like something for Hank Snow. Here's the first draft of the first verse:

> *Last night I gave you roses, soft as velvet, flaming red*
> *You didn't open up the box, you gave them back instead*
> *They looked so red when I gave them to you*
> *But tonight the roses are blue.*

After playing it over and over, I was satisfied it had the right feel. But I needed a chorus lyric that would inspire the melody. I wrote two lyrics and neither worked. The reason why, I told myself, was they were too poetic and folksy. It needed to be simple and on subject. Here's number three chorus:

> *They are blue-oo, the roses are blue-oo*
> *The roses and me.*

I was sure now I was on the right track, if I kept the next verses more country than folk. I put the guitar down and wrote in my diary.

Mary and I have spent the last two weekends together, and have found great delight in each other. And without committing ourselves we have discussed marriage values and personal philosophies in general. I have the feeling she wants to know the depth of my love for her. I have never told her I loved her, though I have said I missed her and wanted to be around her more and more. On Monday my first discontent happened when an older woman came and spent a few hours with me. I think she was the mother of a girl I met in the studio during a session. She hinted about sex and I was vaguely attracted to her, but I got rid of her and immediately became moody and despondent for being even a little bit attracted to her.

Joan came to rehearse and I talked out my mood with her. She thought it was a healthy sign, my being upset with the woman, because of my loyalty to Mary. Later, Janet called to ask if I knew where Mary was. I said no.

At about 7:00 p.m. Mary called and said she had gone shopping for some items she needed. I said I had wanted to see her, but now it was too late. I was going shopping, too. It was a lie. I was sulking over an imagined slight.

On April 2, I picked Mary up to take her to Norman's apartment for dessert. I don't remember the name of the building, but when the elevator stopped and we stepped out, I realized this whole floor was his and Elinor's place. And a classy, tastefully furnished apartment it was. The dessert was excellent, and "Ellie" and Norman were charming. He played records and gave us the grand tour. After we thanked them for their hospitality, we joined Russ and Rod at Foffe, a nice Spanish restaurant on Montague Street. Walter joined us and introductions were made. Russ and Rod bragged on Foffe's martinis, but Mary and I said we didn't like gin, or the olives with it. Russ was quick to suggest we might like Gibsons, vodka martinis made with little pearl onions instead of olives. We tried it, and from then on it became our favorite drink. When we could afford it, we started ordering a Gibson. But neither of us was a big drinker.

Walter told us Marylyn was working, waiting tables, and he was in rehearsal for James Purdy's play, *Color of Darkness*. Russ and Rod fell in love with Mary and took a big liking to Walter's jokes and stories. When he was "on," Walter was, according to Russ, "'Pretty wald" (for pretty wild). Walter's punch line, after telling about strange New York characters he'd met, was, "Town's full o' nuts."

By mid-April I'd been with Mary several times, and each time had been better than the last. I finally told her I loved her. It was a bit difficult to say, but I wanted to say it, and she seemed happy to hear it. I asked her to please come over if I called and said I needed to see her. She said she would. I cried a little as we lay on the bed, but I tried not to let her see it. I felt good after telling her. A few nights later, I cooked dinner for us, and we watched some TV, but couldn't find anything we liked. As we walked to the subway, she asked why I hadn't inquired about what she was going to do next year. I said I didn't know why, except I hoped she'd be living with me. Finally, on the subway steps I stopped and said, "What I really want to do is marry you in the fall." She seemed pleased that I'd said it, and as we sat waiting for the train, she said she was surprised, but not totally. She had seen it coming for a long time. I walked her to her place on East 59th Street, and when I kissed her at her door, she said she loved me. It was the first time she'd said it, and it made me very, very happy.

May 1, 1963

Record data noted in the diary:

"Rev. M. Black" on the Kingston Trio album has sold 250,000 copies.

64 on charts.

The single has sold over 150,000 copies. It is now becoming a solid hit.

8 in Variety / # 15 on Billboard.

"The Girl Who Loved the Man Who Robbed the Bank at Santa Fe and Got Away"

Is # 27 on the charts, becoming a hit for Hank Snow.

Joan and I are set to record next Monday, Tuesday, and Wednesday.

Dick Rosmini will arrange and play on 9 tunes.

Barry Kornfeld has 3 or 4.

The Boys are now giving me $50 a week, and this to be increased to $125 soon, for two years, and after that $150.

Reading this in the diary now, it amazes me. Just a few weeks before, I was borrowing money from Mary to pay the rent. The prospect of real money coming in boosted my spirits tremendously. Being put on a contract that guaranteed steady income made me think I had actually become a professional songwriter. It made me dizzy with enthusiasm.

Our courtship did not exactly continue smoothly the rest of May. Mary quit her job at the public relations firm and headed to the Adirondacks to be a counselor at a Jewish girls' camp. It was mostly my fault. For instance, in one of my speeches following some heavy necking, I proclaimed that she was so perfect in every way she was all women to me. She adamantly replied that she was not ready to accept such a large responsibility and said I didn't really know her. She said she objected to peoples' impression that she was a happy-go-lucky scatterbrain. I argued that such an "impression" did not belong to me. On the contrary, my "definite" impression was that she was as smart as she was beautiful. I was a love-sick puppy dog and had used every adjective I could think of to idolize her. If I included even 20% of it here from my diary, it would make you gag.

In spite of all our arguing and questioning, and my philosophizing, we decided that we were indeed, and for sure, in love. Our minds were made up. I had told her I wanted to marry her in the fall, but we had not yet decided on a specific date. Or, I should say, she had not decided, and I thought I shouldn't push it.

I was so hyper about our declarations of love I couldn't decide if I wanted to work on the wire sculpture, walk to the Met, or do something else. I decided to write to Mary.

June 4

Last night Joan and I went to West 42nd St. to have an album picture made. The photog was sort of scatter-brained and not too imaginative, so I'll be surprised if any of them work. But we'll see. We had to do the pics in a hurry because Joan is leaving tomorrow for the tour with Harry Belafonte, and we'll want to release the album while she's gone. I'm hoping I can send you one before summer's over.

Have you mentioned us, you and me, to your mama? If you have, tell me how she reacted. I guess they both (daddy, too) suspect something is going on. Norman called saying Jerry wants a title for the album. By the way, if we get married in the fall, do you want Fred Ohler or my friend Norris to do the exchanging of the vows?

Norris said the bride usually chooses the minister.
It's up to you.

I love you, C.T. –Billy Edd.

C.T. stands for Carrot Top, which was one of my pet names for
Mary. After writing the letter, I picked up the latest issue of the
West Virginia Hillbilly, not intending to read it unless I saw a short
article in a box similar to the Desert Pete one. There were no
boxes, but a couple of cartoons of outhouses caught my attention.
It got me to thinking about Highcoal and the stories I'd heard
about outhouses. They were a necessary part of life, whether you
were rich or poor, dumb or educated. One minister said he'd
dreamed up some of his best sermons there. It gradually came to
me that these outhouse memories might be worked into a funny,
yet serious, song. I put that hyperenergy I'd been feeling to good
use and started the song "Ode to the Little Brown Shack Out
Back."

When I finished it, and Norman and I had demo'ed it at Mira
Sound, I took it to Dave Kapp himself, the first time I'd been in
his office. He listened to the song, and in his best upperclass New
Yorkese he said, "Billy, we want to have a hit with you, but not
about…outhouses." I was deflated. I didn't bother writing Mary
with the bad news. We had been so upbeat about everything so
far.

I was thinking about going to South Bristol, Maine to visit
Gladden and maybe go out kipper fishing with him a night or
two, but I got a phone call that changed all that. It was from
Burnett Hobgood. He was directing a new outdoor drama in
west Kentucky called *Stars in My Crown*, by Kermit Hunter. He
was in desperate need of an actor who could sing and play guitar.
I would have one of the leading roles. Rehearsals were going
well, he said, but the show would open June 22, so I had to come

right away. They could pay me $50 per week and find me a nice house to live in.

I arrived in Murray, Kentucky, five days before opening night. Burnett, as I called him in Berea, was giving a speech to the cast about how to play their parts with confidence. He said, "If you walk on stage and act as if you own it, you *command* the audience to believe you and keep their eyes on your eyes. Thus, as a man, you could walk on with your fly unzipped and the audience would not notice, and instead of saying, 'Tis better to suffer the slings and arrows of outrageous fortune than to...' you could say, 'Tis better to suffer the eggs and bacon of outrageous fortune than to ...' and no one would notice. So walk and speak with confidence. Own the stage."

He told the cast about my studying at Yale and writing the hit for the Kingston Trio, then asked for their indulgence in spending extra time to help me learn my cues and lines. They were mostly young and full of energy. Willing to cooperate. And after four days of rehearsal, I was ready to go. I could bone up, if necessary, while waiting for my next scene while the play was in progress. But a few times I had to invent speeches. Burnett also asked me to start writing some songs for this scene and that. My role was Mr. Rivers, the spiritual essence of the four main rivers of the area. I could be high minded, loving and gracious, or diabolical and bombastic. New territory for me, knowing deep down I was not an actor. But in spite of that, I tried to "own the stage," as our director had suggested.

I became friends with a young actor who wrote songs and right away wanted me to listen to him play them. His name was Alex Harvey, and he was full of confidence and personality. I took a liking to him instantly—but not to his songs. I said, "Alex, these are the worst songs I've ever heard. Do the world a favor and don't write any more of them." Of course, he thought I was kidding, and to soften the blow, before telling him I meant it, I told him I had written some throw-away stuff myself.

The house they had reserved for me, not free of charge, was very nice. I felt lost in it for several weeks before inviting anyone to come by. So I sat on the couch and wrote songs and letters to Mary. Two songs were good enough to be demo'ed, I thought: "The Waltz of Miss Sarah Green," and "Heart Insurance," which sounded to me like a Jim Nabors song. I had the beginning ideas for several more that included these titles: "The Place of Man," "Gospel Ship," "Bull Rider," and "Ridin' on an Empty Train."

Burnett told me the producers of the drama would appreciate it if I would give some programs to help promote the show. So I took Alex along to a hootenanny, a program featuring folk singers at a local high school. I got a big applause for "Rev. Mr. Black," but an even bigger response when I sang "Ode to the Little Brown Shack Out Back." There were lots of teenagers in the audience, and, in addition to squeals of laughter, some of them yelled out comments about outhouses, causing me to retort to one guy, "I know he's seen one all right," which also got a laugh. Alex played one of his songs, getting good applause, and of course he wanted me to critique it later. I tried not to be too critical, but still truthful about how bad it was. This didn't affect his enthusiasm. He was determined to keep writing songs.

The next day I told Burnett about a play I had in mind, a sort of a hillbilly comedy with moonshine stills and a ridiculous love affair between an old backwoods fisherman and a prim and proper Presbyterian missionary. I was intending to name the play *Fire on the Mountain*, featuring lots of funny songs. Burnett told me the same thing I told Alex about his songs: "Don't waste time writing it. Bad idea from someone who went to Yale Drama School." But, just like Alex, I decided I would write it anyway.

I was delighted to hear from Norman that the Kingston Trio was planning to use some more of my songs and release "Desert Pete" as a single. According to Jerry, if this happened it could mean between $20,000 and $40,000 for me, in addition to the $7,000 already earned from "The Rev. Mr. Black." This was mighty good news. I could pay off some debts and buy a tux for the wedding.

Stars in My Crown ended the first week of August, and I had accumulated a lot of good press for my role as Mr. Rivers and for the songs I had written for several scenes. I put all the articles into an 8x10 envelope to show to Mary. I hung out for several days with Alex after the show closed. I told him what Jerry Leiber had told me: I couldn't use any of his songs, but if he came with one I thought had promise, I would agree to cowrite it with him.

Before I left Murray I was visited by a man and woman from nearby Fulton. She was an official in a group preparing to have a banana festival in Fulton, starting on November 3. They had seen me perform in *Stars in my Crown* and wanted to book me for an appearance to help kick off the festival. Before I could ask what connection Fulton had with bananas, they quickly explained it. Fulton was the major distribution point for bananas in the United States. They came up from New Orleans in reefers containing block ice and were then loaded onto railroad cars with more ice added. From Fulton the bananas headed north via the Illinois Central Railroad and east via the Louisville and Nashville Railroad. They proudly boasted that this festival was a big deal, being covered by national radio and TV. It would be good exposure for me. I said their kickoff would be the third day after my wedding in North Carolina. They said I'd be paid a good fee and would be comfortably put up in nice efficiency. She said, "How often does a couple get to honeymoon, free of charge, at a banana festival?" Of course, I agreed, and signed a contract they'd brought with them.

Back in New York, on September 19, I learned that Joan's and my album, *A New Bag of Songs*, was purchased by Kapp Records and that they planned to release a solo album by me, plus a solo album by Joan. My single, "After Taxes" and "Blistered," was getting good reviews in *Billboard*, which called it "two excellent sides," and by *Cashbox*, which wrote, "Newcomer Billy Edd

Wheeler might break through into the national limelight with this power-packed new release by Kapp." It explained a little of the story line for "After Taxes," and it gave me hope until I read, "The flip, 'Blistered,' is a fast-moving, contagious tear-jerker." This convinced me the writer had not even listened to the song. Both sides of the single were a flop.

For the remaining part of September, I started working on song ideas but made little progress. My mind was on Mary and the wedding. I spent some time with Russ and Rod, playing Scrabble and dining out now and then. I went to a Mets game with Russ, and once when he saw me squinting, he asked, "Do you need glasses?" I said I didn't think so. He said, "What's that left fielder's number?" When I couldn't answer, he handed me his glasses. When I put them on, I was amazed. I could see the guy's number, see blades of grass, and read the billboards. The next day I went to an optometrist, who confirmed that I did, indeed, need glasses. I said, "Can you have a pair ready for me by tomorrow?" He laughed and said, "Maybe in a week."

I wrote to Norris Woodie at Berea and asked him to please let all our mutual friends know I was getting married. I also asked if he would participate in the wedding ceremony, and, oh yes, could I borrow his old Buick to drive to Swannanoa for the wedding? He said yes to both questions. Then I wrote a long and heartfelt letter to Dr. and Mrs. Bannerman. I heard from Mary twice a week. She was busy with wedding plans and ordering our rings. They were gold, featuring two circles joined together. Price: $60 for the two.

November 2, 1963, 4:00PM

The old Elizabeth Williams log chapel was crowded with Mary's and my friends and family, many of whom were Warren Wilson faculty, Dr. Bannerman and Dr. Jensen's staff and coworkers. The chapel was beautifully decorated. Mary's mother wore a stylish hat, and so did Sister. Mary's sister, Janet, was her maid of honor.

My best man, brother Bob, was decked out in a tux. His first, so
far as I knew. I stayed backstage with the Reverend Fred Ohler
and the Reverend Dr. Woodie during the organ preludes. We
took our places at center stage when the processional began, and
I was holding up pretty well. Then Dr. Jensen started singing the
song he had written for Mary and me, and halfway into it, when
the lyric referred to me, holding back tears was impossible.

> *Mary, Mary, joyful good and fair*
> *All who love you join your vow in pray'r*
> *All that is yours to promise, all that is yours to be*
> *God shall bless in every care*
> *Faith, Hope, Honor—these are yours, my son*
> *She who weds you grants a greater one*
> *You are like singing waters born of deep mountain springs*
> *Whose pure theme God lent your song*
> *Ancient moment now as always new*
> *As you marry only once is true*
> *Where in time life may take you*
> *Trust to each the other's quest*
> *Wherein home and man are blessed*

I recovered somewhat during Dr. Woodie's meditation. But
when I saw Mary walk up the aisle on the arm of her father,
her red hair framed in the splendor of white on white, I started
blubbering softly and choking, as if swallowing inner tears to
keep from drowning. In a liquid tone of voice, I whispered my
vows until the final "I do." Norris handed me his handkerchief
just in time for me to kiss the bride. Mary was a solid contrast,
speaking clearly and with confidence. Her poise put me to shame.
Suddenly though, I recovered miraculously and was able to smile
as Mary took my arm and we walked out the aisle toward the
door. A couple of people tossed flower petals into the air over our
heads. Once outside, I felt like shouting, "We're married! We're

man and wife! Ain't it wonderful, yahoo!" And I gave my bride a real kiss. A lot juicier than the stage kiss.

We had a wonderful reception, but the afternoon went by quickly. Before I knew it, it was 5:00 p.m. It would be dark soon, so Mary and I had to get out of our wedding garb and get dressed for the trip to Gatlinburg, where we would spend the night before going on to Fulton, Kentucky, the next day for the banana festival. The old Buick was mostly packed before the wedding, so we were on the road in time to stop at an A&W in Asheville before dark. We dined on burgers, fries, and milkshakes. But my mind was not on the meal. It was on Gatlinburg where Mary and I would consummate our marriage. I was so excited it was hard to keep from speeding. But the up-and-down mountain roads were not conducive to speeding anyway, and Gatlinburg seemed like a hundred miles away. So I asked Mary if it would be OK to stop in Cherokee. She agreed. I'm sure she knew what was on my mind. Hers too, I hoped.

We checked into a large end room with a fireplace. It seemed romantic, but the wood was damp, and it took a while to get a fire burning, testing my patience. Mary opened a bottle of red wine during that time. Finally, and thankfully on my part, we were able to turn the lights down, spread blankets in front of the fire, and make glorious, heart-pounding love. I had dreamed about this moment many times back in Brooklyn. Now the dream was being fulfilled, and I was a deliriously happy man.

When we pulled into Fulton, it was quite a sight to see stalks of bananas hanging everywhere along the streets—on parking meters, street signs, and hanging from limbs on trees. Billboards welcomed one and all to the first ever banana festival in America. Posters were everywhere too, especially in store windows. One of them had my name on it. Our first honeymoon would be in Brooklyn Heights, in the "apartment" Dr. Bannerman described as one room with a nice long hallway. There was a lot of catch-up work to be done on my part with Norman. But Mary was making plans to buy things we needed for cooking and making the place more comfortable. So we walked to a furniture store several blocks away, where she spotted a nice rocking chair. I picked it up, upside down, with the seat on my head, and she helped balance it as I carried it back to 51 Remsen. Those three blocks seemed like half a mile.

Norman surprised me by giving me a large share of one of his own companies: Sleepy Hollow Music, ASCAP. The deal was, he was giving me 190 shares, so that, he said, I would have a publishing company of my own. My lawyer, Al DaSilva, would own 10 shares, representing 5%, and Norman would own the remaining shares in his company, Butterfield Music. I'd had no indoctrination to these publishing matters, but I figured I'd get up to speed when Norman explained it all to me. Our first songs that went into our joint companies were old ones: "Mingo Mountain," "Huckleberry Wine," "Bitter Sweet, Bear Tail" (by Dr. Jensen), and "Love's Running Dry." We demo'ed them at Allegro.

On January 25th, 1964, Mary and I went to hear Judy Henske at the Village Gate, and I loved her. She was full of what I took to be sexual energy, wearing a beaded necklace that hung down between her breasts to the floor. The beads were always in motion from her subtle gyrations. And she told the weirdest stories before each number she sang, and none of them had anything to do with the songs. It was refreshing. Too many singers tell so much about the song they're about to sing, you feel like shouting, "OK, on to the next one!" I'd never seen an act like hers.

Jac Holzman, head of Elektra Records, was backstage, where I introduced myself to him. He said he wanted me to send some more songs to him, saying he loved "High Flyin' Bird" and was going to record it with Judy. A Spanish guitarist was also on the bill, and I was blown away by his performance. Jac said his name was Sabicas, and he was a big seller for Elektra. But he didn't trust American record labels enough to agree to a royalty deal. He demanded a one-time payment of $1,000. "He'd make a whole lot more than that if he'd let us pay him quarterly or semiannually, based on sales."

Jac did record "High Flyin' Bird" with Judy and made it the title of her album. Richie Havens must have learned it from that album, and he sang it at Woodstock. A big band was scheduled to be the first act, but because of the weather they were detained. So "High Flyin' Bird" was the third song Richie sang. This gave it a lot of recognition, but the trouble was, Richie screwed it up. Instead of the phrase, "I used to have an old man (meaning his dad) and he worked in the mines," Richie sang, "I had me a woman, she lived down by the mine." This changed the whole song, and unfortunately a lot of singers learned it from him. Richie's rapid-fire guitar also took the melody out of the song. But one singer, Isaac Guillary, recorded it live in a club in London. He was one hell of a guitarist, and when I heard his version for the first time, I wept. He absolutely nailed it. Janis Ian also loved Isaac's rendition, and that lady has good taste.

For the next two months I gave up writing songs, to let the well fill back up, and started writing *Fire on the Mountain*, my hillbilly musical. I thought I might have it done in time to show it to Burnett Hobgood when Mary and I reported for our roles in *Stars in My Crown*. I told Burnett he had to hire Mary or I wasn't coming back. "Besides, she's an excellent dancer. Take my word for it. She's smooth, graceful, and has the energy to outdance you, me, and two others put together. And…"

He cut me off, saying, "All right already, I'm sold. She's on the payroll. But I don't have a fancy house for you this time. There's some nice trailers for rent, next to a beautiful lake. You'd love it. Lots of cast members will be there to be your neighbors."

I said OK. But I wasn't sure Mary would like the idea. She and I found a small Italian restaurant in the Heights that we took a liking to. And could afford. We shared a wonderful lasagna dish, with a glass of red for her and a chardonnay for me. It didn't have to be Californian. My taste buds had not developed at all by then.

Back in Brooklyn, life got really busy. Norman called to say Faith Whitehill at Leiber and Stoller had received a call from the Lucy Kroll Agency, wanting to know how to get in touch with me. He didn't know what it was about, but told me Lucy Kroll was a big-time agent for well-known writers, playwrights, actors, and such. When I called the number he gave me and told the agency lady who I was, Ms. Kroll picked up the phone. She sounded somewhat like Dave Kapp, but less formal. Her sophistication was oozing with friendliness.

She explained that she was involved with the producers of the first-ever New York Folk Festival, for 1965, and said they wanted me as a singer, but more importantly as writer and narrator. Before I could ask what I would narrate, she said, "I am Carl Sandburg's agent, and Mr. Manheim Fox, and his fellow producers, Sid Bernstein and John Stein, love your *Memories of America* album, as do I. On the third and last day of the festival, they want to produce Carl Sandburg's *American Songbag*, and I have recommended you to synthesize the song bag, and help select the proper folk singers." She went on at length, saying she thought my job would be to create narrations to introduce each song and its singer. But the final decision would be made by Fox and company. At the end of the phone call, I surprised Ms. Kroll by telling her I had written a poem about Mr. Sandburg. She sounded excited and said she had to hear it. So I recited the following for her:

Standing Force
If you ram into an iceberg, you're the one that's hit
Though you may think by moving you are hitting it
If you stumble into Sandburg you may be double crooked
And not know until later the strength of what he's booked
If it is ice or Sandburg you chance to crash into
Wait a while to comment on what ran into who

She was ecstatic. She practically shouted, "It's wonderful. Darling, I suspected you might be the right person for this project. Now I know you are. You and the *American Songbag* are a perfect fit." If you send your poem to me and grant permission, I'll send it on to Carl right away. He'll love it."

She did send the poem to Sandburg, and he told her he loved it. And I did write the narrations that included introducing a dance team from Berea College and performing with them at Carnegie Hall. Some of the folk singers chosen included Grandpa Jones, Jimmie Driftwood, Bob Gibson, Eric Anderson, Dock Boggs, Son House, Mississippi John Hurt, and Bill Monroe. But the biggest thrill Mary and I had was when we went backstage and met Johnny Cash and June Carter. This was before they were married and before we saw them at the White House.

Chapter Fourteen

ODE TO THE LITTLE BROWN SHACK OUT BACK

They passed an ordinance in the town
They said we'd have to tear it down
That little old shack out back so dear to me
And though the health department said
Its day was over and dead
It will stand forever in my memory
Don't let 'em tear that little brown building down
Don't let 'em tear that dear old building down
Don't let 'em tear that precious building down
For there's not another like it in the country or the town

Before we knew it, we were on our way to Murray at the end of May. Rehearsals started for the second season of *Stars in My Crown*. We rented a trailer that was silver and shaped like some of the diners I had frequented for cheap food in New Haven. The floor was a bit grungy, and the single mattresses needed some airing out. Mary spotted some cockroaches, so we needed some kind of spray. Alex Harvey was one of the first to greet us, proclaiming he had a new batch of songs that were really good. He was so positive they were better that I did hope he was right.

He had a winning personality and a great work ethic. He told me that a small publisher in Nashville loved some of his songs and was willing to counsel him in the rewriting of them.

Alex said, "I figured you'd have the big head because of the reviews you got for acting out the Mr. Rivers role. But it don't seem like you're in a braggin' mood."

I said, "Alex, if you have any sense at all, you know I'm not as good as those reviews said I was. Fact is, I just fake it, not having to really act. It's all singing, boasting, and ranting and raving about the evils of the rivers. I'm no actor, and you know it." He smiled, nodding, agreeing with me. I said, "Now, the same goes for your songwriting. You're no good. At least, not yet. But you're so damn pig-headed and enthusiastic about it, you make me, and I'm sure those guys in Nashville think you've got what it takes. Just a matter of time."

On my day off, I found a studio in Murray and did a demo of a couple of songs, "Sister Sara" and "Tie My Rope Around a Tree," an idea from Norris Woodie. When I paid the engineer-owner for the demos and started to leave, he said, "Wait a minute. I got something that might interest you."

He went into a storage room, found a reel, and played it for me in the studio. It just about knocked me down. It was my performance of "Ode to the Little Brown Shack Out Back" from the hootenanny the previous year, complete with the clunkers I hit on the guitar. But the fidelity was good, and the laughter from the audience made the hair on my head tingle, or something like that. I said, "How'd you get this? I didn't see you anywhere."

He said, "I was in another room taping the show. That microphone was my German Neumann mic, the best money can buy. Hence, the great quality." I was absolutely totally blown away. I asked him to make me two copies, and I couldn't wait to send one to Mr. Kapp. When I did, I enclosed a letter saying, "If you won't put this out as a single, please give me a release, and I'll do it myself. I think it's a hit. You can hear the reaction. And people want to buy it."

Within four days I got a telegram from Mr. Kapp, saying, "We're releasing this as a single as soon as we can master it properly and get press releases ready. If it does as well as I think it will, we'll feature it on your album with Joan, with a new title: *Memories of America—Ode to the Little Brown Shack Out Back, with Billy Edd Wheeler and Joan Somer.*

He was true to his word. By February 20, 1965, the single was number three on *Billboard*. Within three months the album was rereleased and was selling well. Mary and I wanted to celebrate and enjoy the moment. We drove back to Swannanoa, where we rented a house on Rainbow Ridge, really close to her parents and within easy walking distance of Warren Wilson's campus. We loved the house and started dreaming out loud about wanting to build a home of our own there someday, and the sooner the better. But the truth was we didn't even have enough money for a down payment on a nice house. Not yet.

Being back in the mountains, close to family and friends, put me in a songwriting mood stronger than I'd felt in a long time. Remembering a decapitated mountain that we'd seen in West Virginia, I wrote a strong and graphic protest song, "They Can't Put It Back."

> *Down in the valley 'bout a mile from me*
> *Where the crows no long fly*
> *There's a great big earth-moving monster machine*
> *Stands ten stories high*
> *The ground he can eat is a sight, takes a hundred tons at a bite*
> *He can eat up the ground, it's a fact*
> *But he can't put it back*

It's full of images of destruction, the bare bones of hillsides spoiled by acid, fish floating belly-up in creeks and rivers. But once, at a party at Lawson Hamilton's house in Berea, Kentucky, his wife Jean (called Momma Jean) said she'd heard of it and asked me to sing it. I refused, telling her she wouldn't like it. After all, Lawson was a strip miner. She insisted, saying it couldn't be that bad. The guests too urged me on. So I started singing, and by the time I was halfway into it, she began gasping, as if in horror, and finally jumped up and left the room crying. Lawson said, "Billy Edd, we can put it back and, by god, we will put it back!" Lawson said he put a thousand dollars per acre in escrow with the government in West Virginia, and he didn't get that money back until they were convinced the land was being reclaimed. This was before MTR, mountain top removal, where they used dynamite for blasting. He was a man among men, a leader, and extremely generous, giving big bucks to colleges, hospitals, and churches. He was also a music lover.

And then I wrote a song that protests in a gentler mode. It mixes in a couple's love that begins to fail because of new roads coming in, bringing more bad than good with them. I called it...

The Coming of the Roads

Now that our mountain is growing with people hungry for wealth
How come it's you that's a-going and I'm left alone by myself
Once I had you and the wildwood, now it's just dusty roads
And I can't help from blaming your going on the coming
The coming of the roads

I got goose bumps up and down my spine and arms every time I played the song, the first time that had ever happened. I took it to be a sign that it just might be the best song I'd ever written. I played it over and over 'til Mary got tired of it. I made a demo of it in Asheville, along with "They Can't Put It Back," and sent them to Norman.

Since Mary and I knew we could not afford to build the house of our dreams, we thought we should at least look for a piece of land. So we went to see Hardy Davidson, and he led us up the hill to where he had a small rock cabin. It was where he spent a lot of time just to get out of the big house and play the violin, away from his two sisters, I supposed. The acreage below it reached down to Bee Tree Road, about two miles from Warren Wilson. Hardy figured the cabin and the piece of land below it was about two and a half acres.

When we asked if he'd sell it to us, and what it would cost, he said, "Well, you can have it for the bargain price of twelve hundred and fifty dollars."

I said, "But Mr. Davidson, the old cabin has no kitchen or bathroom." He shook his head, as if that didn't matter, and stuck to his price.

We thought we could afford the $1250, even if we had to get a bank loan. Dr. Bannerman was a member of the board of directors of the Bank of Swannanoa, owned by the Bank of Asheville, which might be helpful. It was. The loan would be approved by the bank's president when he received the final price from Mr. Davidson. I said, "But he's already named the price, right off the bat, without thinking twice about it."

Jim nodded with a smile. "That's the problem. He's a Davidson, and they value their land. Let's wait and see."

Sure enough, when we told Hardy the loan was approved, he said, "Well, let's step it off and see what we're talking about." When he was done stepping, he said, "I'll let you have it for twelve hundred and seventy-five dollars. Still a bargain, I figure."

We brought Mary's parents out to see the cabin. To me it looked pitiful, but Mrs. Bannerman thought it showed promise and would be a great place for us to live while waiting for a nice house to go up. There was enough land for some creative landscaping. Her artist's eye could see a garden space for vegetables, flowers, and colorful shrubbery.

We got word that *Fire on the Mountain* was opening within weeks at Danville's Pioneer Playhouse, so we timed our stay in the Smith house to enjoy it as long as possible before heading to the premiere. We drove to Berea and spent the night with the

Drukkers. Judy was very impressed with Mary, and Mary was impressed with their house. When she kept admiring a certain chest with a beautiful marble top, Judy said, "Someday when it's my time go, I'll put your name on it."

Mary said she thought that was a beautiful gesture of friendship and said, "But we don't want to take possession anytime soon." Judy cackled with laughter. We enjoyed one of Judy's special breakfasts, and as we drove on to Danville, Mary said Judy reminded her of her mother, the way she entertained with "elegant simplicity."

It was a lively evening at Pioneer Playhouse. Before speeches by a few local dignitaries, Colonel Eben Henson introduced us to the director, Constance Phelps, and leading actor, Jim Varney, famous for his funny ads on radio and TV. His character was a little slow on the uptake—maybe dumb-but-lovable is a better way of saying it—the kind of local yokel who leans into your window, trying to act cool, and the window slams down on his knuckles. His famous phrase was, "Know whut ah mean, Vern?" I was told this was his first starring role, and he was born to play the character of Uncle Jesse. Or maybe he *was* Uncle Jesse. The dialogue was so over the top "hillbilly," it was farcical. But I think I'd hit on a mother lode, for I knew lots of educated people who liked to talk hillbilly. Actually, I do it myself.

The actors got into their roles one hundred percent, a couple of men in overalls, carrying shotguns and wearing false beards, like George Clooney in *Oh Brother, Where Art Thou?* The whole cast was dressed outlandishly. At least two of them were barefooted. And the choreography was, as you might guess, also over the top. But fun, as were the songs. It was that fun element delivered with energy that made the show a crowd pleaser. The love element, with Uncle Jesse trying to romance the Presbyterian missionary, was implausible, but just believable enough in a few scenes to create heart-touching "Ahhhs" from the audience, in spite of the way they both hammed it up.

When they first met, she looked down on him as an uneducated backwoods fisherman, especially when they shook hands and she got fish scales on her hand. The show got a standing ovation and great reviews the next day.

It was a bit hard for Mary and me to leave our dream worlds and drive back to the real world of Brooklyn. But the energy of the city kicked in soon, and I was eager to talk to Norman and The Boys to see what condition my condition was in—to borrow a line from Mickey Newberry's fine song. It looked pretty good. Norman said Judy Collins loved "The Coming of the Roads" and declared it to be my newest best song ever. She was planning to put it on her album, *Judy Collins' Fifth Album*. He said, "Dave Kapp wants you to do your next album in Nashville, with a man named Paul Cohen producing. Paul has picked out a couple of tunes by other writers, songs with a bit more pop flavor. But Jerry wants you to include "Tonight I'm Singing Just for You" that you wrote with him."

So off I went to Nashville and checked in at the Music Row Holiday Inn, which is not its formal name. The pickers, producers, and their friends called it that because they liked the bar area. It was on West End Avenue, just a couple of streets over from the Row. Paul Cohen was very laid back, and so was the arranger for the session, Cliff Parman, a veteran of hundreds of sessions. The musicians were veterans, too. Grady Martin played guitar, and a blind man, Hargus "Pig" Robbins, played piano. A West Virginia guy, Charlie McCoy, played harmonica. He could make that instrument talk, it seemed, when he got a chance to shine. But most of the time he played rhythm, content to be a part of the group sound. The drummer was a household name, but I've forgotten it.

My favorites of the tracks were "The Waltz of Miss Sarah Green," "Tonight I'm Singing Just for You," "Hillbilly Bossa Nova," and "Ode to Granny," a follow-up to "Ode to the Little Brown Shack Out Back." I never got comfortable singing the three outside songs. But Mr. Kapp chose to put two out as a single, "Burning Bridges" on the A side and "On the Outside Looking In" on the B side. Both were too sugary and pop for my taste. Maybe OK for a crooner.

Paul and Cliff entertained me each evening after sessions. Jimmy Kelly's one night, and the second night we drove out to what seemed like the boonies. Maybe because they served alcoholic drinks without the required brown bags. It had a real nightclub atmosphere, with lots of single women available for dancing. But we three were too busy gabbing about the session, and I was tired, having spent lots of nervous energy at Columbia Studios. On the way back, we were passing by a big industrial building, and I said, "I wonder what they make there?" Cliff yelled out, "about ten million a month" and laughed like crazy. I liked him, but in the studio he was scared to death of Grady Martin. When he approached Grady to suggest a certain guitar break, the arrangement shook in his hands. Grady would shrug his shoulders and with sleepy eyes say, "Sure. Whatever." None of the veteran pickers got excited about anything, except Charlie McCoy. He was into it and didn't mind showing it.

The sessions went faster than anticipated, so I had an extra day in Nashville. I went to the RCA building, hoping to see Chet Atkins, but Mary Lynch told me he was out of town. So Cliff and I used the time to write a song based on an idea he had: "The Doves of San Morray." The songs from the Nashville sessions were released on the album *The Wheeler Man / Billy Edd*. Dave Kapp wrote in a letter to me: "Everyone here likes the title, and I think it will help to establish your name more firmly. I wish you would write the liner notes for your LP. I know you can do it, and I think it would be well for you to begin to express yourself from the platform of the liner." Again, I was touched by his determination to help my career, in spite of limited sales. But sadly, it didn't kick up much dust, and the single also went kaput.

Early in 1966, I flew back to Nashville to record *Billy Edd Wheeler / Goin' Town and Country*. The songs included my

cowritten one with Cliff Parman, "The Doves of San Morray."
My version of the "Coming of the Roads" was on the album, but
for some reason the album included internationally known songs,
like "September Song," by Kurt Weill and Maxwell Anderson,
that had been sung by the likes of Bing Crosby and Frank Sinatra,
Ella Fitzgerald and Eartha Kit. What on earth did Paul and Cliff
think I could bring to the songs? I felt intimidated just trying to
get through it, with those legends hanging heavy on my shoulder.
Same with "Sounds of Silence," from the first folk-rock album
ever, sung beautifully by Simon and Garfunkel. Imagining that
Mr. Kapp had suggested those songs, I didn't try to muster up
enough balls to argue with the producers.

Paul and Cliff wined and dined me again after the sessions,
and I drank a couple of rum and Cokes too many. I was not
prepared to jump out of bed for breakfast, but the phone rang,
jarring me out of a deep slumber. It was 7 a.m. "Hi, this is Chet.
How 'bout some breakfast?"

I woke up quickly. "Yeah, great, Mr. Atkins, I'd like to. Uh,
where?"

He said, "The Hole in the Wall. I'll pick you up in say, fifteen
minutes?"

I said that would be great and dashed to the wash basin. I
didn't have time to shower, but the cold water I splashed on
my face helped wake me up a little. The Hole in the Wall was
just that. Barely enough room for a wide counter and a few
narrow tables. The server, I assumed, owned the place and did
the cooking. He and Chet traded insults, Chet about the bad
food and the owner about Chet's being too stingy to afford a
full meal. "Oh, he can afford it all right. Just eats like a bird on a
diet." When the owner was taking care of some other customers,
Chet said, "Good session?" I told him yes. He said, "Paul's a good
producer."

I said, "How'd you know I was in town?"

He said, "Word gets around."

I told him I had come by RCA on my last trip to say hello, but he was out of town. "Yeah, Mary Lynch told me." That was about the extent of our conversation. Chet paid a lot of attention to his one egg, one piece of sausage, and toast.

On the way back to the Music Row Holiday Inn, Chet said in his usual sleepy tone of voice, "I thought the trio did a good job with Reverend Black." Before I could get the words out to thank him, he cut me off, saying, "Bring me some more songs." That was his way of saying goodbye. As I closed the door I said, "OK. Thanks for breakfast."

Lots of things were going on in addition to my recording and songwriting. Mary was in touch with her mother almost biweekly. She had taken our rock cabin on as a project. She was having a mini kitchen installed, plus a tiny bathroom with a phone-booth-sized shower stall. A dirt drive was carved out in the field below that reached to Bee Tree Road, along with a water line put in by Asheville's water department.

Meanwhile, I met Jim Friedman at the Gaslight when he performed some of his original songs. I'd never heard of him, but because of Judy Collins, Dick Rosmini, and others, he had heard of me and seemed eager to cowrite. He was the hippiest guy I ever met. He was unshaven, smoked pot, and wore old clothes that were allergic to washing machines. His pad was a reflection of his image and smelled like it could use some air freshener. His talk was New York hippie too, with "Man" this and "ya-know, man" that. And he bragged about shoplifting groceries. But when he played his old piano, too big for his small space, his sleepy eyes sparkled and made you forget about everything but what he was playing and singing.

I found him to be poetic and charming, a dreamer like me. I wanted to write with him, and he was all for it. Our first song was about how great West Virginia was. We had visions of its doing for the mountain state what "My Old Kentucky Home" did for Kentucky. But it didn't. The next one, however, showed lots more promise. It was about a woman who wore "Bright Yellow Ribbons and Burgundy Hair." I loved it, but it never got recorded until my next album.

I got some song lyrics from Alex Harvey, and one of them, "The Edipunt Song," was very clever. It seemed childish, of course, since it was how a young kid might pronounce elephant, but I thought kids would love it. I encouraged him to work some more on it—offering a couple of suggestions—and then send it to me. I thought if he hooked it, I'd consider recording it myself, thinking it might add variety and help the album break out in new territory. That's how you rationalize as a songwriter, trying to justify a goofy idea, knowing it's all cock-and-bull. I also thought it wouldn't hurt if I put "High Flyin' Bird" on the album. There was no way Judy Collins or Jac Holzman at Elektra would consider it competition. But hearing it as a master cut, as opposed to the quick demo, might give them some ideas.

"Self Portrait
Head On"

Billy

March 15
1952

I know I'm not a great artist, but I love doing it. I didn't have a great
voice, either, but I never let it keep me from singing! On these pages
I share some of my visual art, starting with a 1952 self-portrait.

Inspired by the poetry of Kahlil Gibran, this is how I looked as a mystic in
a past life when I was big buddies with a good-looking Shirley MacLaine.

River of Earth with Tom and Huck, an oil painting from my Thomas Hart Benton phase

A bit of my yard art:
Chagall's 7-ft
circus dancer

Queen of the Nile – a 60 pound rock

Another self portrait

Mountain Hay Time, an oil painting inspired by a Tim Barnwell photograph

Love Dust, oil painting on canvas

Bending Birches, oil painting by Billy Picasso-Kandinski

Dog in a Mint Julep Moon, oil painting by Billy Picasso

Bird Woman with Artist and Cat, oil painting by Billy Picasso

Son Travis & Hardy, 1980, Swannanoa, North Carolina

Fun at Harvest. Using corn silk for a mustache to imitate Baron Von Snodgrass in my largest oil painting ever in those early days.

Johnny Cash and the Ragged Old Flag (a work in progress). From a photo by the late Hugh Morton, owner of Grandfather Mountain in western North Carolina.

Chapter Fifteen

IN YOUR SPANISH EYES

I look into your Spanish eyes and this is what I feel
For the first time in my lifetime I know it's real
And there's an old Spanish tune out of the clear blue
That's like a love song I hear each time I'm near you
It says I love you, mi vita, I love you

I could tell myself not to try so hard to make you mine
But I might as well tell the moon and stars not to shine
I think about you every night and all the day long
For you'll live forever in my heart and in my love song
It says I love you, mi vita, I love you

You gave me your love
True love never dies
I live and I love
In your Spanish eyes

Chet Atkins used to play a hauntingly beautiful melody on the guitar. He said it was an old well-known tune in the public domain. "Why don't you write a lyric for it," he suggested. I did, and we recorded it in his basement "studio." Actually his workplace. I found the lyric with both our names on it, with the copyright listed as 1978, Sleepy Hollow Music (my ASCAP company). I think because he didn't create the melody, he didn't want his name on it. But I thought his version of the song meant his name should be there.

In the fall of 1966 Mary and I decided it was time to get out of New York. Leiber and Stoller were going to discontinue my weekly salary, and I figured I could drive to performing gigs out of Swannanoa easier than New York. I would still receive royalties from The Boys and performance income from ASCAP. Plus, I had the premonition that I might write a real play. *Fire on the Mountain* had earned me some money and satisfied my desire to write. I felt extremely lucky for its success, but it was a novelty.

The rock cabin still looked rustic, but inside it was homey and livable. Mrs. Bannerman's artistic touch was everywhere in that small space. We had a new rollaway bed to sleep on, and next to the windows on the south side, something similar to a tabletop, with hinges, could be raised and serve as a dining table, three feet deep and five feet wide. We had small tenants in the attic, so for a while we heard the patter of little feet while in bed at night. And one day I heard the thump of something landing on the ledge outside of the north side windows. I looked out to see a very large black snake. It had obviously been eating well. We assumed there were also mice, squirrels, and possibly bats living up there.

Alex Harvey was sending songs more often now. I would critique them, send them back, and his Nashville guys would publish them. After a while I tired of this and told Alex that since he was not receiving advances from those guys, I wanted to be his publisher. I said I could not guarantee a weekly, or even a monthly advance, but I would help all I could. He had been on salary as a bandleader and music teacher at a high school. Before too long, he quit the teaching job and moved to Swannanoa, where he bought a house on Rainbow Ridge. It was not fancy, but the price was right. Now he was my neighbor, and we started collaborating a lot.

In 1967 I recorded *Paper Birds* in New York, the album title taken from a song cowritten with Samantha Tan. It was dreamy and poetic, causing one reviewer to write, "Wheeler's new

outing shows the influence of psychedelia." Produced by Barry
Kornfeld, it included "Here, There, and Everywhere" by Lennon
and McCartney, Tim Hardin's "Reason to Believe," and the song I
wrote with Jim Friedman, "Bright Yellow Ribbons and Burgundy
Hair." I had critiqued Alex's "The Edipunt Song," but not enough
to be credited as a writer on the song with him. "High Flyin'
Bird" was on the album, as well as "They Can't Put It Back." On
the cover of *Paper Birds* was a portrait of me painted by my buddy
Remo Bramanti. He didn't flatter me. I liked it.

Norman called me with the great news that Johnny and
June had recorded "Jackson" and it had reached number two on
Billboard. If nothing else happened that year, 1967 was a success.
Nothing that great did happen, but I felt that my premonition
about writing might be coming true when my friend Ewel
Cornett called to ask if I would be interested in penning an
outdoor drama for Beckley, West Virginia, about the Hatfield and
McCoy feud. I told him I'd have to think about it.

The idea of West Virginians shooting each other to pieces just
for the hell of it didn't appeal to me. It was the image deal again. He
tried to convince me there was more to it than that, but I still balked.
He said, "Well, at least research it. You may not get the commission
anyway. Some board members remarked that they were not sure
they wanted the guy who wrote and sang songs about outhouses to
be their playwright." He ended the conversation with a giggle.

I drove to Beckley and spent time in their library. There were
several books about the feud, and one in particular, *The Hatfields
and the McCoys*, by Virgil Carrington Jones, seemed to be the best
documented. It was published in 1948 by the University of North
Carolina Press at Chapel Hill and made several mentions of a love
affair between young Johnse Hatfield and Roseann McCoy. That
piqued my interest big time. I thought instantly about Romeo
and Juliet, caught between two families that hated each other. The
death toll resulting from the Hatfield and McCoy feud was not as
high as I had imagined, and this pleased me, too.

Ewel took me to dinner, and as I told him about my research and how pleased I was with the documentation, the character sketches, and the love affair.

He started snickering. "I knew damn well you couldn't resist it," he said. "It's a playwright's dream. And the beauty of it—some of the family members are still alive and available for interviews. Hell, Johnse Hatfield's mother lives right here in Beckley. She's old, of course, but her mind is sharp as a tack."

I said, "If you get me a good commission it would be helpful. But what about those board members who…"

He cut in and said, "When I told them you studied playwriting at Yale, that did it. They want to open in 1970. But that gives us plenty of time to research, and the board will need time to work up a contract."

I was really inspired, and even before signing the $10,000 contract, Ewel assured me it was a done deal. The check would be forthcoming. In the meantime, he started to gather names of folks who might be helpful. The first interview was with a man who wore several hats: preacher, lawyer, businessman, and writer. From the instant we entered his office, it was clear he admired the Hatfields much more than the McCoys. He referred to Johnse as a lady's man, calling him the "bull of the woods." I said, "Reverend, you wear so many hats, how do you manage to get anything done?"

This brought a twinkle to his eye. He said, "I have my tricks to keep clients from rambling and loitering, wasting time. I have them sit in that chair facing the glare of the window. The back edge of the chair is slanted and smooth, causing their bottoms to slide forward. The instant they start to hitch back upright, I jump up, say 'Thank for you coming,' and usher them out the door."

I said, "That's pretty crafty for a preacher." He said, "Sometimes business takes priority over salvation. Thank you for coming. This way out." We laughed, and he did too. I purchased a copy of Jones's book and started writing down names of main characters and a very rough outline of the script. Things had gotten busy.

Later that year things got even busier. My single "I Ain't the Worrying Kind" went to # 68, and was then covered by O. C. Smith, who had better luck with it. Johnny Cash released my song "Blistered" as a single. It didn't do as well as "Jackson," but it got a lot of airplay and reached the charts. I got the urge to write poetry, and started devoting a lot of time to it. I also managed to go back to Beckley, where Ewel and I started roaming farther out into the country, sometimes following leads and sometimes just winging it. Over in Kentucky we met the Reverend Henry Clay Parsons, a mountain preacher. He turned out to be one of the richest lodes I mined. He was in his 90s, a true man of the cloth, but he loved a lusty expression. He had worked for William Anderson "Devil Anse" Hatfield, cutting, trimming, and sliding big timber to his saw mill. He was very eager to help us, and his memory for dates was astounding.

The occasional parties, trips to West Virginia, and poetry writing were put on hold when I got a call in May that would send my life and Mary's in a different direction. It was from a man at United Artists Music in New York named Murray Deutch, who informed me that UA had purchased my writing contract from Leiber and Stoller. This surprised me, and I wondered why Norman had not contacted me about it. I supposed he had nothing to do with this deal with UA. Maybe it surprised him, too. Mr. Deutch welcomed me and surprised me further by asking if I'd had any business experience. I told him about being alumni director at Berea College, with a staff and a budget, if that meant anything. He said it did. He wanted to hire me to go to Nashville and establish a UA music publishing company there. I'd have an office in the same building as their record producer, Bob Montgomery. I'd draw a salary and have my own secretary. If I agreed, they would draw up a new writing contract, extending the time limit. I would be receiving advances similar to what I'd gotten under my contract with The Boys.

I agreed wholeheartedly, and when it was signing time, I told him about Alex Harvey. I said I could bring him along with me, if UA wanted to put him under contract as well, but I needed $10,000 to cover my investment in him. Mr. Deutch agreed. He wanted us to move to Nashville right away. Mary had to make plans to close up the house and have it looked after, inform the bank, the church, her parents and our friends, while I drove to Nashville, checked in with Bob Montgomery, and went house hunting. Of course, Mary would have to approve the house, the location, and what the rent would be, so I had to use good judgment.

I was excited and happy, actually almost giddy, over this move. I wanted to get to know Nashville and people like Chet Atkins, West Virginian Little Jimmy Dickens, Eddy Arnold, and Canadian Hank Snow. I wanted to see if I could fit in like they did, as folk-oriented as I was. And the fact that I was getting *paid* to move there was—as Aunt Jennie was heard to say—the berries above the persimmons.

By the end of June we had found a nice house on Outer Drive, near 100 Oaks shopping center, in what I would describe as a middle-class neighborhood. The neighbors across the street were genial and welcoming. But the drive from there to UA's offices, upstairs in the Fender Building, took twenty minutes, sometimes more, when traffic was bad. This was something I had to get used to. Fortunately, the Fender Building was right across the street from RCA's Studio B, on 17th Avenue South. The big RCA Building was next door.

My first day at the office was exciting. Bob Montgomery couldn't have been any friendlier, and I knew his PR man, Ed Hamilton, would be easy to work with. I had some catching-up to do regarding Bob's credits. I knew he produced Bobby Goldsboro, but that was about it. I didn't have a secretary yet, but I had plenty to do without one. My next album, and last for Kapp Records, was going to be coproduced by me and Paul Cohen.

One of the songs was going to be "Let the Big Cat Jump," from another of Aunt Jennie's sayings: "If you're going to hang, don't worry about drowning, just let the big cat jump." It would also include one I wrote with Alex Harvey, "Ain't That Livin'." Dave Kapp wanted the title to be: *BILLY EDD WHEELER / I Ain't the Worrying Kind*, despite my so-so single and O. C. Smith's cover. He justified it by saying it had the power of association going for it.

Under the excitement of this sudden move, I felt a bit like an imposter, taking on a major job in Country Land without paying any country music dues. I hired Della Rowland, wife of guitarist Danny Rowland, to be my secretary. Danny and I, with John Darnal, would start doing gigs. John was a literate musician, played a sweet viola, and was also an arranger. They called my musicianship "three chords and a capo."

The big debate in Bob's office was about the new CBS country show, *Hee Haw*. Bob didn't think it would succeed, saying it made fun of country people. Ed Hamilton said it was a hit, total corn pone, yes, but fast moving and fun. I agreed with Ed. It didn't take long to pronounce the show a hit, and not just with country audiences. The show was popular in New York, Boston, Chicago, and other big markets. I congratulated Ed and offered to take him to lunch. My ulterior motive was to ask him to tell me about the boss, Bob Montgomery. And he did, without hesitation. He said, as a kid in Lubbock, Texas, Bob was good friends with Buddy Holly. They even teamed up when they were kids for the *Buddy and Bob* show. And later, as adults, Bob wrote "Love's Made a Fool of You" for Buddy. He also wrote "Misty Blue."

I said, "I'm impressed." Ed said, "And he wrote the damn thing in twenty minutes." I shook my head in disbelief. "Oh yeah," Ed went on. "He said it was a fuckin' gift." I thanked him for all the info, calling him a regular encyclopedia. He shrugged. "It's my job. My only talent's my memory. I'm not creative like you guys."

Just before we left, Ed said, "Bob Montgomery's every bit as good a producer as a songwriter. He took Bobby Russell's

'Honey' to #1 with Bobby Goldsboro, and Bobby's made a career
of it, singing it on every damn show in America."

Trying to find a way to compliment Ed, I said, "I wonder who
lined him up for those shows and promoted him and the song to
high heaven?"

He shook his head, as if waving me off. "I helped a little. But
I tell you, I got tired of 'Honey.' Too damn saccharine for me. But
don't tell Bob I said that."

As we walked along on the way back, Ed said, "By the way,
you play golf?" I said I did, but wasn't too good at it. He said,
"Don't matter. Lots of these big artists play golf, and playing with
them's a great way to plug songs and find out who's looking.
Bob's pretty good, but I'm like you. I do like it, but good I ain't."
I liked Ed, pegged him as a straight shooter, and what a resource
he was! I got my money's worth out of that lunch.

Running United Artist Music was pretty boring. The songs I
received from New York were movie themes and pop stuff. It was
hard to get them cut in Nashville, so I spent a lot of time writing
more poetry. After a few weeks, I started feeling guilty for doing
it on company time. I told myself it was time to start writing
songs in earnest. Ed's talk about golf made me remember playing
with Dub Parker at Biltmore Forest Country Club in Asheville,
a man who owned a knitting mill in Old Fort. Dub had a friend
playing with him who, he told me, had married a rich lady
who also owned a mill. As the game progressed, just to make
conversation, I said to his guest, "I hear you married into money."
As soon as I said it, I thought I'd screwed up. Before he could
interpret it as criticism, I said, "And I think that's fine. I reckon it's
just as easy to love a rich woman as a poor one."

He didn't comment immediately, but after pondering on it, he
said, "Let me tell you something, Billy. Anytime you marry into
money, you *earn* every damn penny of it." He didn't say it angrily or
with a scowl. Just matter of fact. It had resonated in the songwriting
section of my brain, but I got caught up in the golf betting and

forgot to write it down. Now, I thought, it was ripe for the picking, thanks to Ed. I called it, "Gimme Back My Blues." It was about a man who was down and out until he married the daughter of a rich coal field king in West Virginia. Life was good, he thought, until his wife Imogene started letting him know who ruled the roost. He couldn't drink beer, smoke cigars, or do anything for fun without her fussing at him. He finally came to the conclusion that she was half Indian and half bulldog—either on the warpath or lying around the house, sitting on her tail end a-growling.

Well, breakfast in bed ain't too bad for your head
If you lying there enjoying the snack
But it ain't so much fun if you're the one carryin'
And she's propped up in the sack
My Mama she told me, don't you marry for money
You're better off with holes in your shoes
So I'm gonna run, being rich ain't no fun
Hey-hey Judge, just gimme back my blues

A man came into the office one day and showed me two songs. He sang their praises so loudly as I listened to his demos that I had to ask him to be quiet and let me listen. I said to him, as nicely as I could, that I didn't like them well enough to accept them for publication. I smelled liquor on his breath as he turned red in the face and almost shouted, "Well, why don't you like 'em? They loved 'em over at Acuff-Rose." He was a big guy and I thought he might take a swing at me, so I spoke calmly, telling him, yes, they were good songs, but just weren't what I was looking for. Of course, I wanted to say, "If they loved them so much at Acuff-Rose, why are you bringing them to me?" But I didn't.

Later, another man came in who was quite a contrast to the red-faced guy. He was mild-mannered, yet had an aura of confidence about him. He introduced himself as Barry Etris, from down near Atlanta, and he had a nice song called "Reuben James." And that was the problem with the song, too nice. After I listened to it twice. I said, "Barry, I really like this song, and your Reuben James is a fine man. But there's hundreds of men in the phone book who are nice men. So what? Your description of him is fine. But something's missing. If you'll work on it and bring it back, I'd love to hear it. But do me a favor. Give me the first shot at it after you rewrite it, OK?" We shook hands and he said he'd be back. I believed him.

He turned to leave, then turned back and said, "I loved your 'Ode to the Little Brown Shack,' and the Judy Collins cuts. There's a bar on Peach Tree Street in Atlanta that features folk music all the time. I'm sure they'd love you. I know the manager, if you're looking for a gig."

I told him I wasn't, but I probably needed to sing now and then to keep the vocal cords loosened up. I said, "If you're of a mind to, call your manager friend. I've never been to Atlanta, and if he's got a slot for me anytime soon, I'll give it a shot."

In August, Barry Etris called to tell me his manager friend was eager to book me for a two-night appearance at his folk club. He gave me the number, and when I called, I liked the sound of the manager's voice. The money wasn't good, but it would be a new performing environment for me, and the manager had a deal with the brand-new Hyatt Regency. I'd get the room free, plus free beer while I was performing. I said OK, and two days later I lit out for Atlanta.

I found the Hyatt before the club on Peach Tree Street, and when I walked inside I couldn't keep from looking up. The rooms were on all sides, giving me the feeling I was outside because of the greenery hanging down from banisters. It smelled good. The elevators were all glass, shaped like big tubes sliding up and down. Very modern and beautiful. Just seeing it was worth the trip.

At the folk venue on Peach Tree, I was surprised at how many people knew my songs because of Judy Collins and Judy Henske. I heard names like Woody Guthrie and Pete Seeger mentioned, and John Jacob Niles, famous for "I Wonder as I Wander." This was a hip crowd. I had heard many people refer to the Kingston Trio as "commercial folk," but this group seemed to be all inclusive, with no such gripes. It really pleased me that they liked my versions of "Coal Tattoo," "The Coming of the Roads," and "The Reverend Mr. Black," better than all those stars. They were great listeners, too, without much chatter when I was singing. It was noisy otherwise. Smokey, too, but not all of it from cigarettes.

A nice-looking couple I'll call Fred and Janet, better dressed and older than most of the audience, cornered me after my second set. My first thought was, "Oh damn, they're going to bore me and keep me from table hopping," But they started with Fred asking if I wrote poetry, since most of my songs had the ring of poetry about them, as well as the way I talked. This surprised me.

Janet said, "I bet your favorite poet is Robert Frost." I just stared at her. "And I imagine many of your poems have some of his quiet power and country imagery about them."

I shook my head in disbelief and smiled. But instead of agreeing with her immediately, I countered with, "I also like T. S. Eliot, when I'm in certain moods."

She smiled and said, "I doubt that. You're just showing off."

I laughed big and said, "Fred, are you going to let her keep reading my mind?"

He said, "I'll tell you if you'll let me buy you a beer." I asked if he came here often, and he nodded.

I said, "Then you know I get free beer."

He said, "You got me. I also know you get a free room at the Hyatt." I smiled, and he went on. "We're staying at the Hyatt, too, and I'm wondering if you'd like to have a drink with us and talk some more about poetry."

I looked at Janet. "No, I'm outclassed. She'd beat me to death. But thanks for the invite. I think I'll stay here and get high, you know, just breathing."

I got up to leave, but she asked me to hold on a minute. She produced a card, and, as I took it, she asked, "Who's my favorite poet?" I said, "Emily Dickenson." She smiled and looked me over, as if reading me from top to bottom. Then she and Fred walked out.

I went to the bar and the manager said, "I saw them give you a card." I said yeah. He said, "They do it all the time. But they've never scored."

I asked what he meant by that, and his answer was, "Did you read the card?" I shook my head and held the card to the light, reading: Droke House Publishers, Anderson, South Carolina. I said, "I'll be damned," and rushed out the door.

They hadn't walked far, so I caught up quickly and said to Janet, "Was I right about Emily?" She nodded. I said, "Then why didn't you admit it, and why didn't you tell me you were publishers?"

She smiled and said, "You were playing too hard to get, and cute."

I barked out, "Cute?"

Fred jumped in with. "She's competitive, but I'm not. Do you want to join us for that drink?"

Riding the elevator to the top floor of the hotel was fantastic. You're standing out in space as the world below, and all around you, gets quickly smaller, dream-like. Fred and Janet were amused.

I said, "I felt like a kid on a space ship." Their room was really a suite, I assumed, with lots of space, and a nice bar area. Fred asked what I'd like to drink, pointing to a well-stocked glass cabinet. I said, "rum and Coke." He used his key and picked out a Jamaican rum and a can of Coke. Their supply of vodka and bourbon was already on the counter.

I said, "The publishing business must be lucrative in Anderson, South Carolina.

Fred said they were doing all right, and added, "But we do it for love and hope to at least break even. As for Anderson, yes, it's a small town. But our distributor is Grosset and Dunlap, on Madison Avenue. It's a small world, Mr. Wheeler."

I said, "Billy Edd, please. No mister."

Janet asked, "Have you been writing a lot, Billy Edd?"

I told her I had, quite a lot. I said, "My favorite short poem of Emily Dickenson's was...I can't remember the title, but I can recite it, OK?" She nodded. I said, "He drew a circle that shut me out, heretic, rebel, a thing to flout. But love and I had the wit to win. We drew a circle that took him in."

She said, "Bravo, I love that one too. Could you recite one of yours?"

I said, "I can recite dozens, but here's one of my tributes to Mr. Frost called 'Accepted Invitation':

He went to clean the pasture spring, inviting me along, a mere boy thing with 'you come too,' although he thought I wouldn't accept.' There's more verses, but I'll end with this one that's next to last: 'How many wells I've looked into since then are quite a few. But I keep coming back to his place to see if spring water still suits my taste.'"

She said, "I can hear Frost in that one. Do you have enough poems to fill up a book of say, a hundred and fifty pages?" I lied and said yes. She emitted a thoughtful "Hmmm," and looked at Fred.

He said, "Give me an idea of your topics. Sort of an on-the-spot synopsis."

I said, "The poems are about mountain preachers, squirrel hunters, coal miners and their wives, a philosophy of life told in musical and dance terms by a music teacher. For instance: '*A thought can set a sound in motion, and a sound with thought behind it can fill the wind. Every singer must learn to relax deep in his throat, but all relaxation begins in the head. And to sing one must first learn to dance, because all of life is a dance. All of life is a tune.*' It's four pages long. There's poems about equal rights, gentle protests, character sketches, mountain legends and superstitions. I can see the book divided into three parts, Music Lessons, Dance Lessons, and a mixture of Nashville songs, lyrics and more lyrics. Now, if you'll let me take a break for a rum and Coke, I'll tell you the title of the book, and why."

They actually applauded. And Fred said, "That's the best damn presentation I've ever witnessed. We want your book, right, honey?"

She said, "If you're going to curse, I will too. It'll be a damn great book. And yes, we want to publish it."

After the rum and Coke, I finished up by saying, "Shakespeare said, 'It's a wise father that knows his child.' In West Virginia, it's a wise child that knows his father. I didn't meet mine until I was a young teenager. Many people called me a bastard child. Others were kinder and called me a woods colt. That's what I'd like to be the title of the book. *Song of a Woods Colt.*" They both said they loved it. Fred and Janet assured me that if I got the poems to them soon, they would publish the book in 1969. Janet took down my info for the contract and asked me to send her all the biographical material I could find, including articles, record reviews, awards, and letters. She needed it for inside the front and back covers. She said, with my permission, she would refer to me as West Virginia's Robert Frost.

Barry Etris came down to catch my show the second night, and I introduced him to Fred and Janet, explaining to them that he was the reason I was there. After the shows, they invited both of us up for a goodbye drink, during which time they thanked Barry for making it all possible. I could tell it pleased him highly. At one point he asked their permission to show me his ideas for a rewrite of "Reuben James." They agreed and pretended not to listen to my short session with Barry in which I told him it still needed work. Coming back to the party, he said, "I hope you folks will be as hard on him as he's been on me." Of course, I told them I was sure he would make it work. But I wasn't. I just hoped against hope that he would. On the way back to Nashville I thanked the gods of coincidence again. And also the gods of being at the right place at the right time.

In November, the most exciting thing happened since Mary and I got married. She told me we were going to have a baby. I went absolutely crazy with joy. I thought about it day and night, my mind flooding with ideas for songs. I talked about it during interviews on radio and performing on TV. We called our families and sent cards. I was so revved up I wrote poetry like crazy, mostly on my own time, but if an idea came at the office,

I had to put it down with at least a few lines. I was determined to send enough poems to Fred and Janet for *Song of a Woods Colt* before the end of the year. Dreaming about the baby, I assured Mary I would help change diapers and take turns getting up at night for nursing from a bottle. The nursing part gave me an idea for a song for Hank Williams, Jr. I pictured a man whose wife leaves him without any warning, and he doesn't know why. So he gets drunk and cries in his beer. In the chorus he says:

> *Put a nipple on my bottle, bartender*
> *Warm my whiskey and be a baby's friend*
> *A baby can cry and tonight when I get high*
> *I'm gonna be a baby again.*

It seemed too far out to me, but Hank loved it. He recorded it and the label was making plans to release it early in the new year. I gave the news to Murray Deutch at UA, and he was elated.

Chapter Sixteen

HAVING A BABY

Morning's come at last, I look into the glass
I smile and say my name but it's not me, I'm not the same
And I'll never be again, for there's something in the wind
We're going to have a baby

On a day too cold for me to even think of playing golf, Bob
Montgomery said he needed me to make a foursome with
Bob Beckham and Bob Jennings for a round at Hillwood
Country Club. Bob Beckham was the head of Combine Music
Publishing, and Bob Jennings was a songplugger for Acuff-Rose
Publishing. Montgomery and I were going to play as a team
against the other two Bobs. Jennings' nickname was Stumpy, so
that made it a little easier managing all those Bobs!

It was too warm for snow, I thought, but by the second nine,
here it came. I figured the other guys would call it off, but, as we
stood on number ten tee, all three Bobs pulled a pint of whiskey
out of their bags and took drinks. Bob Montgomery handed his
bottle to me. "Have a swig. Keep you warm."

I said, "But if it keeps snowing, how we gonna find our golf balls?"

He said, "We'll start using colored ones," and handed me a red
one and an orange one.

I shook my head at him. "You guys are crazy."

Our bet was one dollar a side. If you won both sides, you got an extra dollar. Bob Beckham kept badgering Montgomery to increase the bet. I said to my partner, "I'm a beginner and haven't had much playing time. I don't mind losing three bucks, but I'm not in the mood to contribute more to Mr. Beckham's personal charity."

Bob said, "Better not call him 'Mister.' He'll think you're light on your feet, or he'll call you a cocksucking Yale bird. Beckham doesn't mince words."

I said, "Us West Virginia hillbillies don't take kindly to insults. And I'm big as he is."

Bob said, "I think he likes you. You didn't chicken out, and you don't make excuses and try to explain why you missed every shot."

We finished the eighteen holes and that whiskey *did not* keep me warm. My hands were frozen, but I enjoyed those guys and felt grateful to be invited. After we went into the club, thawed out, and had coffee and a snack, Beckham ordered more whiskey. He had a discernible buzz going, but he didn't look drunk. He lit a cigarette, took some deep puffs, and said, "Wheeler, I know you didn't lose intentionally out there. You're not a hustler. But I got a feeling you're gonna be damn good. You got a sweet swing and a good temperament. I'll even give you strokes, if you'll play with us again."

I said, "Thanks, Mr. Beckham."

He chuckled and looked suspiciously at Montgomery. He said, "That cocksucker put you up to the *Mister* shit, didn't he?"

I smiled and said, "How many strokes?"

He laughed and said, "We'll see."

As I started to walk out with Montgomery, Beckham called out, "If you get tired of writing for UA, I got a front row seat for you at Combine."

Outside, Bob Montgomery said, "I told you he likes you. And you watch, Stumpy'll take you out with Chet Atkins when it warms up. He worships the ground Chet walks on."

I drove to Beckley, West Virginia, and Ewel introduced me to the members of the board that soon would be called Theatre

West Virginia. Photographers from the *Charleston Gazette* and the
Beckley newspaper took pictures as the chairman handed me
a $10,000 check for the "research and writing" of *Hatfields and
McCoys*. I told them about my ideas for the script and songs, with
Ewel providing melodies and arrangements. I would not stray
far from documented facts, but might take some liberties with
character development and love songs for Roseann. I would use
humor to balance violence. And I assured them the drama and
music would be ready for the premiere in 1970.

By the first of December, I mailed my typewritten poems
and lyrics to Fred and Janet at Droke House, Anderson, South
Carolina. In 1969 I would be a published author, a man of letters.
Whoopee! Mary and I celebrated my birthday on December 9
by looking at house plans. We had enough money to qualify for
a loan, hoping to have a nice house to move into by the time my
job at United Artists ended in 1970. A cozy home, too, for our
child. Would it be a boy or girl? It didn't matter. It would fill our
hearts with love and joy.

After Christmas, we drove to Central City, Kentucky, to see
Sister and Arthur's house there. Brother Bob was there, and we
all visited Shelby Gene, Nell Jane, and kids, and he showed us
through his large IGA store, where Sister was working, weighing,
wrapping, and putting meat out into display cases. She loved
having something to do, plus being able to make a modest salary.
Her favorite story was about a lady customer asking her where to
buy Tampax. Sister thought she said thumb tacks and asked if she
wanted the kind you push in with your thumb or drove in with a
hammer? The lady seemed stunned for a second, stared at Sister as
if she were crazy, then turned and hurried away, shaking her head
until she was out of sight.

Nineteen-sixty-nine found me busy from the git-go. The
great Bob Montgomery was producing my new, and final, album
for Kapp, with Norbert Putnam on bass, Billy Sanford on guitar,
Larry Butler playing piano, and Scottie Henson picking banjo.

It pleased me that Bob let me pick the songs, and I was pleased further to learn that Don Tweedy was to be my arranger. I loved his fantastic arrangement for Bobbie Gentry's international hit, "Ode to Billie Joe." Don also played flute and did a speaking role on my song, "The Coon Hunters," about several guys gathered around the fire, drinking moonshine and listening to their dogs. During a break, Don told about the coon hunter with a wooden leg who got so drunk, with all the others, he dozed off and his leg got into the fire. Later, when the dogs hit a hot trail, he was the first one up and running into the darkness. After about ten yards, he yelled back, "Watch out, boys! Every other step there's a big hole."

I recorded three songs by Doug Kershaw, the crazy Cajun who also played fiddle on my session. I'd become friends with him, and he got me officially recognized as an *Honorary Coon Ass*. I received a really funny song from two Charleston, West Virginia architects, Blankinship and Johe. The song, "The Interstate Is Coming through My Outhouse," was inspired by my "Ode to the Little Brown Shack Out Back." I loved it, and so did audiences.

But my favorite on the *Nashville Zodiac* album was "Mississippi Magic," by the Baptist minister, the Reverend Will D. Campbell. I had met him when he came to lecture to a packed house at Warren Wilson College. Author of the book *Brother to a Dragonfly*, he had quite a following among Nashville music folks. The book was about his coming to grips with the death of his younger brother and his relationship with some Klansmen that he forged after working alongside Martin Luther King as an early leader in the Civil Rights Movement. His religious mantra, as I understood it, was "Be reconciled." When asked how he ingratiated himself with Kluxers, he said, "by emptying their bedpans."

The Reverend Will told me he loved traveling with Bobby Bare, and I heard he married Waylon Jennings and Jessi Coulter on stage at a big bar in Nashville. I visited him at his home in

Mt. Juliet, Tennessee, and listened to him talk as he did some
gardening. He sipped a little moonshine from time to time and
offered me a taste, but I begged off, telling him truthfully it was
too strong for me. Even the high-dollar, charcoal-mellowed kind
I bought from a moonshiner friend in Swannanoa was too strong.
Mary and I served it to special friends or tourists, who swore they
liked it better than brandy. I admired that moonshiner because,
like Jenis Cottrell, he was self-sufficient and grew everything he
needed in his garden, same as the Reverend Will. But most of all,
I love the down-to-earth equal rights preaching Will does in his
song, "Mississippi Magic."

> *That Mississippi magic is Mississippi madness now*
> *Whites don't like black people, blacks don't like whites no how*
> *On that I-Central railroad ridin' way on up the track*
> *Met a doll in Chicago, said I ain't never going back*

> *Spoken:*
> *She say, where you from, Sport, Mississippi? I say, yeah, that's right,*
> *Mississippi. She say, why ain't you going back? You like the blacks*
> *or the Kluxers? I say I like the blacks and the Kluxers. She say,*
> *what are you, some kinda radical? I say, no Doll, I ain't no radical.*
> *I just like ever'body, and the blacks and the Kluxers are somebody.*

> *Sung:*
> *But that Mississippi magic is Mississippi madness now*
> *Whites don't like black people, blacks don't like whites no how*

> *Spoken:*
> *She say, hold on, Sport, what about when you're dead? You*
> *going back then? Yep, going back then. Going back home. They*
> *gonna love me when I'm dead. She say, no man, they ain't never*
> *gonna love you. You better stay up here and lie beside me. I say,*
> *oh yeah they gonna love me when I'm dead. They gonna come*

*in for miles around to that old Hartman Funeral Home there in
McCloud City. They'll stand around my coffin all night. They'll
say, ole Will was a good ole boy. He just had some crazy ideas.*

Sung:
Then that Mississippi madness, be Mississippi magic again.
{ *Oh, we was born we was all kin, when*
 we dead we be kinfolks again.

Spoken:
*Uncle Bob Tolbert, he'll shake his head and say,
don't he look natural. Aunt Susie, she'll say, Lord
Jesus, child, he looks just like he oughtta talk.*

Barry Etris came in with yet another rewrite for "Reuben
James." I said, "Man, I hope you've got it finished at last. But let
me take a look at it."

I think he broke into a sweat watching me read it. I took my
time, just to be polite, but when I looked up and shook my head,
he said, "Aw, shit." He walked around shaking his head as if in
despair. He threw up his hands and said, "Well, that's the best I
can do. There's no more gas left in the tank."

I said, "Barry, I'm sorry. You're the most persistent songwriter I
ever met, but what can I say?" He shrugged his shoulders. Then I
said, "Wait a minute. I take that back. Alex Harvey's got you beat.
I told him to give it up, but he didn't listen. Now he's proving
me wrong and writing some good stuff. How's about I put you
two together and see what happens? You up for that?" He nodded
with enthusiasm, smiling brightly, and said yes. I told Barry I'd
check with Alex and let him know.

When I caught up with Alex, he said he was working on a
song with Larry Collins, but thought it was almost finished. Said
I could go ahead and tell Barry to come back in a few weeks. I
gave him a copy of the lyrics to "Reuben James" and challenged
him to come up with a gimmick, a new twist. He glanced at the

lyric and seemed lost in thought, but I knew it had nothing to do with the lyric. He said, "I had a row with Murray Deutch." Before I could get on his case for going over my head, he went on. "Now, don't get pissed. I didn't want to bother you…I guess I should've…I asked him for a raise. He didn't like my tone of voice, I guess, and told me to go to hell." I was angry at Alex, but I sucked it up and just shook my head. I told him to give me a date for Barry, and we'd talk about him and Mr. Deutch some other time.

In June, I was invited to participate in the Acuff-Rose golf tournament down at Mt. Juliet State Park, about forty miles south of Nashville. I played a practice round with a big songwriter named Jerry Chesnut, and his partner, Lamar Fike, who had a belly as big as Santa Claus. Jerry wore a broad-brimmed hat that looked big enough to camp out under. He had a great sense of humor, so we had a big time swapping jokes. We hit it off so well we decided to try writing a song together. His office was next to Columbia Studios on 16th Avenue South. The first time I went there, all set to write, he said, "Why don't we get something to eat first?" That became our routine, with Lamar usually tagging along.

When we got back to the office, he asked if I had an idea. I said, "Yeah. Well, maybe."

He looked at Lamar and said, "How 'bout leaving us alone for a bit, OK?" Without a word, Lamar left. I asked Jerry if Lamar had a job. He said, "Naw, he's trying to be a song publisher; got an office next to mine. He's Elvis's gofer, when Elvis is in town. Elvis likes him but fires him a lot, and Lamar has to work at the car wash 'til Elvis feels sorry for him and hires him back. But anyway, what's your song idea?"

I said, "This guy is trying to forget his ex and does OK until it gets late. The first line is: How come when it's late, sometimes I can't keep from hating myself for loving you."

Jerry was silent for about fifteen seconds. Then he said, "How come when it's late, sometimes I even hate myself for loving you."

I said, "Yeah, that's better. I love it." We came up with some more lines and decided the title was "It's Midnight." In a joking manner, he said, "This songwriting wears my country ass out. Hard way to make a living, ain't it?" He laughed and said, "Let's take a break and think about it."

After I put Alex and Barry together, they came in to my office within a week with a damn good lyric and a tune to go with it. Alex's idea was to let a black sharecropper raise Reuben James, after Reuben's mother died giving birth to him. It starts out, *"Rueben James, in my song you'll live again, and the phrases that I rhyme are like footsteps out of time, the time when I knew you, Reuben James."* I loved it, and after they tweaked it a couple of times, we demo'ed it, and I placed it with Kenny Rogers.

Jerry Chesnut called and asked if I'd like to play golf again. I asked who with. He said, "Me and you and Lamar."

I said, "Jerry, I don't think so. After seeing Lamar hit the ball… well, he can't hit it out of his shadow. It's a pretty big shadow, I know, but…"

Jerry cut me off, saying, "He's taking our song to Elvis, as soon as we finish it, and I've got some pretty good lines in mind. Whatta you say?"

I said, "I'm not going if Lamar can't go with us!" His booming laugh was so loud I had to hold the phone away from my ear.

He continued, "You ever played at Harpeth Hills?"

I told him I hadn't, but my clubs were in the car. He said, "We'll pick you up. They got good sandwiches and fries, so we can eat a bite before we tee off, OK?"

I had a scorecard on my cart, and, just out of curiosity, I decided to keep Lamar's score. On the first par five I asked him what he shot. "Thirteen," he told me. I said, "Lamar, I counted your strokes. You had a fifteen. You whiffed the ball three times."

He looked at me, disgusted, and said, "Well, goddamn, if you're going to play pro rules…"

Jerry winked at me. "Give him a twelve. We won't count whiffs, right?" After the match I tallied Lamar's score and it was over 100. When Lamar went to the bathroom, Jerry said, "Who gives a shit? He's taking our song to Elvis."

Back at Jerry's office, he had some good lines ready for "It's Midnight." On one new line I said, "*Where is all my self-control…*" and Jerry finished it with, "*I'm burning way down in my soul, and needing you.*" Then, together, we wrote, "*Wishing I could be the man I try to, hating me for wanting to be with you, knowing you don't love me like you used to…but it's midnight…and I miss you.*"

I sang on the demo, and Lamar took the song to Elvis. When he came back from Memphis, he said Elvis liked it and was going to cut it at his next session in 1970. We took Lamar to Jimmy Kelly's, and he ate two steaks and a mess of fried cornbread. Jerry and I agreed it was money well spent.

When brother Bob called to say his dad had died, I felt sorry for him. They were close, and I used to secretly envy him for that. My hatred for Arthur had mellowed somewhat when Mary and I went to visit them in Central City and I saw how well they all got along. Arthur would put his arm around Sister as they sat on the couch, and she seemed to enjoy it. She obviously had been able to bury any memories she had of his physical and mental abuse. But I hadn't.

July 24 Mary and I went to Vanderbilt Hospital and she was given an epidural the morning of the 25th. I stayed with her until she went into labor in the afternoon. Then I watched through a viewing window as the baby was born, but could hardly see because of the tears flooding my eyes. In a private recovery room, where Mary looked tired and sweaty, but all right, there were more tears and celebration. She named the baby Lucy, after her mother, Lucile, and I thought it was perfect. I said, "I get to name the next one, if it's a boy, OK?"

I let her and Lucy rest and went to get my 8 mm camera. When I returned, baby Lucy was nursing, and I started filming.

Mary tried to cover her breasts, but I shook my head, saying it didn't matter. I got some great footage. After we went home and a routine developed, I was true to my word. When Mary thought it was OK to start letting Lucy nurse from a bottle, I got up and fed her at night. I would prop her up in the corner of an overstuffed chair and take flash pictures that made her cry, waking Mary up. After some serious scoldings, I knocked it off. I was so happy I wrote another song, called "Little Lucy." Here's a pinch of it:

> *Used to be where it was at for me was cruising and running wild*
> *Then I stood by the side of my woman at the birth of a baby child*
> *They picked her up & wiped her off & spanked on her little behind*
> *At the first yell my tears fell, ooo she blew my mind*
> *Little Lucy we're so proud, you make us laugh and cry*
> *You keep growing, I'll keep crowing, while granddad's stepping high*

I got wind that Alex had scheduled a demo session at Woodland Sound, across the river from downtown. I couldn't believe he would do something like that behind my back, so I drove over and walked into the studio while Alex was on the mic. I listened to him sing a song whose melody sounded a lot like "Amazing Grace." I thought, if you're going to steal something, steal something good. But it was different enough, so no problem, especially with a lyric like I was hearing: *"Delta Dawn, what's that flower you have on? Could it be a faded rose from days gone by? And did I hear you say he was meetin' you here today to take you to his mansion in the sky."* Just from that snatch, I knew this was a good song. When Alex finished singing, he came into the control room and was surprised to see me. He ignored me while he listened to the playback. By then I was positive this was a hit song. I told the engineer, "Make me a copy and bill United Artists for the session."

Alex got red in the face and blurted out, "I thought you were my friend."

I said, "I am your friend, Alex, but I'm not going to lie for you. You're a UA writer, the last I heard." He repeated his story about what Murray Deutch said. But I told him, as far as I was concerned, he was still under contract to UA. Back in the office, I called Mr. Deutch, told him about the song and how I was positive it was a hit. I said, "Alex says you told him to go to hell, and he took it to mean you let him go."

He said, "Can you get him back?" I told him yes, but it would cost him some money, like a raise or something. He agreed.

A couple of weeks before Christmas I got a great present from Fred and Janet at Droke House. My poetry book, *Song of a Woods Colt,* came in the mail, a whole box of them. The cover by Illustration Design of Nashville was fantastic. Mary and I had a lot to be thankful for—a baby, a book, and a new house under construction. We took little Lucy and the book to Swannanoa to spend Christmas with Mary's parents, who went crazy over their granddaughter. I can't remember what they thought of the book, but I remember the love and joy in the air.

Nineteen-seventy came in with blasts of icy winds and frozen landscapes, not just in the mountains but Nashville, too. I had a backpack sort of baby carrier ready for taking Lucy for walks, though the weather didn't allow it for weeks. But the music business was hot, for me at least, as well as for my writers and cowriters. "Delta Dawn" was recorded by thirteen-year-old Tanya Tucker, and it launched her career. Of course, it helped Alex's career also. He and I remained friends, and I was best man at his first two weddings. Kenny Rogers's release of "Reuben James" as a single added more luster to Alex's rising star.

Elvis Presley released "It's Midnight," and to celebrate its going to number five on *Billboard,* guess what Jerry, Lamar, and I did? Yep, we went to Jimmy Kelly's. I had another song idea, but Jerry didn't want to talk about it while we ate. Another reason might have been Lamar's presence. There have been instances where several people are talking about a song idea, and when one guy dots an i or crosses a t, he gets a piece of the song, without contributing anything substantial. That probably would not have happened with the three of us. Jerry may have just wanted to concentrate on celebrating. It wasn't every day you got a cut by Elvis.

A few weeks later, Chet called and said, "I have a guy here I think you'd like to meet." I hurried over to his office, where he introduced me to San Francisco poet, Rod McKuen, who held a copy of my book in his hand.

He said, "I'm one, too. Except in France they call us love children instead of woods colts."

I had a copy of his 1967 best-selling book of poetry, *Listen to the Warm*, and loved it. I told him how excited I was to meet him. I said, "I like love child."

He said, "I like woods colt. Both are better than bastard."

I congratulated him for winning a Grammy the previous year for Best Spoken Word recording. I heard it sold sixty million copies. In some reviews he was called the "King of Kitsch." But I loved his songs, and so did Frank Sinatra, Barbara Streisand, Johnny Cash, and Perry Como. I was impressed, too, that so many people of note checked in with Chet first off when they came to town.

As the premiere of *Hatfields and McCoys* approached, Mary, Lucy, and I moved into a house in Beckley. Several songs needed work, and I kept telling Ewel I wanted to write a dream scene where Devil Anse and Randolph McCoy get together, even though it never happened in real life. Ewel thought it would decrease each leader's stature and look undignified. But I persuaded him to try it and see. He did, and it worked like a charm.

My Yale bud, Gladden Schrock, came down from Maine, and after watching a rehearsal, he told Ewel and me something was missing. We encouraged him to be candid and tell us what it was. He said, "Your audience has invested a lot in the character of Roseann McCoy, but she just disappears after Johnse dumps her. She needs a farewell scene, and I'm thinking, also a song that shows the depth of her sorrow."

Ewel said, "Wow. By god, B. E., I think he's right. Whatta you say?"

I said, "Gladden, you bright sumbitch. I'll think about it. Let's drink some beer for inspiration tonight. You in, Mr. director?"

Ewel frowned and said, "For beer? Ha! You know I don't drink that shit. As far as I'm concerned, you can pour it all back into the horse. But, yeah, I'll tag along and drink something civilized." He was a wine and bourbon man.

In spite of the beer, or maybe because of it, I did get an idea. I would allude to the rose and brier theme of the ballad, "Barbara Allen." I wrote the song the next afternoon, and Ewel started working on an arrangement.

I wrote and edited other major speeches, and Ewel wrote arrangements until a week before opening. The play was the brainchild of the theater's founder and outgoing director, Norman Fagan. It was his idea, too, to seat the oldest surviving son of Devil Anse, Willis Hatfield, and a McCoy lady together, smack-dab in the middle of the audience on opening night. When they were introduced, they stood and embraced, getting a thundering response from the crowd. Willis was portrayed as a three-year-old, which pleased him. The show, with a cast of forty-five actors, was a hit. And it ran every summer for forty-four years.

Back in Nashville, I left the girls and hurried off to Hershey, Pennsylvania to meet the producers of a TV series called *An American Odyssey*. I would be performing with the legendary Merle Travis and Jean Ritchie, along with B. B. King, the great Tom Paxton, and Oscar Brand, who served as host. The show was filmed in a defunct coal mining setting, just twenty miles or so from Hershey. It was the first time I met Merle. He had written the liner notes on my RCA album, *Love*, so I got to thank him in person. He sang his classics, "Sixteen Tons" and "Dark as a Dungeon." I loved just being around him.

When I got back to Nashville, Mary told me she had been talking to Mommy B., who told her our house was really taking shape. The inside wall of the sunken living room was going to be of field stone, twenty-two feet high. We were going to have a beautiful house. I could turn the stone cabin into an art studio and, at last, have a place to paint.

Jerry Chesnut and I started working on my song idea, "Never Again." A couple of lines went like this: *I hope I never ever love anyone this much again. I can't take any more, I've been hurt before, but never ever quite like this time.*

When we finished it, Lamar took it to Elvis, and, when he came back, he said, "Elvis asked me right off, 'Is this about me and Pricilla?' I said, 'Elvis, not every song I bring you is about you and Priscilla.'"

Jerry asked, "Did he like it?" Lamar said he didn't know but thought he might cut it. "I'm not a mind reader," Jerry said, "but you know him better than anybody, so if you think he'll cut it, I believe you."

Lamar smiled from ear to ear, taking Jerry's comment as a supreme compliment. But Jerry didn't really believe it. He told me Lamar made up a lot of stuff to make himself look important and in-the-know. "He's full of shit, and by the way, he's going to have a bypass operation and get rid of about fifty pounds or, who knows, maybe a hundred. Shit, he'll still look like Santa Claus." Elvis did end up cutting "Never Again," and he put it on an album.

When Elvis came to Asheville, North Carolina, in July of 1975 to perform a concert, Lamar Fike invited me to come to the Rodeway Inn in the nearby town of Oteen where Elvis had blocked off all the top floor rooms. Lamar's room was next to Elvis's. I was shooting the bull with Elvis's producer, Felton Jarvis, and two body guards when the phone rang. I picked it up and said, affecting the voice of an English butler, "Mr. Fike's residence. May I be of service?"

The voice I heard, ignoring my idiotic answer, said, "This is Elvis. Put Lamar on." I said, "Oh, Elvis, he just stepped out. This is Billy Edd, and I want to thank you for recording my songs."

He said, "Thank you for writing them. Just tell Lamar to call when he gets back."

Mary and I went to the Civic Center that night and saw Elvis onstage wearing what Lamar called his "gypsy suit." About half way into the first act, Elvis said, "This next song is by a local boy I'm sure you all know…a good friend of mine…" He paused before reaching into his pocket, pulling out a piece of paper and squinting at it for a moment. After a beat he said, "Billy Edd Wheeler." I was pleased, of course, but later, when I asked Lamar about it, he said, "Elvis can't remember names. It could've been Liza Minnelli or some other star, and it would have been the same." (I told him I didn't mind having Elvis carry me around in his pocket.)

Because the show sold out so fast, a second show was scheduled for the next night. I spent some time with Lamar in Elvis's dressing room, and, when we walked up the incline below the stage, I saw an incredible sight. Women of all ages, preteens to grandmothers, were handing things up to Elvis. He took scarves from his neck every two seconds, handing them down to his adoring fans, many of whom were screaming and crying. It was an unforgettable sight.

Chapter Seventeen

LOVE

I remember that spring when you looked up
From combing your hair and asked me what love is.
All I could think was to say you a poem that went:

> *Love is a ploughman turning the sod,*
> *Love is a sinner turning to God.*
> *Love is a gift, but more it's a thought.*
> *Love is wanting to give more than you've got*

Then you said, Well what about us, our love?
And I said: If ever my love for you grows cold
The rivers will run up stream, and cold black night
Will turn snow white, and dreamers will no longer dream.
And I'll spend my days singing love's praise
If I can spend them and end them with you.

In mid-October I took Lucy for the last ride on my back in the neighborhood. Mary and I decided we had to get back to Swannanoa to see our house completed. Another reason was to get away from the casual racism among a few of our friends in Nashville. I went to a recording studio the evening Martin Luther King was killed and heard several guys telling the most crude racist jokes I'd ever heard. One singer-songwriter said, "I'm going to hire a nigger to mow my grass and use him for target practice."

I shouldn't have told Mary. She wanted to leave the next day, but we didn't. But now the time had come. We had studied the final plans, but seeing the house under roof, with rooms taking shape and the twenty-two-foot rock wall half-finished, was very exciting.

Mary's parents had built a house on College View Drive but still lived in the president's home on campus. So Mary, Lucy, and I had a nice house to move into temporarily, with a view of the valley, the Swannanoa River, the college, and blue mountains beyond. The following year, when we moved into our house, we felt like we were living in a mansion. I began to paint in the rock cabin, we renewed old friendships, and we went to church where Fred Ohler, the man who married us, held forth from the pulpit, mixing poetry and quotes from theologians into his sermons that challenged you to think about who you were and what you believed in.

I started playing golf regularly with Dr. Bannerman at Biltmore Forest Country Club, and also tennis, at which I thought I was still pretty good until I met a club member named Frank Fishburne who had a serve I couldn't even touch. We became friends, and one day, being a businessman, he asked me how the music business worked. I told him I wrote for publishers, such as United Artists Music, who gave me advances and, when I came up with a song that made money, they took half and gave me the other half, minus the advances.

Frank said, "Why don't you be your own publisher and keep both halves? You've been around the block."

I said, "I don't get a salary from United Artists now. I need walking around money." He convinced me that he could get Carl Straus, one of Asheville's smartest lawyers, to take my Sleepy Hollow Music company and make it into a limited partnership. He and his best friend, Charles Taylor, who was running for the US Congress, would be my first two investors. Mr. Straus could easily find the others. That's how I became my own publisher. Charlie won his seat in Congress and served us for many years.

I started meeting new men friends and fishing buddies, thanks to Charlie Stafford, in Black Mountain, who played Fender bass in a local band.

A special buddy in Swannanoa was Edsel Martin, a master woodcarver, free spirit, and someone who was never tied down to a job. We played music in his yard while corn, still in the shucks, roasted slowly over a low fire. He played a mean homemade dulcimer, with me on guitar. We fished lots of lakes where he gathered driftwood to use in mounting birds he'd carved and colored. Because he had a wooden leg, he often bragged that he could wade through creeks and just get one foot wet. I admired him so much I wrote two songs about him. One was "Mose Rankin," recorded by Tom T. Hall, who changed the title to "Levi Jones." The other one's about my buddy who's gone but not forgotten.

Edsel Martin
Born and raised in Buncombe County
You couldn't count the dulcimers he's made
His daddy was a fiddler, Edsel he's a whittler
Everyone agrees that he's an artist at his trade

See that hound dog he's a-carving
Listen hard and you might hear him bark
Although he's made of white pine, Edsel cut him so fine
He dreams of chasing raccoons deep in his wooden heart

Hey play Edsel Martin, I'm as high as that Carolina moon
I love to hear you play, it's sweeping me away
Getting down on the Swannanoa on your last ole dollar tune

I went to Nashville to do my 1971 album for RCA, with Bob Ferguson producing. It featured the title song *Love*, with a picture of Lucy and me on the cover.

One day, Wilford "Joe" Johnson, from Black Mountain, knocked on my cabin door, asking if I'd listen to a song he'd written. I said sure, and he played it for me. I told him it had promise, but needed a lot of work. He said, "I did some roofing for a guy who paid me off with a pool table. It's worth a couple of thousand, but if you'll coach me rewritin' the song, I'll sell it to you for five hundred."

I said, "You got a deal."

Daddy B., a lefty, loved shooting pool, so we started a rivalry that carried over to the golf course. He was a fierce competitor. Mary and I usually had a drink or a glass of wine before dinner, and when Mommy B. started joining us, Daddy B. stared at her. She paid him no mind, and within weeks, or maybe months, if we didn't offer him a drink, he'd ask for it. It was hard for me to believe he was my father-in-law, after I'd admired him as a statesman-like president of Warren Wilson. He was referred to by many prestigious writers as a "great man of the South." He ran the college with a firm but gentle hand, working in unique harmony with Dr. Jensen through periods of transition, hard times, and challenges that threatened the school's very existence. When he died in 1976, I wept for him as the father I never had.

Daddy B.

Of all the fathers I have searched for in this world
You were the best. You were my buddy and
My adversary. We warred on the golf course,
Pool table and rug, putting in the living room.

You were the largest man in the smallest body
I ever knew. You were Craggy Mountain in the
Softness of Dogwood Ridge. You were the
General in the cap and smile of a private. You
Were Mr. President in the care and concern of a
Missionary. You rounded out my world.

And just as much as you gave me you, you gave
Me me. Thank you, Mr. President. Thank you,
Craggy, General, buddy, opponent, friend.
Thank you, Daddy B.

I fished, golfed, and painted three years away until January 22, 1973, when Mary gave birth to a son I named Travis. Before he was born, I wished for another little girl to love. I was sure I wouldn't be as thrilled with a boy. But I was wrong (I found you could love a little boy as much as a girl.) I started writing poems about him, and in 1977, I published a book titled *Travis and Other Poems of the Swannanoa Valley / With Some Poems and Prayers by Henry W. Jensen.* Ronald Fowler, a dancer in *Hatfields and McCoys*, painted a great color portrait of Travis for the cover, with gorgeous black-and-white pencil sketches of him and Lucy inside.

Because I was still traveling a lot to Nashville to record demos and soundtracks for plays, Mary and I bought a condo at Versailles Townhomes. It was at 3000 Hillsboro Road, the route Chet took on his way home, so he started dropping in for a drink or a walk around the complex. Sometimes we swapped jokes, and other times we got song ideas we'd write down on the round glass table top in the tiny extension of the kitchen we called a dining room.

On several occasions I drove to Central City and brought Sister back to spend a couple of days with me. I took her to an upscale Italian restaurant called Cirocco's. I had been there many times, so when I introduced her to Mr. Cirocco, he gallantly kissed her hand and welcomed her. She blushed a little and said, "Oh, my." I asked Sister if she'd like a glass of wine with me. She said she might have one if they would combine it with fruit juice.

Then, for the first time ever, I asked her to tell me about my father, Dutch Perdew. She cleared her throat and said, "Oh, well. He liked to have a good time." I said I figured as much, but what else?" She said, "He was the best dancer in West Virginia."

I loved this private time with Sister. Brother Bob found her a small apartment in Berea, and Sister started having a great new life, having lunch almost daily at Boone Tavern Hotel where Bob was the manager. She acquired lady friends who would dine with her, and she began buying nice clothing and loved to dress up. Because the shoes she bought were usually glitzy, we called them her Las Vegas shoes. In 1997 she died from a fall in her apartment. I attended her funeral in Central City, where she was buried on a hillside next to Arthur (I thought about going back several times to sit by her grave and meditate, letting her know I loved her. I never did. I think Sister knew it anyhow)

In 1977 I wrote *Barbry and Willie*, a folk-flavored musical based on the ballad of Barbara Allen and sweet William, with the theme, once again, of the rose and the briar, with some new wrinkles and characters in it. It was the first play produced in Kittredge, Warren Wilson's brand-new theater arts building. The cast was made up mostly of students, with some staff taking roles and supervising set construction. Ted White, student actor and musician, would, some thirty-nine years later, become my son-in-law on New Year's Eve, 2016.

I was still writing casually with Chet and playing a little golf. Back in Swannanoa I was surprised but pleased to get a call from Roger Bowling, the writer of "Lucille" for Kenny Rogers. He had moved out of Nashville to Clayton, Georgia, just across the North Carolina border, in the northeast corner of Georgia where the movie *Deliverance* was filmed. He seemed eager to connect with someone who used to write songs in Nashville but now lived somewhere else. He asked if he could drive to Swannanoa and meet me. I said yes, anytime. But he meant right then, since it was only about forty miles away.

He came, and after a late lunch, we wrote a song called "Fever Reliever" in two hours or so. The idea was that the woman who caused his temperature to rise could also relieve his pain. It didn't sound like a hit song to me, but it was different, and it showed that we would have no trouble collaborating. We became friends, and I visited him often. Eventually we wrote "Coward of the County," a number one hit for Kenny Rogers, and "Long Arm of the Law," which was never a single for Kenny but was included on his *Greatest Hits* album.

I put half of each of these songs into my company, Sleepy Holly Music, and a couple of years later sold it to All Nations Music for a nice chunk of money. It allowed me to pay back my investors and give each of them a gold record for "Coward of the County."

Back in Nashville, Don Light, Jimmy Buffet's manager, introduced me to Russ Miller, a producer for National Geographic Society. Russ explained that he wanted an album with songs and dialogue about Daniel Boone blazing the trail from North Carolina through the Cumberland Gap into Kentucky. I liked Russ, and I loved the idea, but even before I started writing, I knew I had to create a sidekick for Daniel Boone. Russ didn't know if the Society would accept a fictional character. But I told him I would write it so well it would seem perfectly natural and they would love it.

Russ and I rode together to Cumberland Gap, walked in the woods, and visited the museum. I started writing down ideas as he drove, and he seemed pleased to be a witness to the creative process he had set in motion. Before the end of the year, Dennis Burnside had composed an overture based on my songs and arranged all the selections.

> *They call me Chinquapin Jones.*
> *I'm a-livin' in Pennsylvania.*
> *I'm the son of the man up in the moon.*
> *It's true I like to have fun,*
> *But show me a job, I'll get it done,*
> *Me and my buckskin buddy,*
> *Ol' Dan'l Boone.*

National Geographic left the role of Daniel's sidekick intact. He was named Chinquapin (pronounced Chinkypin) Jones. They reasoned that in his travels Daniel Boone must have had a number of friends like him. He was a composite of them all, and I ended up playing the role myself.

A year later, 1979, after *A Song of the Cumberland Gap* came out, I wrote a short play called *All God's Critters* for Carver Optional School in Black Mountain. Every kid had a part. Those in kindergarten, including our son, Travis, were tadpoles. Lucy, nine, played a bird. A Black Mountain lady played a cow, and I dressed like a tramp to sing the role of Mr. Pollution. We drew large audiences of parents, friends, and kids from other schools and were a big success.

A woman in eastern Kentucky known as Widow Combs made a big splash in news outlets by lying down in front of bulldozers to protect her home from landslides. Some rocks from new-cut roads above her had almost crashed into her house. A few good rains, she contended, and her house would be doomed, and maybe her with it. A picture of her being carried off by two policemen, one at her feet, the other at her arms, made her look like a sack of potatoes, her bottom almost dragging the ground. This inspired me to write *Mossie and the Strippers* for a production by Ewell, with Suzanne Heitmann playing Mossie and John "D" Swain playing her husband, a retired coal miner. Both were recruited in New York.

The play was a gamble for both of us. But when it was finished, I was proud of it, and Ewel loved it. He presented it to his board, on which were two men who owned strip mines. But they finally gave in, saying it would be bad publicity for them, but the play said something that needed to be said. Probably with Norman Fagan's help, Ewel arranged for the premiere to be at Culture Center in Charleston, where it got rave reviews. Within weeks, people started writing letters to the editors of newspapers, objecting to some curse words in the play, and a couple of references to farting and belching. Ewel told me he was not surprised. He said, "My friend, this is the buckle of the Bible belt." He had planned to take it to a host of schools, but all dates were canceled.

In Nashville, I hosted a series of TV shows called *Country Suite*, produced and written by Myles Harmon and Larry Murray, with a lot of great guests that included John Hartford, Joan Baez, Don McLean, Kris Kristofferson, and the former Monkee Michael Nesmith. I think Arlo Guthrie was a guest too. If not, I wanted him to be. After Don did his show, we went to a bar at the hotel, and he told me his inspiration was Pete Seeger, who had come to his high school to talk and perform. Don was riding high with "American Pie," and told me he was making more money than he'd ever dreamed of, thanks to Mister Pete.

I met Mickey Newbury at a golf tournament and was thrilled to hear him sing his songs, like "American Trilogy," "Frisco Mabel Joy," and "How I Love Them Old Songs." Nobody could sing them like he did, with his golden voice. He told me several times I should get to know Susanna and Guy Clark, so on one trip I did call, and Susanna said she and Guy wanted to meet me, saying they loved my songs.

But it was a bad time. Her dad had just died, and they were hoping to go to the funeral. Then after a pause she said, "On the other hand, come on. It might cheer us up." When I got there, I was introduced to their guests, Townes Van Zant ("Poncho and Lefty") and Billy Joe Shaver, who wrote "Honky Tonk Heroes" and "Old Five and Dimers Like Me." Billy Joe had lost part of one finger working at a sawmill. But it didn't bother his picking. Townes said it was Elvis who inspired him to start playing guitar and writing songs. He said, "Elvis is making millions, has lots of cars and girls, and all he does is play the guitar and sing." I overheard Susanna talking to Guy in the kitchen, wondering how on earth they were going to be able to go to the funeral.

This was back in their lean times before her "Come from the Heart," written with Richard Leigh. To me, it was one of the most beautiful songs ever to come out of Nashville. I stepped into the kitchen and said, "Excuse me. But could y'all use a couple hundred bucks? You can pay me back when you start writing more hits, OK?" Susanna almost cried, and they both hugged me. I didn't really consider it a loan—just one songwriter helping another—but years later, in their gravy days, they handed me two hundred dollars.

I had met songwriter Paul Craft at several events produced by NSAI, the Nashville Songwriters Association International. When he heard that Chet was often coming by the Versailles to pick with me and a protégé of his, Muriel Anderson, he wanted an invite. Paul wrote the Ray Stevens hit "It's Me Again, Margaret," and Bobby Bare's "Dropkick Me, Jesus (through the Goal Post of Life.)" Despite the funny title, it was one of the best-written songs I'd ever heard.

Muriel was small of stature but was an exceptional guitarist, which explained why Chet was promoting her. He acknowledged she was good but could get better. Much better. Paul and I started referring to her as "The little one." We all sat around the glass table and entertained each other. Sometimes people dropped in uninvited, girls and guys, who would sing along or just gawk at Chet. Not much drinking went on. We didn't need it to stir up the fires in our heads, hearts, and picking fingers. I partied a lot, too, at various places—the Holiday Inn with Beckham and company, my friend Jim Vienneau's office, and at the condo next door to the great finger picker, Chip Young, owner of a studio and in demand as a musician. He gave me a copy of his latest album, *Thumb Fun*.

After I'd stayed for several weeks in a row, just playing around, gabbing and drinking with buddies, Mary called and asked when I was coming home. She said, "The kids need you." She could have scolded me, as I'd heard wives scold their husbands back at

Highcoal. I deserved it. But she didn't. She didn't have a mean
bone in her body. Her statement made me realize I needed them,
and her, twice as much as they needed me. A thought came to me
as a question: "What greater calling in life can a man have than to
be a good husband and a good father?" I thought I would make
that simple pronouncement at the end of this book. But it seems
more apropos to say it now, and let the ending fend for itself.

In the '80s I got busy again. *The Glass Christmas Tree,* about
child labor at the turn of the century, with music by Ewel, was
produced by Stage One, Louisville Kentucky's Children's Theatre,
directed by Moses Goldberg. The stunning set was based on a
glass factory in West Virginia. Blinko?

Bird on the Wing, with Bob Morrison and Haila Stoddard, was
a country music play that gave me the rare opportunity to work
with that grand lady of Broadway. Haila introduced me to Mrs.
James Thurber when I went with them to see *A Chorus Line.*
Haila was producing *I Do! I Do!* at the Elitch Theatre in Denver,
with John Raitt playing the role originated by Robert Preston.
Of course he's almost as famous for being the father of singer and
guitarist Bonnie Raitt. Mary and I went to lunch with John, and
as Mary was wont to do, she tried to sample a morsel from John's
plate. He picked up his fork and in a threatening tone said, "You
touch my plate, lady, and I'll stab your pretty little hand." We both
thought he meant it. Later, when he was in a better mood, up
to his neck in the wading pool of a grand old castle overlooking
Denver, he said, "It pisses me off that my daughter makes more
money than I do." *Bird on the Wing* flopped at Wright State
University, as directed by my other Yale bud, Walter Rhodes. But
it wasn't his fault. The play wasn't that good. But Haila, whose first
role on Broadway was as an ingénue in *Tobacco Road*, made out just
fine when she cowrote and coproduced *A Thurber Carnival.*

In 1985 I got a call from Loyal Jones, and before he told me
why he called, he had to tell me a joke. As I listened and laughed,
his joke reminded me of a joke I just had to tell him. This went

on and on for half an hour. I said, "Loyal, we need to put these into a book, and the title just came to me: *Laughter in Appalachia*.

He said, "Aw, who'd want to buy a joke book?"

I said, "I don't mean the cartoony kind you see in airports. We'd include funny tales, real mountain humor, sayings, and stories you can relate to."

He was silent for a moment, and then I heard some excitement in his voice. "We could have a humor festival, invite some well-known storytellers, but also anybody with a joke to tell. I could apply for a grant." I said I would donate some bucks, also, to give to the teller of the best joke or tale, original or traditional, best funny song or old ballad, and so on. Our first festival included storytellers Roy Blount Jr., Joe Bly, and Bob Terrill of Asheville, The Earl of Elkview, West Virginia, and amateurs, young and old, from many states, including California.

August House in Little Rock, Arkansas, published *Laughter in Appalachia* in 1986, and it's still in print. We followed with more titles, and I started going to book fairs. In 1992 I went to a big fair in Bowling Green, Kentucky, promoting our third book, *Hometown Humor*. It was upstairs in a huge room. My table was in a corner, but all the action was in the opposite corner, which seemed like it was fifty yards away. Someone told me the author was Robert James Waller, autographing his mega hit, *Bridges of Madison County*. I went over and waited until the crowd thinned, then stepped to his table and said, "Mr. Waller, I have your book, and I love it. I just wanted to shake hands."

He said, "I saw you way over there. What's your book called?"

I told him and said I cowrote it with Loyal Jones. He said, "And you are?" When I told him, he said, "Holy smoke!" Then jumped up and gave me a big hug, saying, "I love 'Coming of the Roads.' Come on, I want the photographer to take our picture. Then we can talk." And talk we did, swapping addresses and phone numbers. Before we parted he said, "I'm so glad you like my book. It didn't get good reviews, you know."

I said something like, "Well, millions of your fans proved the reviewers wrong." I didn't sell many books that day, but my ego and I left Bowling Green feeling warm and fuzzy.

Then another big event happened that year, reminding me of where, and who, I came from. My biological father, James L. "Dutch" Perdew, died in 1986 at the age of seventy-eight. Johnny Protan, former sheriff of Boone County, West Virginia, called to invite me to the funeral. I told Johnny I didn't think I'd go—I hardly knew Dutch. "Your sister'll be there," he said. "My sister?" I didn't know I had one. He said, "Well, your half-sister. Her name's Jewel and she lives in Ohio." I told him I'd be there. I called brother Bob and we drove to Whitesville on January 2, 1986. I met my half sister, Jewel, at the Armstrong Funeral Home, and her mother, Dutch's wife, Vernie Chingle Perdew. I had a guilty conscience because everybody was looking weepy but me. So I frowned and blew my nose a few times, and it seemed to pass for a show of emotion.

The preacher preached one of those generic, one-size-fits-all sermons without saying a thing about Dutch. He was forced to get personal, though, when he listed Dutch's survivors—daughter, Jewel, wife, Vernie, a sister, Agnes Farley, six grandchildren, and twelve great-grandchildren. Following the service, as people filed by the casket for a last look at Dutch, I stepped out of line to speak to the preacher who seemed to be dozing. "Mr. Price," I said, extending my hand. "I wanted to meet you and say I was disappointed when you read the list of survivors without mentioning me. I'm Billy Edd Wheeler, Dutch Perdew's bastard son." The preacher almost choked, swallowing and muttering *er-ahs*, at a total loss for words. I didn't mean to be malicious. I just wanted to wake him up and let him know I found his research a bit lacking. As for Jewel, we corresponded for a while, but I decided I could do without a half-sister I had nothing in common with, though I did admire her ability to cuss like a sailor.

In Swannanoa, I was getting so many letters and tapes from people wanting their songs critiqued that I decided to create the Great Smokies Song Chase. That way they could all come in person and get professional feedback. I hired critique leaders from Nashville, most of whom had written or produced hit songs. One of my "students" was David Wilcox, a great writer and performer who could have taught me a few things. I made no money except for the year when Chet came and gave me a free concert.

I was ready to quit after four years, but in 1991, Doug Orr, Warren Wilson's new president, asked me to do it one more year. He said he would take it over in 1992, with his friend, Jim Magill, as director. I did, and Doug started *The Swannanoa Gathering* that now, twenty-five years later, is a great success with 1,500 registrants from dozens of other countries. It is regarded as the premiere folk gathering in the world. I think part of the success of The Gathering was because Doug and his wife, Darcy, were folk singers themselves. Their recent book, *Wayfaring Strangers: The Musical Voyage from Scotland and Ulster to Appalachia*, was a *New York Times* best seller. Doug coauthored the book with Scotland's Fiona Ritchie, host of NPR's "The Thistle and Shamrock," and Darcy acted as art editor.

The success of The Gathering should not overshadow Doug and Darcy's service as president and first lady of Warren Wilson College for nineteen years, during which great improvements were made. New friends and supporters came on board, and the college enjoyed educational recognition, prestige, and financial success. Student enrollment also increased. The Orr years proved to be great years, and the good news is that they are still actively involved with the school.

Ewel had become a fairly regular actor at the Derby Dinner Playhouse in Clarksville, Indiana, just across the river from Louisville. Through him I became good friends with the director and coowner, Bekki Jo Schneider. I don't know how it happened, but Bekki Jo commissioned me to write an original musical, with

Ewel and Dennis putting music to my lyrics. It was about five old guys who met every week at a knitting mill owned by one of them. They played cards and talked about how virile they used to be, but how they were now pretty much over the hill. Except for one of the five, who was very sexually active. He bragged that his hormones still rocked and rolled like Mexican jumping beans. He told them constantly they were in a rut and eventually convinced them that they needed a woman in their lives. He started giving them lessons on how to pick up girls, resulting in some hilarious scenes that developed under Bekki Jo's encouragement and theatrical eye.

When the play was finished, with Dennis's great arrangements, the rehearsals began. There's an old chestnut that says, *You can't get blood out of a turnip.* Well, Bekki Jo did. It took a brilliant director and the choreographer, Barbara Cullen, to meet the challenge of creating moves for a bunch of old codgers. But I thought the show was fun. It drew big crowds that left the theater audience smiling and laughing.

Chet kept being invited to lend his name to golf tournaments all over the place, like the *Country Gentleman* at Callaway Gardens, Georgia. Or the *Country Gentleman* at Knoxville. It was amazing how many celebrities came to honor Chet—singers, actors, jockeys, baseball players, golf pros, and instructors who gave free lessons and demonstrations. I opened for Chet at untold dozens of tournaments and other venues. We went with a bunch of friends to Miami one time without it being a tournament. We just wanted to have fun together at a nice golf course. When it was over, Chet and I drove down to Key West to see our mutual friend, Shel Silverstein, whose illustrated children's book, *The Giving Tree*, was a favorite of mine. It was Chet who sent Shel's song "A Boy Named Sue" to Johnny Cash. Shel had a nice girlfriend named Warrene Williams. He was tired that first evening, so he told Warrene to take us out to dinner.

Years later, after she had married well, he caught up with her, and following the formalities, he asked, "So what are you doing this afternoon?" She said, "Shel, I'm married now." He said, "Oh, stop saying that. I should be grandfathered in." What a great line! Even though I first met her in Miami, she now lives in fairly close to me, in Asheville, North Carolina, where she's in real estate.

Once, when Chet performed with the Knoxville Symphony, I was totally shocked and surprised when he stopped playing, stood up, and said, "I'm going to take a break now and have my friend Billy Edd Wheeler come down here and sing for you." I was up high in the cheap seats, so it took me several minutes to wind my way down to the stage, where Chet handed me his guitar, told me to pick a little for them, and walked off. I enjoyed singing for the highbrows. They were very appreciative, especially when I sang "Ode to the Little Brown Shack Out Back." Chet seemed to enjoy putting friends on the spot, especially musicians who were backing him up. He didn't do songs live the way you rehearsed them.

The most unique setting for any of my plays was at the old Cherry Springs Baptist Church next to the McDowell County Cemetery, in Marion, North Carolina, 1993. It was to celebrate the sesquicentennial of McDowell County. The play was called *Voices in the Wind* and had a large cast made up of young and old, black and white actors and singers. I wrote it in the style and format of *Spoon River Anthology*, using folk and original songs. It was directed by Sandra Epperson.

My last collaboration was with a Yale alumnus, Jim Crabtree, producer and director of Cumberland County Playhouse, Crossville, Tennessee. *Wings over Appalachia* was a musical play drawn from my songs, plays, and poetry, as conceived and adapted for the stage by Jim. The book was by Jim and me, with additional music and musical direction by Dennis Davenport. This was a fun project since Jim and Dennis did most of the work, though I did give a couple of concerts to help promote the show.

With my last three outdoor dramas still to be written, I think had matured a little. At least my attitude had changed. Instead of thinking I was doing these folks a favor, I felt honored by their trusting me to make their local legends come alive in flesh and blood on stage. *Young Abe Lincoln* was not just a local legend, of course. Yet it seemed local because it was being staged where Abe had spent fourteen of his formative years right there in Indiana, after coming with his parents from Kentucky. I wrote book, lyrics, and music, with arrangements by Dennis, and it ran for eighteen years at the Lincoln Amphitheatre in Lincoln City.

I was honored by William "Bill" Ellery Jones, president and founder of the Johnny Appleseed Heritage Center in Mansfield, Ohio, who was the first to contact me about writing what would become my final full-fledged outdoor drama. It would be based on Jones's book, *John Chapman, or as Some Say, Appleseed*. To say that Bill, one of the nicest men I ever met, ate, drank, talked, and dreamed about Johnny Appleseed would not be an overstatement. And his enthusiasm was contagious. He drove me to every nook and cranny of all the towns surrounding Mansfield that might have had anything to do with Johnny (I was intrigued by Appleseed, a legendary but real person known as a true visionary, a man of God. His life's work was to plant apple trees but also to teach others how to do it and become self-sufficient.) He loved animals and would not kill anything for food. And when farmers turned overworked and broken-down horses out to die, Johnny would spend his paltry resources to feed and look after them. The play, written again with Dennis's inspiring arrangements, was produced in Ashland, a few miles out from Mansfield, in 2004 and 2005.

Epilogue

HOW DO YOU SPELL APPALACHIA?

"'Snake,' said Eve, 'if you try to deceive I'll throw this apple at-cha.'"
—*Dr. Gordon Ross*

I had to leave Appalachia to see it better. Somehow the myriad paths I chose, usually by chance, landed me in New York where I found that New Yorkers are no different from Appalachian mountaineers. Their slang is just different. (I know Appalachians (amen) who didn't graduate from high school who are brighter and more inventive than many city dwellers I've met.) Fortunately, in the music business, publishers and producers don't care if you speak with a twang or didn't go to school. Just deliver the goods, baby. Come up with the line, the melody, the idea, and you're in. They slap you on the back, buy you drinks, and give you money.

I was touched by that dark miracle of chance Thomas Wolfe talked about in his novel, *Look Homeward, Angel*, except to me it was the *bright* miracle of chance. Time after time it lit up my life and made "new magic in a dusty world." And all those arbitrary decisions I made. Were they really arbitrary? Or was some force, angel whispers maybe, helping me discover the pattern my life was destined to take?

Years ago, when I was in Jay Vern's studio recording my album, *Songs I Wrote with Chet*, Janis Ian dropped in, and Chet asked her to do the background vocals on our favorite song, "Django." On the first playback, I asked Chet if Janis's harmony was perfect on a given phrase. Without listening to it he said, "If she likes it, it's perfect." That impressed me. She and I became good friends over many years, and when I had the chance to introduce her to Warren Wilson College, it thrilled me when she fell in love with it, and with Doug and Jim's Swannanoa Gathering. She has become—along with many other notable singers and musicians—a mentor and teacher to hosts of men and women, boys and girls, who have come from all over the world to listen and learn. And (as Dr. Jensen's alma mater proclaims: *Like a thousand stars by night we shall faithfully lead the way.*)

I want to say I am deeply touched that this place, this Swannanoa, has come to mean as much to Janis as it has to me, Mary, and our family. So much so that she has written a beautiful song that is already being considered a masterpiece, with the title, what else?

Swannannoa
Janis Ian

Swannanoa. I can hear you
call my name upon the wind
If I fall behind, don't worry
You will see my face again
You will see my face again

Swannanoa, I am longing
for my home so far away
I will carry you within me
from the cradle to the grave
From the cradle to the grave

And the mountains and the mist
and the white clouds they kissed
And the sweet gum's perfume
in my hair.

When these hard times have passed
I will see you at last
Swannanoa, I'll be home to stay
Oh my darling, I'll be home to stay

SPECIAL THANKS

Doug M. Orr, for wise counsel and feedback, especially related to editing, and for writing a thoughtful and informed introduction.

Janis Ian, for sharing her wisdom and no-nonsense advice while in the middle of a project of her own, not to mention writing a beautiful foreword, and for giving permission to use her newest masterpiece, the song, "Swannanoa."

Richard Bellando, Warren Wilson and Berea College graduate, for help with research involving staff and students of both institutions.

My wife, Mary, for having a better memory than mine for fifty-five years, and for adding humor to the project by telling people I'm writing a book of fiction and calling it a memoir.

Lucy Wheeler, my daughter who's helped trouble-shoot when my computer files have done disappearing acts or acted crazy, driving me crazy, too.

Shelby Stephenson, Poet Laureate of North Carolina, for reading early chapters and giving his blessing, saying he "Wouldn't change a thing."

Gladden Schrock, my old Yale bud, for his five-page treatise on how not to write a memoir.

Walter Reed, my other Yale bud, for supplying names and spellings of all our teachers.

George Brosi, long-time editor of the magazine *Appalachian Heritage*, for his critique of an earlier version of the memoir, with tips on artful ways to describe people uniquely. Loyal Jones, for details about the Council of Southern Mountains, as well as who taught what courses at Berea College.

Travis Stemeling, assistant professor of music history at West Virginia University, for a period of constant feedback and encouragement.

My aunt, Shirley Faye, the only "sister" I ever had, for supplying family information, dates and places, and some juicy and informative anecdotes. (She's a year younger than me.)

Brother Bob Stewart, for refreshing my memory of coal camp days, with names and dates.

Chuck Neese, retired Nashville music publisher, for supplying names of singers, writers, and producers I'd forgotten, along with the songs involved. And for his sense of humor.

Mary McMahon, for reading an earlier version, offering positive criticism, and for volunteering to do proofreading.

Russ Cheatham, former professor of criminal justice at Cumberland University, for great tips on editing, and for encouragement.

Samuel Scoville, retired academic dean and professor of English at Warren Wilson, for literary research.

My lawyer, Chris Horsnell, selected by his peers as a candidate for best lawyer in America in areas of entertainment, television, and copyright law, for looking over my contract.

Sally Biggers at Black Mountain Digital Media, for scanning photos for the book.

Kurt Schotthoefer, for finding songs I couldn't find, complete with lyrics.

David Manning, who did an excellent editorial read and made some fantastic suggestions.

And finally:

Scott B. Bomar, my editor at BMG, for listening patiently to my gripes and suggestions, contract-wise, from the git-go, and for attending to them with assurances that have made the writing easier and worry-free. For helping with clearances and for convincing me that BMG was the way to go.

BILLY EDD WHEELER'S DISCOGRAPHY

CHARTING SINGLES AS A SONGWRITER:

(Artist / Song / Co-Writer(s) / Date / Label & Release
Number / Chart Position)

Mike Clifford / "What to Do With Laurie" / Jerry Leiber, Mike
Stoller / 12-29-1962 / United Artists 557 / #68 pop

The Kingston Trio / "The Reverend Mr. Black" / Jerry Leiber /
4-6-1963 / Capitol 4951 / #8 pop, #15 R&B

Hank Snow / "The Man Who Robbed the Bank at Santa Fe" /
Jerry Leiber, Mike Stoller / 4-27-1963 / RCA Victor 8151 /
#9 country

The Kingston Trio / "Desert Pete" / 8-3-1963 / Capitol 5005 /
#33 pop

Billy Edd Wheeler / "Ode to the Little Brown Shack Out Back" /
11-28-1964 / Kapp 617 / #3 country, #50 pop

Johnny Cash and June Carter / "Jackson" / Jerry Leiber /
3-4-1967 / Columbia 44011 / #2 country

Nancy Sinatra and Lee Hazlewood / "Jackson" / Jerry Leiber /
6-24-1967 / Reprise 0595 / #14 pop

Billy Edd Wheeler / "I Ain't the Worryin' King" / 8-24-1968 /
Kapp 928 / #63 country

Johnny Darrell / "I Ain't Buying" / 9-21-1968 / United Artists
   50442 / #27 country

Bill Willbourn and Kathy Morrison / "Him and Her" /
   1-11-1969 / United Artists 50474 / #44 country

Hank Williams Jr. / "Baby Again" / 2-22-1969 / MGM 14024 /
   #16 country

Johnny Darrell and Anita Carger / "The Coming Of The Roads" /
   4-12-1969 / United Artists 50503 / #50 country

Billy Edd Wheeler / "West Virginia Women" / 5-3-1969 /
   United Artists 50507 / #51 country

Johnny Darnell / "River Bottom" / 9-13-1969 / United Artists
   50572 / #23 country

Billy Edd Wheeler / "Fried Chicken and a Country Tune" /
   9-13-1969 / United Artists 50579 / #62 country

Johnny Cash / "Blistered" / 11-22-1969 / Columbia 45020 /
   #4 country, #50 pop

Del Reeves / "Son of a Coal Man" / 5-23-1970 / United Artists
   50667 / #41 country

Johnny Duncan / "Baby's Smile, Woman's Kiss" / 11-27-1971 /
   Columbia 45479 / #12 country

Billy Edd Wheeler / "200 Lbs. O' Singin' Hound" / 7-29-1972 /
   RCA Victor 0739 / #71 country

Elvis Presley / "It's Midnight" / Jerry Chesnut / 10-26-1974 /
   RCA Victor 10074 / #9 country

Jerry Reed / "Gimme Back My Blues" / 11-11-1978 / RCA
   11407/ #14 country

Kenny Rogers / "The Coward of the County" / Roger Bowling /
   11-17-1979 / United Artists 1327 / #1 country, #3 pop

Billy Edd Wheeler / "Duel under the Snow" / 11-17-1979 /
   Radio Cinema 001 / #94 country

Roy Clark / "Chain Gang of Love" / Roger Bowling /
   12-15-1979 / MCA 41153 / #21 country

Roger Bowling / "Diplomat" / Roger Bowling / 5-31-1980 /
    NSD 46 / #78 country
Roger Bowling / "Long Arm of the Law" / Roger Bowling /
    8-23-1980 / NSD 58 / #52 country
Billy Edd Wheeler with Rashell Richmond / "Daddy" /
    6-20-1981 / NSD 94 / Jerry Duncan, Betty Gibson /
    #55 country
Johnny Cash / "The Reverend Mr. Black" / Jerry Leiber /
    1-23-1982 / Columbia 02669 / #71 country
Jim Wyrick / "Memory" / Roger Bowling / 2-26-1983 / NSD
    157 / #85 country

ALBUMS
(Title / Year / Record Label, Release #)
Billy Edd: USA / 1961 / Monitor, MF-354
Billy Edd and Bluegrass, Too / 1962 / Monitor, MF-367
A New Bag of Songs / 1964 / Kapp, KL-1351
Memories of America / Ode to the Little Brown Shack Out Back /
    1965 / Kapp, KL-1425
The Wheeler Man / 1965 / Kapp, KL-1443
Goin' Town and Country / 1966 / Kapp, KL-1479
Paper Birds / 1967 / Kapp, KL-1533
I Ain't the Worryin' Kind / 1968 / Kapp, KS-3567
Nashville Zodiac / 1969 / United Artists, UAS-6711
Love / 1971 / RCA LSP-4491
Some Mountain Tales About Jack / 1972 / Spoken Arts, SA-1113
Appalachian Dulcimer Music (Edsel Martin, with guitar and
    production by Billy Edd Wheeler) / 1973 / Southern
    Highlands Handicraft Guild, PRP-33431
Sings His Favorite Original and Traditional Folk Songs / 1974 /
    Southern Highland Handicraft Guild, BEW
My Mountains, My Music / 1975 / Sagittarius, SR-1975

A Song of the Cumberland Gap (In the Days of Daniel Boone) / 1978 /
    National Geographic Society, 07809
Wild Mountain Flowers / 1979 / Flying Fish, FF-085
Asheville / 1982 / Sagittarius, SR1282
*Gee-Haw Whimmy Diddle and Other Folk and Original Southern
    Mountain Tales* / 1984 / Southern Highland Handicraft Guild,
    BE-114
What a Way to Go / 1993 / Sagittarius, SR 12932
Songs I Wrote with Chet / 1994 / Sagittarius, SR1994
Songs and Legends of the Outer Banks / 1996 / Kitty Hawk,
    KHR1996
The Best of Laughter in Appalachia: Live from Berea, Kentucky (with
    Loyal Jones) / 1999 / Sagittarius, SR1999
Milestones: A Self Portrait by Billy Edd Wheeler / 2001 / Sagittarius,
    SR2001CD
New Wine from Old Vines: Billy Edd Wheeler Uncorked / 2006 /
    Sagittarius
Songs of Doc Jensen: Like a Thousand Stars by Night / 2008 /
    Sagittarius

PLAYS & MUSICALS
(Title / Year / Venue / Location)
Fire on the Mountain / 1965 / Pioneer Playhouse / Danville, KY
Hatfields and McCoys, with Ewel Cornett / 1970 / Beckley, WV
Barbry and Willie / 1977 / Warren Wilson College / Swannanoa,
    NC
A Song of the Cumberland Gap / 1978 / Folk Opera for National
    Geographic
A Song of the Cumberland Gap / 1979 / stage play / Pineville, KY
All God's Critters / 1979 / Carver Optional School / Black
    Mountain, NC

Mossie and the Strippers / 1979 / the Culture Center,
    Charleston, WV
The Glass Christmas Tree, with Ewel Cornett / 1983 / Stage One,
    Louisville, KY
Bird on the Wing, with Haila Stoddard & Bob Morrison / 1987 /
    Wright State University / Dayton, OH
Young Abe Lincoln / 1987 / Lincoln State Park / Lincoln City, IN
Wings over Appalachia, with Jim Crabtree / 1990 / Cumberland
    County Playhouse,
Crossville, TN
Voices in the Wind / 1993 / McDowell County Cemetery /
    Marion, NC
What a Way to Go, with Ewel Cornett and Dennis Burnside /
    1994 / Derby Dinner Playhouse / Clarksville, Indiana
Johnny Appleseed / 2004 / Johnny Appleseed Heritage Center /
    Mansfield, Ohio

POETRY
(Title / Year / Publisher)
Song of a Woods Colt / 1969 / Droke House, distributed by
    Grosset & Dunlap
Travis and Other Poems of the Swannanoa Valley / 1977 / Wild
    Goose, Inc.

BOOKS
(Title / Year / Publisher)
Laughter in Appalachia, with Loyal Jones / 1987 / August House,
    Inc.
Outhouse Humor / 1988 / August House, Inc.
Curing the Cross-Eyed Mule, with Loyal Jones / 1989 / August
    House, Inc.
Hometown Humor, with Loyal Jones / 1991 / August House, Inc.

More Laughter in Appalachia, with Loyal Jones / 1995 / August
    House, Inc.
Real Country Humor / 2002 / August House, Inc.
A Song to Kill For (first published as *Star of Appalachia*) / 2003 /
    Infinity.
Kudzu Covers Manhattan, with Ewel Cornett / 2005 / Fighting
    Dove Productions